The Best
Totline
NEWSLETTER

Compiled by Jean Warren
Illustrated By Kathy Kotomaimoce

TOTLINE®
BOOKS

Warren Publishing House
Everett, WA

We wish to thank the teachers, childcare workers, and parents whose names appear on page 390 for contributing some of the activities in this book.

Editorial Staff
    Managing Editor: Kathleen Cubley
    Editor: Gayle Bittinger
    Contributing Editors: Susan Hodges, Elizabeth McKinnon
    Copyeditor and Proofreader: Mae Rhodes
    Editorial Assistant: Kate Ffolliott

Design and Production Staff
    Art Manager: Uma Kukathas
    Book Design: Sarah Ness
    Book Production/Layout: Lynne Faulk
    Cover Design: Brenda Mann Harrison
    Cover Illustration: Kathy Kotomaimoce
    Production Manager: Jo Anna Brock

ISBN 1-57029-045-8

Library of Congress Catalog Number 94-61017

Printed in the United States of America
Published by: Warren Publishing House
              P.O. Box 2250
              Everett, WA 98203

20 19 18 17 16 15 14 13 12 11 10 9 8 7 6 5 4 3 2

Introduction

Welcome to *The Best of Totline*! This giant book is filled with my favorite activities, songs, and articles from the past 15 years of the *Totline* newsletter.

Many teachers look over the selection of outstanding Totline books and ask me, "If I can just buy one, which book do you recommend?" That was always a difficult question to answer—until now. *The Best of Totline* is the perfect book to start with because it has a sampling of the kinds of materials you will find in a variety of Totline books.

The Best of Totline is divided into 12 chapters, one for each month of the year. Each chapter is filled with art activities, learning games, stories and rhymes, science and self-awareness activities, movement games, music, and seasonal themes. Each chapter also comes with two pages of teaching-aid patterns to accompany a story or an activity for that month. And as with all Totline books, the activities in this book are developmentally appropriate for 3- to 5-year-olds, and they use readily available materials.

I wish you the best of luck in your profession. I hope *The Best of Totline* will make your job easier and more rewarding.

Jean Warren

Contents

January

Cotton Ball Snowpal

Cut two large circles out of white butcher paper, making one slightly larger than the other. Place the circles on a table. Pour small amounts of glue into shallow containers. Let your children dip cotton balls into the glue and place them all over the circles. Have them continue until the circles are completely covered with cotton balls. When the glue dries, hang the circles on a bulletin board with the larger circle on the bottom, making a "snowpal." Decorate the snowpal with facial features and clothing cut out of construction paper.

Variation: Instead of gluing the cotton balls on butcher paper, have your children press them on large circles of clear self-stick paper.

Snow Scene Mural

Cut a house shape out of construction paper and glue it on blue or black butcher paper. Pour small amounts of glue into shallow containers. Place the butcher paper on a table. Let your children dip cotton balls into the glue and place them all over the butcher paper for snowflakes. Show the children how to fluff out some of the cotton balls and glue them around the house shape to make a snowy lawn. Hang the mural on a wall or a bulletin board.

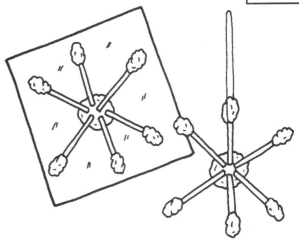

Snowflake Printing

Cut snowflake shapes out of plastic-foam food trays. Add extra detail to the snowflakes by making indentations in the plastic foam with a pencil. Make a handle on the back of each shape with masking tape. Give each of your children one of the snowflakes. Have the children paint across the fronts of the snowflakes with thick white tempera paint. Then press the shapes onto blue paper to make snowflake prints.

Floating Snowflakes

Cut cotton swabs in half. Give each of your children a 4-inch square of aluminum foil with a small amount of glue in the middle of it. Let each child select six of the cotton-swab halves. Have the children arrange the cotton swabs on their foil squares to form snowflakes as shown in the illustration. When the glue dries completely, let the children peel their snowflakes off the foil. Attach a loop of thread to each snowflake and hang it in a window or from a mobile to make a Floating Snowflake.

Winter Snowflakes

Help each of your children glue three craft sticks together as shown to create a snowflake with six points. Attach a loop of thread to each child's snowflake for hanging. Let each child paint one side of his or her snowflake with white tempera paint. While the paint is still wet, have the child hold the snowflake over a box, sprinkle it with white or silver glitter, and shake off the excess. When the paint has dried, have the child repeat the process on the other side of his or her snowflake.

ART • Winter Scenes

Snow Scenes

Collect holiday cards with snow scenes on them. Let each of your children select one of the cards. Have the children cut off the backs of their cards (or cut them off yourself). Set out small containers of glue and small brushes or cotton swabs. Have the children paint glue all over their cards. Then let them sprinkle salt on the glue. When the glue dries, the salt will look like sparkly snow all over the cards.

Frosty Pictures

Give your children construction paper and crayons. Let them use the crayons to create winter scenes or designs on their papers. Make a solution of half Epsom salts and half water. Have the children use wide paint brushes to cover their pictures with the Epsom salt mixture. As the mixture dries, shiny crystals will appear on the children's papers, making Frosty Pictures.

Snowflake Jars

Give each of your children a small baby food jar and a sheet of waxed paper. Have the children tear their sheets of waxed paper into tiny pieces and put them into their jars. Help each child fill his or her jar with water and tighten the lid securely. Have the children shake their Snowflake Jars and let them watch the waxed paper "snowflakes" dance and fall to the bottom.

Inkblot Pictures

Give each of your children a large piece of paper that has been folded in half and then unfolded. Point out the two sides of each paper. Ask the children to paint pictures or designs on only one side of their papers. As they finish, have the children fold their papers in half, with the paint inside, and rub across the outsides of them with their hands. Let each child open up his or her paper to discover the identical, but opposite, picture on each side.

Spiral Art

Find an old, working record player turntable and place it on a table. Punch a hole in the middle of several paper plates. Set out the paper plates and some felt-tip markers. Let one of your children select a paper plate and a marker. Show the child how to place the paper plate on the turntable so the hole in the plate is over the spindle. Start the turntable and let the child gently rest the felt-tip marker on the paper plate. As the plate rotates, spiral designs will appear on the paper plate. Repeat for each child. (Be sure to supervise your children at all times when electrical appliances are in use.)

Rolling Paint

Collect several empty roll-on deodorant bottles. Clean out the bottles and fill them with tempera paint. Let your children roll the bottles on large pieces of paper to create designs. Encourage them to experiment with different ways of moving the bottles.

Snowpal Sequence Cards

Photocopy the snowpal sequence cards on page 36. Color and cut out the cards. Cover them with clear self-stick paper for durability, if desired. Using the cards, tell your children a story about making a snowpal. Lay each card down as you tell the corresponding part of the story. When all the cards are displayed in a row, review the story, stressing what happened first, second, third, and last. Then mix up the cards and let your children put them back in the proper order as they retell the snowpal story.

Heads and Tails Matching Game

Photocopy and cut out the animal heads and tails cards on page 37. Color and cover them with clear self-stick paper, if desired. Have your children find all the heads, all the tails, and then find the matching pairs.

Heads and Tails Lotto

Make two photocopies of the animal heads and tails cards on page 37. Cut one copy into cards. Use the other copy as a gameboard. Cover the cards and game board with clear self-stick paper for durability, if desired. Let your children take turns placing the game cards on top of the matching pictures on the gameboard.

Mitten Match-Ups

Cut pairs of mitten shapes out of various textures of fabric. Mix up the mittens and let your children take turns finding the matching pairs.

Variation: Keep the mittens in a laundry basket and let your children hang them in pairs on a clothesline.

Flannelboard Snowpals

From white felt, cut three large circles, three medium-sized circles, and three small circles. Then cut three top hat shapes out of black felt. Have the children place the large circles in a row on a flannelboard. Let them place the medium-sized circles above the large circles. Then have them place the small circles above the medium-sized circles. Let the children add the top hats to make snowpals. Then mix up all the circles and hats and let the children make the snowpals all over again.

Mirror Snowflakes

Cut small paper snowflakes in half. Give each of your children one of the snowflake halves and a small rectangular mirror. Show the children how to hold their mirrors beside their snowflake halves to create whole snowflakes. Help them discover that they can make new snowflake patterns by moving their mirrors.

Counting Candles

Let your children take turns making a "birthday cake" by pressing playdough into a plastic container or a small baking pan. Set out some birthday candles with the wicks cut off. Have the child making the cake tell you how many candles he or she would like on it. Then help the child count out that many candles. Or put some candles on the cake and have the child tell you how many are on it.

Building Blocks

Place six square building blocks on a baking sheet. Show the block setup to one of your children. Then give the child directions such as these: "Put one block on each corner of the baking sheet. Put five blocks in a row. Make six blocks into two rows. Put two blocks in one stack and two blocks in a second stack; now put the same number of blocks in a third stack. Use five blocks to build a short stack and a tall stack."

Counting Sets of Two

For each of your children, cut a large numeral 2 out of heavy paper. Collect a variety of small objects to be glued on in sets of two such as paper clips, rubber bands, cereal pieces, buttons, cotton balls, and yarn pieces. Put each kind of object into a separate bowl. Give each child one of the paper numbers. Then let the children glue the objects on their numbers in sets of two.

Stamping Numbers

On each of several sheets of paper write the numerals from 1 through 10 in a row. Give each of your children one of the numbered sheets, a rubber stamp, and an ink pad. Sing the song below and have the children stamp on top of each number at the appropriate time.

Sung to: "Ten Little Indians"

One little, two little,
Three little rubber stamps.
Four little, five little,
Six little rubber stamps.
Seven little, eight little,
Nine little rubber stamps,
Ten little rubber stamps.

Kathy McCullough

Stamping Patterns

Use rubber stamps to create a simple pattern on the top half of a piece of paper. Give the stamps and the pattern sheet to one of your children and ask him or her to duplicate the pattern.

Variation: Let the children create their own patterns with the rubber stamps. Encourage them to explain their patterns to you.

Letter Stamps

Write each of your children's names on a separate piece of paper. Let your children find letter stamps that match the letters in their names and stamp them below the letters on their papers.

The Pancake Man

Adapted by Jean Warren

Once upon a time there was a farmer and his wife who lived with their daughter on a large farm.

One morning the wife was making pancakes for breakfast. She mixed up the batter and heated up the skillet. She poured a large circle of batter into the pan and a smaller circle of batter close to the top of it. Then just for fun, she added more batter to make two arm shapes and two leg shapes and plopped on blueberries for eyes and a mouth.

She flipped the pancake over and was getting ready to put it on a plate when the pancake started to move. Suddenly it stood up, hopped out of the pan, jumped to the floor, and then ran out the door.

As it ran past the wife, she heard it cry, "Run, run, fast as you can. You can't catch me—I'm the Pancake Man."

The wife tried to catch him, but she couldn't.

He ran past the daughter, but the daughter couldn't catch him.

He ran past the farmer, but the farmer couldn't catch him.

He ran past the cow, but the cow couldn't catch him.

He ran past the dog, but the dog couldn't catch him.

He ran past the cat, but the cat couldn't catch him.

He ran and he ran and he ran. Has anybody seen that Pancake Man?

Huff and Puff's Snowy Day

By Jean Warren

Huff and Puff
Went out to play,
One bright and sunny
Winter's day.

Far below
The children sighed,
"Where is winter?"
They all cried.

Their skis were waxed,
Their bobsleds, too.
There was no snow!
What could they do?

Their mittens were ready,
Their snowsuits, too.
Where was the snow?
Boo-hoo, boo-hoo!

Huff and Puff
Watched their plight,
Then slowly floated
Out of sight.

Up, up they went,
Where the cold winds blow,
And filled their pockets
Full of snow.

Then back they came,
Down, down, so low,
Tossing out the
Cold, white snow.

The children shouted and
Jumped with glee!
Snow and more snow was all
They could see.

They climbed on their sleds
And rode down the hills,
Laughing and waving,
Enjoying their spills.

They pulled on their skates
And danced on the ice.
Whirling and twirling
Was ever so nice.

Huff and Puff watched
And decided to try
Gliding and spinning
Up in the sky.

They whirled and they twirled,
With great flips and flops.
They slid down the mountains,
Then spun on their tops.

They had a great time.
The children did, too.
Winter was fun with
Snow things to do!

The children were happy,
And they wanted to say,
"Thanks for the snow,"
In their own special way.

So they built a big snowpal
With arms stretched high,
Waving "thank you"
To their friends in the sky.

Then Huff and Puff
Came back down low
And covered the ground
Once more with their snow.

Then back up they went
To their home in the sky,
Waving their arms
In a final goodbye.

Walking in the Snow

Let's go walking in the snow,
   (*Do actions as rhyme indicates.*)

Walking, walking on tiptoe.

Lift your right foot way up high,

Then your left foot—keep it dry!

All around the yard we skip,

Watch your step, or you might slip.

Adapted Traditional

Icy Winter

Icy you and icy me,

Icy branches on each tree.

Icy patterns on the glass,

Icy steps we have to pass.

Icy walks and roads galore,

Icy wintertime once more.

Icy vines upon the wall,

Icy scenes I now recall.

Help your children discover that *icy*
could also be read as *I see.*

Jean Warren

Snowy Surprise

Sometimes the snow falls at night when I'm sleeping.
   (*Lay head on hands, palms together.*)

I'm so surprised when I awake.
   (*Stretch and yawn.*)

I look out at the world around me.
   (*Look around.*)

It looks like a frosted cake.
   (*Lick lips.*)

Diane Thom

Small or Tall

Talk with your children about how they would feel if they were smaller than everyone else. What problems might they have? What would be easier? Then ask them how they would feel if they were extremely tall. What problems would they have then? What would be easier?

Answers and Questions

Play a game with your children by giving them an "answer" and having them think up a "question" that fits the answer. For example, if you said, "The answer is three," the children might reply with "How old is Katie?" or "How many apples are there?"

Hint: You may need to give your children many examples of this game before they catch on to how it is played. Or you may wish to begin playing this game by having your children give you the answers while you make up the questions.

Seasonal Words

Play a seasonal word-recognition game with your children. Start with just two seasons—winter and summer. Mention a word, such as sled, snow, mittens, sun, swimming, or warm, and have the children tell you which season the word is connected with. Add seasons as your children's abilities allow.

Mirror, Mirror

While you read the following poem, have one of your children look in a mirror and act out the motions.

I look in the mirror and what do I see?

A very wonderful, special me!
    (Point to self.)

With pretty eyes all shiny and bright,
    (Point to eyes.)

My smile shows my teeth all pearly white.
    (Smile and point to teeth.)

It certainly is great to be

This very wonderful, special ME!
    (Hug self.)

Ann M. O'Connell

This Is Me

Lay large pieces of butcher paper on the floor. Have each of your children lie down on one of the papers. Then trace around the children's bodies with a crayon or a felt-tip marker. Let the children paint their features and clothes on their body outlines. Encourage the children to talk about themselves as they create their images.

Thumbs Up

This activity fosters an awareness of self and others and explores some of the ways in which we are the same and different. Have your children sit in a circle and practice the thumbs-up response for yes and the thumbs-down response for no. Then have the children respond accordingly when you ask such yes or no questions as: "Did you play with blocks today? Are you wearing blue? Do you like hamburgers? Do you have a sister?"

My Interests

Give each of your children a piece of construction paper with his or her photograph glued to it and the title "(Child's name)'s Interests" written on it. Let the children add to their papers such items as magazine pictures or drawings of their family members, friends, favorite foods, and things they like to do. Display the collages around the room.

Feelings

Cut out magazine pictures of people showing different emotions. Show the pictures to your children and ask them to name the feeling they think the person in each picture is showing. Encourage the children to talk about why someone might feel that way.

Puppet Talk

Make a hand puppet out of an old sock or a paper bag. Give the puppet to one of your children. Ask the child questions for the "puppet" to answer. Children often express themselves more freely when "talking" through a puppet.

My Own Snack

Set out bowls of cut-up fruits and vegetables. Give your children small plates or bowls. Let them make their own snacks by choosing the fruits and vegetables they want.

Evaporation

For each of your children, use a permanent felt-tip marker to mark a line and the child's name on the side of a clear-plastic cup. Set out several small pitchers of water. Give the children their cups. Have the children use the water pitchers to fill their cups up to the lines. Let them place their cups around the room. Have them observe their cups of water over the next several days. What is happening to the water levels? Where is the water going? Explain to the children that the water is *evaporating*. Evaporation occurs when particles of water become warm enough to turn into vapor and escape into the air. How could the children make the water in their cups evaporate faster?

Condensation

Collect two jars and their lids. Fill one jar with ice water and the other jar with room-temperature water. Screw the lids on tightly. Place the jars on a table. Show the children the jars. Ask them to describe what is happening to the outsides of the jars. Point out that only the jar with ice water inside has drops of water on the outside. This is called *condensation*. Condensation happens when the water particles in the air, called vapor, become cold enough to change into drops of water.

Absorption

Collect a variety of materials that will absorb water, such as fabric, cotton balls, and newspaper, and a variety of materials that will not absorb water, such as plastic, aluminum foil, and waxed paper. Give each of your children a small piece of each kind of material, a cup of water, and an eyedropper. Let the children put several drops of water on each of their material pieces and observe what happens. Which material absorbs water best? Which materials do not absorb water at all?

Orange Cups

Cut oranges in half. Let your children carefully remove the orange segments from each half. Save the segments for eating later. To make each Orange Cup, poke four holes near the top of an orange rind. Fasten a piece of string through each hole and tie the strings together at the top. Let your children fill the Orange Cups with birdseed and hang them on a tree.

Bread Feeders

Let your children use cookie cutters to cut shapes out of slices of stale bread. Have them spread peanut butter on the bread shapes and sprinkle on birdseed. Insert a pipe cleaner through each bread shape to make a hanger. Help the children hang their completed Bread Feeders on a tree.

Suet Bags

Cut 6-inch squares out of nylon netting. In a large bowl, let your children mix together suet (available from a butcher) and birdseed. Have the children place a spoonful of the suet mixture in the middle of each nylon-netting square. To complete each bag, bring the corners together and tie them with a string. Let the children hang the Suet Bags on a tree.

Getting Started

Have your children lie on the floor and form a beautiful blanket of snow. Next, have them pretend that children are rolling them up to make large snowballs until they become so large they have to stand up and become snowpals. Now take them on a winter adventure as you lead them through the following activities.

Snowpals

Explain to your children that because they are snowpals, they must stand frozen and stiff. Then tell them that one day, the sun shines a little warmer, and they begin to thaw slightly. Call out body parts for the children to start moving. Have them begin moving these parts slowly until their whole bodies are moving.

Marching and Skating

Tell your children that the snowpals are so excited they can move that they start marching, skipping, and running all around. Then let them pretend to join some winter skaters at a frozen pond and skate around the room.

Melting

Pretend to be the sun and shine down on the snowpals. Tell the children that they get weaker and weaker as it gets hotter and hotter, until they gradually melt away. Encourage the children to melt slowly and gracefully to the floor.

Jumping Footprints

Find an old flannel-backed, vinyl tablecloth. Use a permanent felt-tip marker to draw left and right shoe shapes in a jumping pattern on the vinyl side. (Start with a very simple pattern, such as feet together, feet apart, feet together, feet apart, as shown in the illustration.) Place the tablecloth on a carpeted floor. Let your children jump along the pattern, moving their feet according to the positions of the shoe outlines. As the children become more skilled, make progressively harder jumping patterns for them to try.

Hula Hoop Designs

Give your children several hula hoops. Ask them to place the hoops on the floor in a path. Then let the children take turns moving along the hoop path. Encourage each child to move differently by asking him or her questions such as these: "How would a rabbit get to the end of the path? How would a baby get to the end? Can you dance to the end? Can you go backward to the end?"

Kick Bag

Stuff an old drawstring bag with crumpled newspaper. Fasten the end closed and hide the string inside the bag. Have your children remove their shoes and take turns gently kicking the bag all around the room.

Cheer the Year

Sung to: "Row, Row, Row Your Boat"

Cheer, cheer, cheer the year,
A new one's just begun.
Celebrate with all your friends.
Let's go have some fun!

Clap, clap, clap your hands,
A brand new year is here.
Learning, laughing, singing, clapping,
Through another year.

Susan M. Paprocki

New Year's Here

Sung to: "Frère Jacques"

Crash your cymbals, toot your horns,
New Year's here! New Year's here!
A time for happy drumming,
New birthdays are coming.
New Year's Day! New Year's Day!

Betty Silkunas

Celebrate

Sung to: "This Old Man"

Celebrate
The new year,
Blow your horn and give a cheer.
Clap your hands together,
Stamp your feet and say,
"Have a happy New Year's Day!"

Susan Hodges

Ni Hao Song (Hello Song)

Sung to: "Happy Birthday"

Ni hao (nee how) to you,
Ni hao to you.
Ni hao, ni hao,
Ni hao to you.

Elizabeth McKinnon

Chinese New Year Song

Sung to: "London Bridge"

See the lion dance and prance,
Dance and prance, dance and prance.
See the lion dance and prance
On Chinese New Year's Day.

Additional verses: Hear the firecrackers pop;
Hear the drums go boom, boom, boom; Hear the
cymbals clang, clang, clang; See the children
laugh and clap.

Elizabeth McKinnon

Martin Luther King

Sung to: "Mary Had a Little Lamb"

Who was Martin Luther King,
Luther King, Luther King?
He was a man who had a dream
That we would all be free.

Martin Luther gave a speech,
Gave a speech, gave a speech.
He wanted all of us to live
In peace and harmony.

He won the Nobel Prize for Peace,
Prize for Peace, Prize for Peace.
For his love for all the world
And for you and me.

Josette Brown

Snowflakes Falling
Sung to: "Mary Had a Little Lamb"

Snowflakes falling from the sky,
From the sky, from the sky.
Snowflakes falling from the sky
To the earth below.

Watch them as they dance and whirl,
Dance and whirl, dance and whirl.
Watch them as they dance and whirl,
Soft, white winter snow.

Judith McNitt

Ice and Snow
Sung to: "Jingle Bells"

Ice and snow, cold winds blow,
Hop aboard our sleigh.
Oh, what fun it is to play
Winter games today.
Ice and snow, cold winds blow,
Let's be on our way.
Oh, what fun it is to play
Winter games today.

Betty Silkunas

Frost
Sung to: "The Farmer in the Dell"

The frost is on the trees,
    (Point up.)
The frost is on the ground,
    (Point down.)
The frost is on the window,
    (Make window with hands.)
The frost is all around!
    (Make circle with hands.)

The frost is very icy,
    (Shiver.)
The frost is very bright,
    (Cover eyes with hands.)
The frost is very slippery,
    (Slide one hand over the other.)
The frost is very white!

Lois E. Putnam

Put on Your Mittens

Sung to: "Up on the Housetop"

Put on your mittens—it's cold I fear—
    (Pretend to put on mittens.)

Now that winter snow is here.
    (Hug self and shiver.)

Play in the yard and when you're done,
    (Pretend to make snowballs and stomp around.)

Pull off your mittens, one by one.
    (Pretend to remove mittens.)

It's fun to play in the snow!
    (Pretend to toss armfuls of snow.)

It's fun to play in the snow!
    (Pretend to toss armfuls of snow.)

Play in the yard and when you're done,
    (Pretend to make snowballs and stomp around.)

Pull off your mittens, one by one.
    (Pretend to remove mittens.)

Barbara Paxson

I'm a Friendly Snowpal

Sung to: "I'm a Little Teapot"

I'm a friendly snowpal, big and fat.
Here is my tummy and here is my hat.
I have two funny eyes and a carrot nose.
I'm all snow from my head to my toes.

I have two bright eyes so I can see
All the snow falling down on me.
When the weather's cold, I'm strong and tall,
But when it's warm, I get very small.

Susan M. Paprocki

On My Sled

Sung to: "Frère Jacques"

Belly flopping, never stopping,
On my sled, on my sled.
Riding down a snowy hill,
What a giggle, what a thrill!
On my sled, on my sled.

Betty Silkunas

Lacing Cards

Cut brown posterboard into teddy bear shapes and punch holes around the edges. Then let your children lace pieces of colorful yarn through the holes.

Alphabet Bears

Cut 26 teddy bear shapes out of heavy paper and write a different alphabet letter on each one. If desired, cover each bear with clear self-stick paper for durability. Then let your children practice putting the bears into alphabetical order.

Sorting and Counting Bears

Set out a collection of teddy bears. Ask your children to sort the teddy bears by categories such as color, size, and those wearing bows. Then have the children count the number of bears in each category.

Weighing Bears

Review the concepts of heavy and light by having one of your children hold a different teddy bear in each hand. Ask, "Which bear feels heavier? Which feels lighter?" Or let your children use balance scales to compare the weights of their teddy bears.

Bear Puppets

Give each of your children a paper lunch sack. Let the children create teddy bear faces on the sacks by gluing on scraps of colored construction paper and decorating with felt-tip markers.

Teddy Bear Parade

Play some marching music and set out a collection of teddy bears. Let each of your children select one of the bears to hold while marching around the room.

Teddy Bear Rhyme

Let your children pretend to be teddy bears as they recite the following rhyme and act out the movements.

Teddy bear, teddy bear, turn around,
Teddy bear, teddy bear, touch the ground.
Teddy bear, teddy bear, reach up high,
Teddy bear, teddy bear, touch the sky.
Teddy bear, teddy bear, touch your shoe,
Teddy bear, teddy bear, I love you!

Traditional

THEMES • Time for Peace

Martin Luther King Jr.

January is the month when many people celebrate the life and triumphs of Dr. Martin Luther King Jr. This is a wonderful opportunity to focus on activities that promote peace. Peace education includes any activity that fosters children's self-esteem and promotes cooperation and nonviolence. The following activities are just a start.

Peace Mural

For each of your children, cut a dove shape out of white construction paper. Set out paintbrushes, bowls of glue, glitter, and white feathers. Let the children use the brushes to spread glue on their dove shapes. Then have them decorate their doves with glitter and feathers. When the dove shapes are dry, let the children tape them up around the room.

Martin Luther King

Sung to: "I'm a Little Teapot"

Martin Luther King, they always say,
Thought of friendship every day.
And he always wanted you and me
To live together peacefully.

June Meckel

Positive Statement Poster

With your children, brainstorm a list of "Good Feeling Statements." Examples might include "You're nice" or "I'm glad we're friends." Write these statements on a chart and display the chart in the room.

What If?

Ask your children "What if?" questions about problems that commonly arise. Try questions such as these: "What if you want to play on the swing, but your friend won't get off? What if there's one cookie left and three of you want it?" Help your children come up with peaceful solutions to these problems. Then encourage the children to think of more problems for the group to try solving.

We Know How to Get Along

Sung to: "Mary Had a Little Lamb"

We know how to get along,
Get along, get along.
We know how to get along
Every single day!

We take turns and share a lot,
Share a lot, share a lot.
We take turns and share a lot
While we work and play!

Kathy McCullough

THEMES • Doctors and Nurses

Medical Kits

Fold a large piece of black construction paper in half. Cut a medical kit shape out of the paper as shown in the illustration. Make one for each of your children. Give each child one of the kits and a variety of medical items such as a tongue depressor, a cotton ball, an adhesive bandage, and a cotton swab. Let the children glue or tape these items inside their kits.

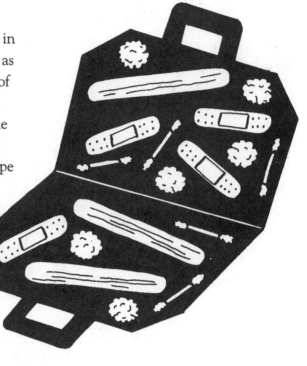

I'm Happy That I Am a Nurse
Sung to: "My Bonnie Lies Over the Ocean"

I'm happy that I am a nurse,
I help to make people well.
I'm happy that I am a nurse,
It makes me feel just swell.
I am a nurse,
I help to make people well, well, well.
I am a nurse,
I help to make people well.

Substitute *doctor* for *nurse*.

Jean Warren

Doctor or Nurse Visit

Invite a doctor or a nurse to visit your group. Ask the visitor to bring along several medical instruments such as a stethoscope for listening to hearts, a reflex hammer for checking reflexes, and a light for looking into eyes and ears. Ask your visitor to talk about such things as caring for cuts and bruises and practicing healthy habits. If possible, arrange for him or her to bring disposable face masks (or other disposable items) to hand out to the children.

Good Health Story

Collect a variety of items that promote good health such as a comb, a bar of soap, a facial tissue, an apple, a jump rope, and a small pillow. Place the items in a large bag. Have your children sit with you in a circle. Start telling a "good health" story about a child or an animal character. Then let the children take turns removing items from the bag and holding them up. As they do so, incorporate the items into your story. Continue until all the items have been used.

Good Health Posters

Let your children help make Good Health Posters to display around the room. For example, on a large piece of construction paper, draw or glue a picture that illustrates washing hands. Add the title "Wash Hands." Let the children decorate the poster by gluing on soap bar wrappers. Other poster ideas include using facial tissue (decorate with real tissues), eating nutritious foods (decorate with canned fruit and vegetable labels), exercising properly (decorate with pictures of outdoor play), and avoiding dangerous substances (decorate with Mr. Yuk stickers).

Snowpal Sequence Cards

Refer to page 12 for directions.

Heads and Tails Cards

Refer to page 12 for directions.

February

Heart Collages

Cut several sizes of heart shapes out of different kinds of paper. Let your children make collages by gluing the hearts on large pieces of white construction paper. Encourage the children to experiment by overlapping some of their hearts.

Painted Glitter Hearts

Let your children fingerpaint with red tempera paint on heart-shaped pieces of paper. While the paint is still wet, have the children sprinkle glitter on their hearts.

Ink Hearts

For each of your children, use a water-based black felt-tip marker to draw a large heart shape on a paper towel. Set out small bowls of water. Give each child one of the paper towels and a paintbrush. Have the children brush water over the black lines of their heart shapes. The dye in the black ink will begin to bleed, leaving rings of color around the hearts.

Easy Lace Valentines

Give each of your children a piece of red or pink construction paper with a heart shape drawn on it. Show the children how to place self-stick hole reinforcement circles around their hearts to make fancy "lace" edgings.

Variation: Let your children use a hole punch to punch holes around the edges of white paper hearts. Have them glue their hearts on pink or red construction paper.

Heart Necklaces

Cut small hearts out of red construction paper. Punch a hole near the top of each heart shape. Cut plastic drinking straws into 1-inch lengths. Cut yarn into 18-inch lengths. Tie a straw section to one end of each piece of yarn. Wrap the other ends of the yarn pieces with tape to make "needles." Give each child one of the yarn pieces and several hearts and straw sections. Show the children how to string their hearts and straw sections on their yarn. As each child finishes his or her necklace, tie the ends together.

ART • Doily Fun

Doily Rubbings

Collect several paper doilies with interesting designs. Use loops of tape to attach the doilies to a table. Have your children place thin sheets of paper over the doilies and make rubbings of them with crayons, pencils, or chalk.

Doily Hats

Set out a variety of colored doilies, ribbons, and glitter. Give each of your children a paper plate. Have the children decorate their plates by gluing on the doilies, ribbons, and glitter. When the glue has dried, staple crepe paper ties on each plate to make ready-to-wear Doily Hats.

Doily Designs

Set out doilies, construction paper, paint, and paintbrushes. Let your children arrange the doilies on top of sheets of construction paper. Have them carefully paint over the tops of their doilies. Then help them remove the doilies to reveal the designs left on their papers.

Handy Valentines

Cut large heart shapes out of red construction paper. Set out the hearts and large white doilies. Fill a shallow container with red tempera paint. One at a time, have your children place their hands in the red paint and then press them on the doilies. When the paint is dry, let the children glue their doilies to the red hearts.

Heart of Love

Cut white paper into 8-inch squares. Give each of your children one of the squares and have them draw pictures of the people they love. Cut a large heart shape out of red butcher paper. Have the children glue their pictures to the heart. When the glue dries, hang the heart on a bulletin board and decorate it with the words "We Love You."

Pussy Willows

Draw a tree with many branches on a large piece of blue butcher paper. Hang the paper on a wall or a bulletin board at your children's eye level. Set out bowls of puffed rice cereal and shallow containers of glue. Let your children dip the pieces of cereal into the glue and arrange them on the tree branches to make Pussy Willows.

Heart Number Necklaces

Cut heart shapes out of red, pink, and white construction paper. Punch a hole at the top of each heart. Hide the hearts around the room and let your children hunt for them. After the children have found all the hearts, have them take turns bringing their hearts to you. Count the hearts with each child and write a different number on each one. String the hearts on a piece of red yarn to make a Heart Number Necklace for the child to wear.

Mailbox Game

Cut heart shapes out of red construction paper. Use a hole punch to make from one to five holes in each heart. Make five mailboxes by cutting slits in sturdy cardboard boxes and numbering them from 1 to 5. Have your children take turns selecting a heart, counting the number of holes in it, and "delivering" it to the corresponding mailbox.

Roll a Heart

Cut small heart shapes out of red construction paper and put them in a basket. Give each of your children a piece of construction paper with nine squares drawn on it. Have the children sit at a table. Select one child to begin. Have that child roll a die to see how many hearts he or she can take from the basket. Have the child place the hearts on his or her paper, one in each square. Let the next child roll the die and place the appropriate number of hearts on his or her paper. Continue, letting each child have a turn, until one of the children has covered all his or her squares.

Extension: When the game is over, give each of your children nine hearts. Let the children glue their hearts in their squares. Hang the finished papers on a wall or use them as placemats.

Variation: Use heart stickers instead of construction paper hearts.

Counting Hearts

Number index cards from 1 to 10. Give each of your children a paper plate and a plastic bag filled with 10 paper heart shapes. Have the children sit in a circle. Place a numbered index card in the middle of the circle. Have the children count out on their paper plates the same number of hearts. Have the children put their hearts back in the bag before you set out another numbered index card. Continue the game until all the numbered cards have been used.

How Many Hearts?

Place several candy hearts in a baby food jar. Let each of your children guess how many candies are in the jar. When everyone has guessed, empty the jar and count the candies together. Change the number of hearts in the jar and play the game again.

Variation: Instead of candy hearts, use heart-shaped erasers or buttons.

Match the Hearts

Remove the numbered heart cards from an old deck of playing cards. Cut each heart card in half so that the number shows on both halves. Let the children take turns matching the corresponding numbers.

Special Delivery

Let each of your children make a simple valentine for each of the other children in the group by decorating paper heart shapes. Hand out paper sacks or large envelopes and have your children decorate their sacks or envelopes to make valentine holders. Help the children write their names on their valentine holders and have them place their holders on a table. Then let each child pass out the valentines that he or she made by putting one in each of the other children's holders.

Heart Line-Up

Cut three to five heart shapes out of construction paper, making each one slightly larger than the one before it. Mix up the hearts and place them in a pile. Let your children take turns lining up the hearts by size to discover which one is the largest.

Heart Match-Ups

Cut 8 to 12 medium-sized hearts out of posterboard or construction paper. Then cut each heart into a two-piece puzzle. Make sure that each heart is cut in a different way. Have your children join each set of puzzle pieces together to make Heart Match-Ups.

Box Fun • LEARNING GAMES

Button Box

Gather a variety of buttons of different sizes, shapes, colors, and materials. Place the buttons in a box. Show the box to your children. Let the children think of as many ways to sort the buttons as they can.

Feelie Box

Cut a hole large enough for a child's hand in one end of a shoe box. Place an object inside the box and put on the lid. Have one of your children put his or her hand through the hole in the box, feel the object, and try to guess what it is. After the child guesses correctly, put a new item in the box and let another child have a turn.

Hint: To make the game easier, show your children several items. Hide the items and put one of them into the box for the children to guess.

Writing Boxes

Spread a thin layer of salt on the bottom of each of several shallow boxes. Let your children draw or write in the salt with their fingers. Have the children shake the boxes to start over again. If you prefer, use fine white sand (available at most garden centers) instead of salt.

Huff and Puff on Groundhog Day

By Jean Warren

Huff and Puff one winter's day
Floated past where groundhogs stay.

They saw a hole and peeked inside,
"Oh, look! A groundhog," they both cried.

The groundhog knew that it was time
To begin her yearly climb.

Up, up she went, up to the top—
But suddenly she had to stop.

"Oh, dear me," she started to cry,
"I see the sun up in the sky.

"Oh, dear me, what can I do?
If I go out, my shadow will, too!"

Huff and Puff heard her cry.
They linked their arms and flew up high.

They called their friends to join their fun.
Soon the clouds covered up the sun.

The groundhog saw the sun disappear
And knew that now she had nothing to fear.

So out she popped—this time to play.
Now she knew that she could stay.

The ground was hard, the day was cold,
But she was happy, and she was bold.

She ran and ran all around,
Enjoying every sight and sound.

She saw all the signs of spring,
Crocuses, buds, and other things

And said, "How very lucky am I
To have such good friends in the sky.

"Thank you for my early fling.
Thanks, Huff and Puff, for the gift of spring!"

Groundhog Puppet

Fold a paper plate or a construction paper circle in half. Photocopy the pattern on page 69. Place the pattern on top of the folded paper plate and cut along the dotted lines. Make the groundhog and her shadow appear and disappear by folding them up and down. Use the puppet to help you tell the story on this page.

The Valentine Tree

I know a very special tree
That lives among the pines.
It has no leaves upon its boughs—
It just grows valentines.

It grows some pretty red ones,
And others that are blue.
It grows some fancy lace ones
With flowers on them, too.

It grows some little pink ones,
And great big ones of green.
It grows the nicest valentines
That I have ever seen.

One day I walked up to it
And shook that special tree.
Down fell a big red valentine
Especially for me!

*Adapted by Jean Warren
from a story by Marion Schoberlein*

Five Paper Valentines

Have your children help you with the following rhyme by filling in each blank with the appropriate word. Help them gradually learn more and more of the rhyme until they can repeat it all by themselves.

I have five little valentines, not one more.

I'll give one to Mother, and then I'll have _____.

Four paper valentines are all that I see.

I'll give one to Dad, and then I'll have _____.

Three paper valentines all bright and new.

I'll give one to Grandma, and then I'll have _____.

Two paper valentines—this is lots of fun!

I'll give one to Grandpa, and then I'll have just _____.

One paper valentine, and I know what to do.

I'll give my last valentine to no one but _____!

Jean Warren

Thousands of Valentines for Hundreds of Friends

By Susan M. Paprocki

Valentine's Day was not far away. The children in Bobby's class all had ideas about the kinds of valentines they were going to share with their friends, but Bobby had BIG PLANS. He said, "I have thousands of valentines for hundreds of friends!" The other children looked at Bobby. He must be confused, they thought. No one has hundreds of friends. And how do you carry thousands of valentines? After all, the valentines were going to be placed in decorated shoe boxes. And thousands of valentines wouldn't fit in a shoe box. IMPOSSIBLE!

The next two days before the party were busy ones. The children talked about caring, sharing, and friendship as they made their valentines.

"How do we show our friends that we care about them?" asked the teacher.

"By sharing," said Mike.

"And by taking care of them," added Bobby. "On Valentine's Day I'm going to take care of hundreds of friends."

"There he goes again," thought the other children.

Valentine's Day finally arrived. Bobby placed his mysterious box on the table along with the others. The other children looked closely at it and decided it wasn't big enough to hold a thousand valentines. Bobby just smiled. He was the last to share the contents of his decorated box.

"We have to go outside first," Bobby said. The other children and the teacher were puzzled, but they put on their coats and hats and followed Bobby to the schoolyard. Once outside, they watched Bobby as he carefully uncovered his valentine box.

"It's filled with seeds—thousands of seeds!" shouted Becky.

"Why, those seeds are birdseed, children," the teacher explained.

"The birds are my special friends," said Bobby. "It is cold in February, and I can show my friends that I care by giving them food during the cold winter."

Bobby let each child spread some birdseed on the ground. He kept the rest in his valentine box and placed it on the windowsill. He knew that he and the other children would enjoy watching the birds feast on his valentines for many weeks to come. And he had indeed shown that he had thousands of valentines for hundreds of friends. He cared and shared, and that is what Valentine's Day is all about.

Qualities

Play a game with your children by finding objects with different qualities. Name a quality, such as soft, hard, smooth, rough, cold, hot, small, large, empty, or full, and have the children look for something in the room with that quality. Repeat as long as interest lasts.

Rhyming Riddles

Make up rhyming riddles about various objects. Have your children try to guess what the objects are. You may wish to try some of the following examples.

- I am thinking of something that is straight or curly and rhymes with chair. What is it?

- I am thinking of something that is fuzzy and soft and rhymes with hat. What is it?

- I am thinking of something that can sink or float and rhymes with coat. What is it?

Rain Watching

Make a rain gauge by using a permanent felt-tip marker to mark inch measurements on the side of a clear-plastic jar. Place the jar outside. Each day, have your children bring the jar inside to check for rainfall. Keep track of the rainfall on a chart.

Variation: Instead of making a rain gauge, make a snow gauge and keep track of snowfall.

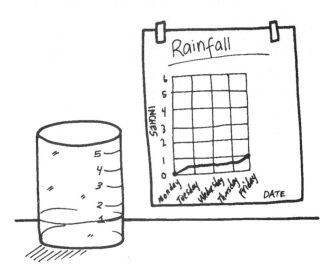

Wind Watching

Hang some ready-made windsocks and wind chimes outside where your children can see them. Let the children watch the windsocks and chimes swing and sway when the wind blows. Can they tell which direction the wind is moving? How hard is the wind blowing?

Storm Watching

Thunder and other sounds associated with storms can be scary for young children. Find a nature tape with storm sounds on it (many libraries have these) or tape-record your own storm. Let your children take turns listening to the tapes. Show the children how to turn the volume down and up so they can make the storm as quiet or as loud as they want.

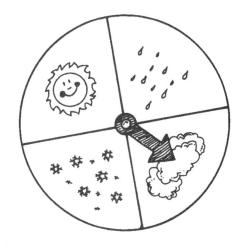

Weather Wheel

Photocopy the weather wheel and arrow patterns on page 68. Glue the weather wheel and arrow to heavy paper and cut them out. If desired, color the wheel and arrow and cover them with clear self-stick paper. Attach the arrow to the wheel by pushing a brass paper fastener through the black dot. Each day, show the wheel to your children and let one of them point the arrow to the picture that represents the day's weather.

Weather Chart

Select a calendar with large squares (or make one yourself). Cut sun, cloud, raindrop, and snowflake shapes out of construction paper. Each day, let one of your children select the appropriate weather shape and attach it to that day's square on the calendar. At the end of the month, help your children make a graph showing the number of cloudy days, sunny days, and so on.

Weather Wear

Collect an assortment of clothes for various kinds of weather. Have three or four of your children dress up in the clothes. (Be sure each child is wearing clothes for one particular kind of weather.) Then have the children show their Weather Wear to the group. Ask the group to guess what kind of weather each child is dressed for.

Listen to Your Heartbeat

Bring in a stethoscope and let your children use it to listen to one another's hearts while sitting quietly. Encourage them to describe the sound the heart makes as it beats. Let them listen to one another's hearts after doing jumping jacks. What differences can they hear in the heartbeats? Talk about how our hearts need both rest and exercise in order to stay healthy and strong.

Which Heart?

Display a picture of a real heart and a picture of a valentine heart. Let your children tell you which kind of heart the following sentences apply to. Make up your own sentences as desired.

- Your heart beats 90 times a minute.

- Mom likes the glitter heart I made for her.

- Your heart keeps blood flowing through your body.

- We give hearts to each other on Valentine's Day.

Healthy Heart Collage

Discuss the importance of eating a variety of foods to make our hearts and bodies grow strong. Then provide each of your children with a drawing of a human heart. Let the children glue magazine pictures of different kinds of foods around the heart drawing.

Variation: Let your children use food stickers or rubber stamps to decorate their papers.

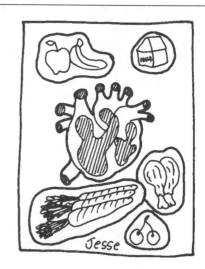

Measuring

Give your children a ruler, a tape measure, or a yardstick and have them measure things in the room. They can measure the floor or the tables. Cut pieces of yarn to match the lengths of different objects around the room. See if the children can figure out which piece of yarn goes with which object.

Scales at Work

Many workers in the community use scales in their work. Gather as many different kinds of scales as you can. Try to find some that measure in ounces only and some that are larger. Have the children guess what kind of object would be appropriate to measure on each scale. Ask the children if they know how much they weighed when they were born. Find things in the classroom that weigh about the same amount to show the children.

Paper Cup Balance

Cut the middle section out of the bottom of a wire coat hanger and discard it. Cover the sharp ends with masking tape. Punch two holes in the rims of each of two paper cups. Attach a 6-inch piece of string to the holes in each of the cups. Hang the cups from the cut ends of the coat hanger and bend up the ends of the hanger to keep the cups from falling off. Place the top of the hanger on one finger and put a small object in each cup. Have the children tell you which item is heavier.

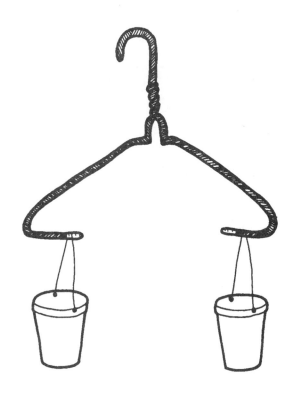

Too Many Valentines

Have your children sit in a circle. Choose one child to start walking around the group as you recite the first two verses of the rhyme. At the end of the second verse, have the child who is walking point to another child to join him or her while you continue with the third and fourth verses. Repeat until everyone is walking around in a circle.

One mail carrier
Walking down the street,
Delivering the mail
And stamping (his/her) feet.

Too many valentines!
What could (he/she) do?
(He/She) called another carrier,
   (Child points to another.)
"Come help, too!"

Two mail carriers
Walking down the street,
Delivering the mail
And stamping their feet.

Too many valentines!
What could they do?
They called another carrier,
"Come help, too!"

Jean Warren

Valentine Mess

Have your children pretend that they are making valentines when all of a sudden, someone opens the door. A gust of wind blows in and knocks over their glue and scatters their valentines. Have them pretend that as they try to pick up their valentines, their feet stick to the floor and their hands stick to whatever they touch. Then ask them questions such as these: "How would you walk? How would it feel to be all stuck together? How would you get unstuck?"

Take a Hike

For each of your children, draw a different kind of line on an index card. (See illustration.) Have your children sit in a row along one side of the room. Shuffle the cards and pass them out face down. When you say "Take a hike!" have the children turn their cards over and walk across the room in the manner suggested by the lines on the cards. When the children have completed their "hikes," collect the cards, reshuffle them, and pass them out again. Keep playing until each child has had a chance to try out several cards.

Shadow Dancing

Arrange a bright light to shine on you so that it will cast your shadow on a wall. Show your children what a clever shadow you have. It does everything you do. Show them how you can make your shadow wave, dance, twirl, and even fall down. Then let the children take turns performing with their shadows individually or as a group. Sing this shadow song with the children while they perform.

Sung to: "Skip to My Lou"

Dance, dance, just like me,
Dance, dance, just like me,
Dance, dance, just like me,
Little shadow, just like me.

Additional verses: Raise your hand; Kick your foot;
Bend way down; Flap your arms.

Jean Warren

I'm a Little Groundhog
Sung to: "I'm a Little Teapot"

I'm a little groundhog fat and brown,
Popping up above the ground.
I sure hope my shadow doesn't show,
For if it does, we'll have more snow.

Diane Thom

Where Is Mr. Groundhog?
Sung to: "Ten Little Indians"

Where, oh, where is Mr. Groundhog?
   (Look all around.)
Where, oh, where is Mr. Groundhog?
Where, oh, where is Mr. Groundhog?
Sleeping in his burrow.
   (Pretend to sleep.)

Shh, he's peeking out his hole,
   (Hold index finger to mouth.)
Shh, he's peeking out his hole,
Shh, he's peeking out his hole —
Now what will he do?

OH, NO!
   (Spoken. Hold hands on either side of head.)
Mr. Groundhog sees his shadow,
Mr. Groundhog sees his shadow,
Mr. Groundhog sees his shadow —
Six more weeks of winter.
   (Hold up six fingers.)

Sally Braun

A Great Man

Sung to: "Twinkle, Twinkle, Little Star"

A great man you ought to know,
Lived a long, long time ago.
Abraham Lincoln, the President,
Gave freedom to each resident.
He made the world a better place
For you and me and the human race.

Carol Metzker

George Washington

Sung to: "Yankee Doodle"

George Washington was the first
President of our country.
The people loved him, one and all,
He worked to make our land free.
He led soldiers, that was hard,
For they were cold and hungry.
He said, "Be brave, now don't give up,
We'll build a brand new country."

Vicki Claybrook

Whose Fine Face?

Sung to: "London Bridge"

Whose fine face is on the penny,
On the penny, on the penny?
Whose fine face is on the penny?
Abraham Lincoln's.

Whose fine face is on the quarter,
On the quarter, on the quarter?
Whose fine face is on the quarter?
George Washington's.

Betty Silkunas

MUSIC • Songs About Love

I Love You

Sung to: "London Bridge"

Annie, Annie, I love you.
Yes, it's true, I love you.
Annie, Annie, I love you.
Yes, I do.

Substitute the name of one of your children for Annie.

Jean Warren

Love, Love, Love

Sung to: "Three Blind Mice"

Love, love, love; love, love, love.
See how it grows, see how it grows.
I love my friends and they love me.
We love others and then, you see,
There's more than enough for a family
Of love, love, love.

Betty Swyers

Write a Letter

Sung to: "A-Tisket, A-Tasket"

I love you, I love you.
This is what I must do—
Write a letter to you, love,
And tell you that I love you!

Jean Warren

Valentine's Day Songs • MUSIC

A Valentine Song for You
Sung to: "If You're Happy and You Know It"

Oh, this Valentine's Day song is just for you.

I don't need crayons, scissors, tape, or glue.

Yes, this little song I'll sing,

Hugs and kisses it will bring.

Oh, this Valentine's Day song is just for you!

Becky Valenick

Three Valentines
Sung to: "Mary Had a Little Lamb"

Three valentines I have for you,

Have for you, have for you.

Three valentines I have for you,

Pink and red and blue.

I'll put them in the mail for you,

Mail for you, mail for you.

I'll put them in the mail for you,

Pink and red and blue.

Gayle Bittinger

I'm a Little Valentine
Sung to: "I'm a Little Teapot"

I'm a little valentine,

Red and white.

With ribbons and lace,

I'm a beautiful sight.

I can say "I love you"

On Valentine's Day.

Just put me in an envelope

And give me away!

Vicki Claybrook

Creating the Environment

Most early childhood professionals are committed to creating an environment where boys and girls are treated equally and all children are encouraged to reach their full potential. But what can you do when your girls won't go near the block area, or a boy is taunted when he plays with a doll? Here are some ways to help your boys and girls feel equally welcome, challenged, and inspired in all areas of your room.

Speaking With Your Children

- Ask for a big, strong child, not a boy, when you need help.

- When you notice boys playing in nurturing ways, make a positive comment such as this: "Sam, what a gentle daddy you are." Similarly, commend girls for playing in nontraditional ways with a comment like this: "Laurel really knows how to use that dump truck to build roads."

- Make sure you use gender-neutral terms, such as firefighter, flight attendant, and police officer, instead of fireman, stewardess, or policeman.

- Listen for opportunities to correct stereotypical comments. For example, if a child says, "Look! Joey is playing with dolls just like a girl," you might gently respond, "Our bodies make us boys or girls, men or women—not what we do. Both boys and girls play with dolls."

In Your Room

- Avoid pink for girls and blue for boys in decorations and crafts. Instead, let your children choose the colors.

- If you hang name tags or birthday markers, try to use shapes or real photographs to represent your children instead of stereotypical boy- and girl-shaped patterns.

- Display artwork, posters, and pictures of men and women in nontraditional jobs and roles, such as male nurses, caregivers, and housekeepers and female firefighters, sanitation workers, and construction workers.

- Occasionally, try conducting "boys only" cooking projects or "girls only" woodworking activities.

- Make sure all children have opportunities to perform all classroom jobs.

Make the Housekeeping Area More Inviting to Boys

- Refrain from calling it the "kitchen" or "doll" area. Instead, you might use the terms "housekeeping" and "dramatic play" area.

- Include boys' dress-up clothes and props along with girls' costumes. Provide both male and female dolls.

- Change the area every few months to inspire all children to come and play. You might try setting up an office, a hospital, or a carwash.

Encourage Girls in the Block Area

- Add materials such as scarves, dolls, and pillows.

- Try a "girls only" block time.

- Invite female carpenters, builders, or architects to talk with your children.

Shadow Pictures

Let each of your children take a sheet of white construction paper to an outside area. Have the children hold their papers behind leaves or grass to create shadow pictures with the help of the sun. Because the pictures last only a moment, have the children work in pairs and share shadow creations with their partners.

Shadow Puppets

Cut animal shapes out of posterboard. Attach the shapes to tongue depressors. Shine a light on a wall and let the children move their puppets in front of the light. Show them how to make smaller shadows by standing farther back from the wall. Then let them use their shadow puppets to act out the movements described in the following poem.

There is a little shadow
That dances on my wall.
Sometimes it's big and scary.
Sometimes it's very small.

Sometimes it's, oh, so quiet
And doesn't move at all.
Then other times it chases me
Or bounces like a ball.

I'd love to meet that shadow
Who dances in the night.
But it always runs away
In the morning light.

Jean Warren

Shadow Poem

Write the initial letters of the lines in the following poem on separate squares of paper. Back the squares with felt strips. Then place the letters on a flannelboard to spell "SHADOW" as you read the poem to your children.

Sun is shining, let's go for a walk.

Hurry outside and around the block.

At your side there's a little friend, too.

Does the very same things you do.

Open the door and go inside—

Where, oh, where does my shadow friend hide?

Mildred Hoffman

Shadow Line-Up

Have your children go outside on a sunny day. Have them line up and see if they can identify their shadows. Ask questions such as these: "Can you spot your own shadow? How can you tell it's yours? What causes shadows?"

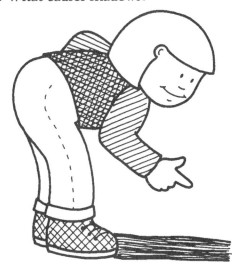

Shadow, Shadow

Sung to: "Twinkle, Twinkle, Little Star"

Shadow, shadow, you are fun.
   (Clap.)
I see you when there's light or sun.
Long in the morning and afternoon,
   (Stand tall.)
Short in the middle of the day, at noon.
   (Crouch down.)
Shadow, shadow, that is you.
When it's dark, oh, where are you?
   (Look around.)

Shadow, shadow, you are fun.
   (Clap.)
I like to see you jump and run.
   (Jump; then jog in place.)
You follow me wherever I go,
On the grass or on the snow.
Shadow, shadow, who are you?
   (Hold palms up.)
I would like to play with you.

Diane Thom

Three-Cornered Hats

Let your children make three-cornered hats to wear for Washington's birthday. For each child, cut a sheet of 9-by-12-inch blue construction paper into three 9-by-4-inch strips. Have the children decorate their strips by gluing on white stars and red circle "cherries" cut from construction paper. Help them add stems to their cherries with a felt-tip marker. Then staple the short ends of each child's strips together as shown in the illustration.

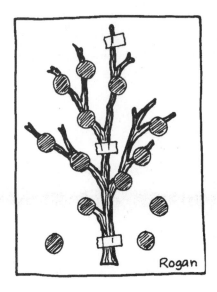

Washington Cherry Trees

For each of your children, glue or tape a twig "tree" to a sheet of white construction paper. Give the children red self-stick dots to use for cherries. Then let them attach the dots to their papers, some growing on the tree branches and some falling off.

Silver Dollar Toss

Let your children act out the legend about George Washington throwing a silver dollar across the Potomac River. Make "silver dollars" by cutting circles out of heavy cardboard and covering them with aluminum foil. Place two pieces of blue yarn several feet apart on the floor for a river. Then let the children take turns tossing the dollars across the river into a plastic dishpan or other container. Count the number of dollars in the container after each round of the game.

Hint: Make the river wider or narrower depending on the ages and abilities of your children.

Log Cabin Game

On a piece of posterboard, trace around a tongue depressor to create a cabin made of six logs. Number the logs from 1 to 6 as shown in the illustration. Select six tongue depressors and number them from 1 to 6 by drawing on sets of dots. Then let your children take turns placing the tongue depressors on top of the matching numbered logs on the gameboard.

Under Lincoln's Hat

Have a black top hat (or decorate a cylindrical oatmeal box to look like one) and five or six small toys or objects ready. Have your children sit in a circle. Place the objects in the middle of the circle and have the children name each one. Then have the children close their eyes as you hide one of the objects under the hat. When the children open their eyes, have them try to guess which object is under Lincoln's hat. Let the child who first guesses correctly hide a different object under the hat for the next round of the game. Repeat as long as interest lasts.

Storytime Fun

Select a variety of familiar picture books to set out at storytime. Talk with the children about how young Abe Lincoln liked to stay up late at night reading by the light of the fire. Explain that he said he loved books because he could always learn new things from them. Encourage the children to tell about their favorite books or stories. Can they find picture books among those you set out that have helped them learn new things? Let the children choose one of the books they think that young Abraham Lincoln might have liked. Then read the book aloud for Abe on his birthday.

Weather Wheel Pattern

Refer to page 53 for directions.

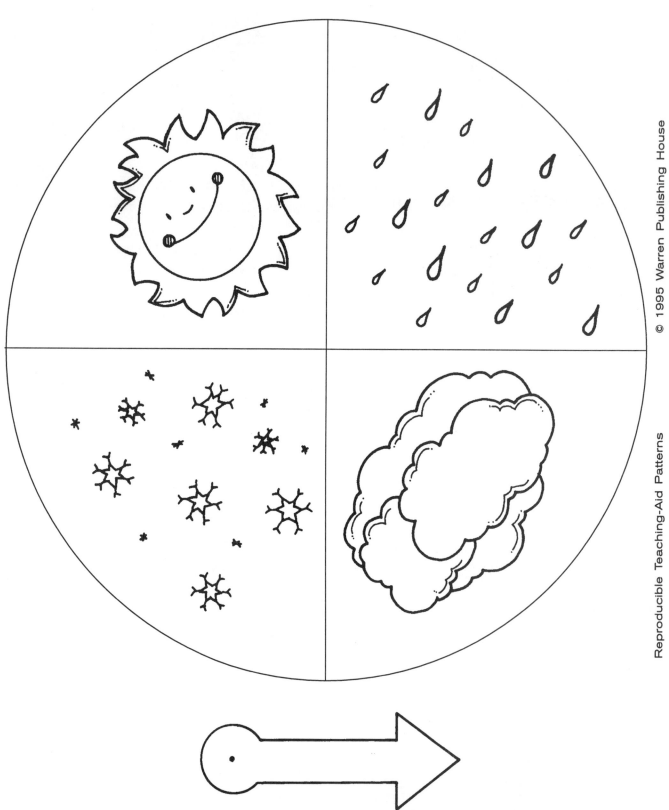

Groundhog Puppet

Refer to page 48 for directions.

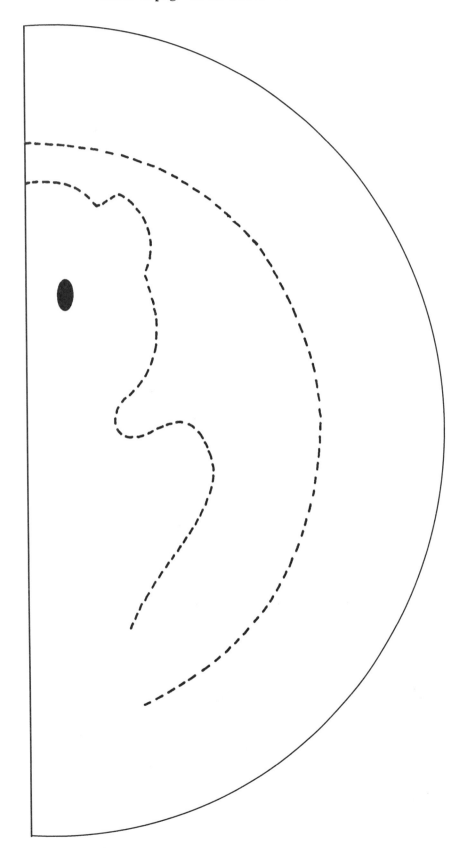

March

Windsocks

Cut cardboard into 1-by-18-inch strips. Bend each strip into a circle and securely tape it in place. Cut crepe paper into strips about 2 feet long. Give each of your children one of the cardboard circles. Let the children tape the crepe paper strips around their circles so the strips all hang down one side. To complete each Windsock, punch two holes in the cardboard circle opposite each other and tie a 3-foot piece of yarn through them. Hang the Windsocks in a windy area and let the children watch the wind make their crepe paper strips dance and sway. Or let the children run outside with their Windsocks floating behind them.

Wind Art

Take your children outside on a windy day. Give each child a piece of construction paper with a few drops of tempera paint on it. Have the children hold their papers up and let the wind blow the paint into designs.

Mrs. Wind

Give each of your children a piece of construction paper. Have the children use crayons to draw pictures on their papers of what they think Mrs. Wind looks like. Then have each child use a small brush to paint glue coming out of Mrs. Wind's mouth. Help the child sprinkle glitter, sand, or salt onto the glue and shake off the excess.

Rudy

Wallpaper Hats

For each hat, you will need two 20-inch squares of wallpaper. Let each of your children select one of the squares. Have the children use small brushes to spread glue all over the backs of their wallpaper squares. Then have them each choose a second square. Help each child place his or her second square on top of the first, backs together. Show the children how to press their squares together from the centers out, to squeeze out any excess glue. One at a time, have the children stand in front of a mirror and place their squares on top of their heads. Help them shape their squares into fancy hats. Tie a string around the band of each hat to help it keep its shape. Remove the hats from the children's heads and let them dry. When the hats are dry, remove the strings and cut the brims of the hats into the desired shapes. Set out flowers, ribbons, fabric scraps, lace, and bows and let the children decorate their hats.

Milk Jug Hats

Clean and dry an empty plastic gallon milk jug for each of your children. Cut off the bottom half of each milk jug and give one to each child. (Save the tops of the jugs to use as funnels at the sand or water table.) Let the children decorate their milk jugs with felt-tip markers, stickers, or colored glue. You may wish to punch holes around the edges of the milk jugs and let the children lace yarn through the holes.

Shamrock Puzzle Mural

Cut a giant shamrock shape out of posterboard. Then cut the shape into puzzle pieces, one piece for each of your children. Put a mark on the back of each puzzle piece with a felt-tip marker. Set out small green squares of construction paper or tissue paper, containers of glue, and cotton swabs. Give each child a puzzle piece. Have the children use the cotton swabs to spread glue all over the unmarked sides of their puzzle pieces. Then have them cover the glue with the green paper squares to create mosaic designs. After the glue has dried, put the shamrock puzzle together on a wall or a bulletin board and add a St. Patrick's Day greeting.

Pot of Gold Mural

Collect construction paper in the rainbow colors (red, orange, yellow, green, blue, and purple). Cut many 1-by-9-inch strips out of each color. Hang butcher paper on a wall or a bulletin board. Cut a pot shape out of black posterboard and attach it to one corner of the butcher paper. Show the children how to tape the ends of the construction paper strips together to make paper chains. Then have each child select paper strips of one color and make a chain with them. Attach the paper chains to the butcher paper to make a rainbow shape that ends in the "pot of gold." Add a construction paper leprechaun shape and construction paper shamrock shapes to the mural, if you wish.

Art Paper

Let your children use crayons, pencils, chalk, and fingerpaint on pieces of wallpaper. Encourage the children to experiment and explore the effects of the various drawing tools on different wallpaper surfaces.

Texture Collages

Cut wallpaper of various textures into small pieces. Let your children glue the wallpaper pieces on construction paper to make Texture Collages.

Rubbings

Place smooth-surfaced sheets of wallpaper over textured surfaces such as a sidewalk, the side of a building, bricks, carved wood, or leaves. Let your children rub the paper with crayons, pencils, or chalk to create textured designs.

Artwork Placemats

Mount your children's drawings directly on pieces of wallpaper. Or use a craft knife to cut frames out of the wallpaper pieces. Mount the drawings on the backs so that they show through the frames. Cover the artwork and wallpaper with clear self-stick paper. Let the children use their Artwork Placemats at snacktime.

LEARNING GAMES • Nature Games

The Shape of Nature

Let your children collect twigs and blades of grass. Show them how to use the twigs and grass to form squares, triangles, rectangles, and circles.

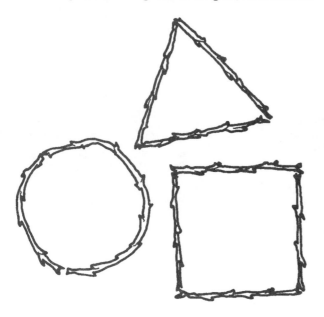

Counting Nature

Set out three different flowers and ask your children to guess which one has more petals. Then let the children count the petals of each flower.

How Big Is Nature?

Collect a variety of measuring tools such as a yardstick, a retractable tape measure, a collapsible carpenter's measure, fabric tapes, and several rulers. Let your children use the tools to measure things like sticks, tree trunks, leaves, and flower stems. Let them decide which measuring tools work better than others on certain things. Then ask them what they measured and which tool worked best.

Leprechaun Math • LEARNING GAMES

Counting Gold

Collect several small rocks. Spray paint the rocks gold in a well-ventilated room away from your children. Allow the paint to dry. Place some of the "gold" pieces in a pot. Have the children guess how many gold pieces are in the pot. Then have them count the pieces of gold. Repeat with a different number of gold pieces.

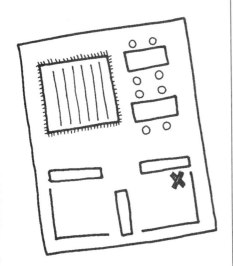

Finding the Gold

Draw a simple map of your room on a piece of paper. In your room, hide the pot of gold from the Counting Gold activity on this page. Put an X on the map at the spot where the gold is hidden. Give the map to two or three of your children and let them work together to find the pot of gold.

Weighing Gold

Collect a variety of sizes and shapes of rocks. Spray paint the rocks gold in a well-ventilated room away from your children. Allow the paint to dry. Set out the pieces of "gold" and a scale. Let your children take turns weighing the gold. Help them read the numbers on the scale as needed.

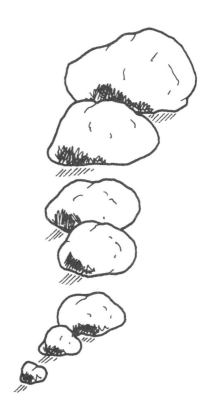

Sizing Up Gold

Set out the rocks from the Weighing Gold activity on this page. Have your children arrange the gold pieces in order from small to large.

Number Kites

Cut five large kite shapes out of felt. Cut the numerals 1 through 5 out of felt. Glue a different numeral to each kite shape. Attach a yarn tail to each kite and place the kites on a flannelboard. Cut 15 bow shapes out of felt. Show your children the kites. Help them identify the numbers on the kites and place the appropriate number of bows on each yarn tail.

Shamrock Search

Collect three or four coffee cans. Cover each one with a different color of construction paper. Cut several shamrock shapes out of each color of paper. Hide the shapes around the room. Let your children hunt for the shamrock shapes. When they find the shapes, have your children put them into the matching colored coffee cans.

Hat Sort

Set out a variety of hats. Look at the hats with your children and talk about how they are alike and different. Have them guess when or why each hat is worn. Put the hats into a large box. Let the children take turns deciding how to sort them. For example, the hats could be sorted according to the season they are worn in; if they are worn for work or for play; if they are worn by children or adults; or by color.

Color Flannelboard

Cut shapes, such as fish, hearts, stars, and kites, out of red, yellow, and blue felt. Ask your children to place just the red shapes, just the yellow shapes, or just the blue shapes on a flannelboard. Or place different colored shapes on the flannelboard and ask the children to place matching colored shapes next to them.

Flannelboard Positions

Cut a rectangle and a circle out of different colors of felt. Place the rectangle on a flannelboard and put the circle above it. Ask your children to describe the positions of the shapes by saying sentences such as these: "The rectangle is under the circle," or "The circle is above the rectangle." Rearrange the shapes and have the children describe their positions again.

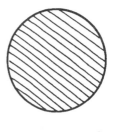

Number Flannelboard

Cut the numerals 1 through 5 out of felt. Ask your children to line up the numerals on a flannelboard in the correct sequence. Or place sets of felt shapes (three stars, two diamonds, etc.) on the flannelboard and ask the children to place the corresponding numerals next to them.

When March Hats Blow

When I hear March winds blow,
I look up in the sky.
Instead of things like birds or planes,
I watch the hats fly by.

Each one different from the last,
Every color do I see.
Some are big and some are small,
As they fly by me.

Here comes a blue hat flying by,
Now a yellow hat in the sky.
Next a red hat on its way,
Then a brown hat flies away.

Green and black, orange and white,
Even purple—what a sight!
I like it when there's rain and snow,
But most of all when March hats blow.

Jean Warren

Cloud Story

As you read the following story, let your children fill in the blanks.

Puffy clouds floating by, making pictures in the sky.
The big one looks like a _____.
The one over there makes me hungry,
Because it looks like _____.
The next one is as round as a _____.
That one looks like a stuffed _____.
The one I like best looks like _____.
Puffy clouds floating by, making pictures in the sky.

Jean Warren

Wind Tricks

Photocopy the flannelboard patterns on page 100. Cut out the patterns. Color the patterns and cover them with clear self-stick paper, if desired. Attach a piece of felt to the back of each pattern. Cut a hill shape out of felt. Arrange the patterns on a flannelboard. As you recite the following rhyme to your children, move the patterns accordingly.

The wind was full of tricks today.
It blew my brother's hat away.
It made the trees bend and dance.
It made the leaves twirl and prance.
It chased our paper down the street.
It almost blew me off my feet!

Adapted Traditional

Five Little Leprechauns

Photocopy the flannelboard patterns on page 101. Cut out the patterns. Color the patterns and cover them with clear self-stick paper, if desired. Attach a piece of felt to the back of each pattern. Arrange the figures on a flannelboard. As you read the rhyme to your children, move the figures accordingly.

One day out walking,
I happened to see
Five little leprechauns
Coming toward me.

They ran to a house.
They ran through the door.
I managed to catch one.
Then there were four.

Four little leprechauns
Climbed up a tree.
I caught another.
Then there were three.

Three little leprechauns
Hid in a shoe.
I caught another.
Then there were two.

Two little leprechauns
Started to run.
I caught another.
Then there was one.

One little leprechaun
Ran to his gold.
He grabbed some coins—
Then stepped out bold.

"Give back my friends,
   And I'll give you this gold."
So I set them all free.
Now my story is told!

Jean Warren

Five Umbrellas

Five umbrellas stood by the back door.
The red one went outside—then there were four.

Four umbrellas pretty as can be.
The blue one went outside—then there were three.

Three umbrellas with nothing to do.
The green one went outside—then there were two.

Two umbrellas not having much fun.
The yellow one went outside—then there was one.

Just one umbrella alone in the hall.
The purple one went outside—and that was all!

Jean Warren

One Little Daffodil

One little daffodil had nothing much to do.
Out popped another one—then there were two.

Two little daffodils were smiling at a bee.
Out popped another one—then there were three.

Three little daffodils were growing by the door.
Out popped another one—then there were four.

Four little daffodils were glad to be alive.
Out popped another one—then there were five.

Five little daffodils were wearing golden crowns.
They danced in the breeze in green satin gowns.

Jean Warren

Mother Nature's Gift

A Native American Folktale Adapted by Jean Warren

One day while Mother Nature was out working in her garden, she heard the sound of angry voices. It was two of her children, the Sun and the Rain, arguing about which one of them was most important.

"I am the most important!" shouted the Sun. "Without me nothing would grow!"

"No, I am most important!" shouted the Rain. "Without me nothing would grow!"

Back and forth they argued, each one sure that he was more important than the other.

At last Mother Nature grew tired of listening to them quarrel. To teach them a lesson, she sent the Sun to one side of the world and the Rain to the other side.

Soon there was peace and quiet again, and Mother Nature went back to her work. At first, the Sun and the Rain didn't like being separated. But then they decided that this would be the perfect chance to prove which one of them was most important.

Day after day, the Sun shone down on one side of the world while the Rain poured down on the other. Before long the land on the Sun's side was dry and bare, and on the Rain's side there were terrible floods.

When the Sun and the Rain realized what they had done, they were sorry. They went back to Mother Nature and apologized. "We know now that neither of us is more important than the other," they said. "We need each other, and the world needs both of us to help the plants and animals grow."

Mother Nature was happy that the Sun and the Rain had learned their lesson. To celebrate, she decided to give the world a special gift.

Across the sky she painted an arc of beautiful colors—red, orange, yellow, green, blue, and purple. "The world needs both my children, the Sun and the Rain," she said. "Whenever they decide to visit the world at the same time, this arc will appear in the sky. When the world sees the rainbow, it will know that my children are happy working together."

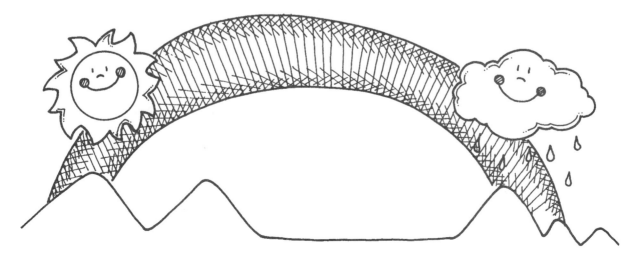

Wind Experiments

On a windy day, let your children go outside and experiment with the wind. Take out several pairs of objects such as a piece of paper and a book, a leaf and a tree branch, and a balloon and a ball. Ask the children why the wind moves some of the things but not the others. Let the children observe the weight of objects compared to the strength of the wind.

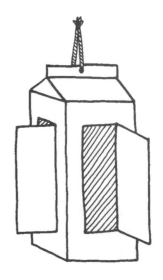

Wind Catchers

For each of your children, collect a cardboard milk carton. Cut off the bottom of each carton and cut a "door" in each side. (Make sure the doors open in the same direction.) Fold the doors of each carton open and let your children paint the cartons with a mixture of powdered tempera paint and liquid soap. Punch a hole in the top of each carton and tie a piece of string through it. Hang the finished Wind Catchers outside and watch them twirl.

Bag Kites

Have your children make beautiful kites to fly on a windy day. Provide each child with a small paper bag. Let the children decorate their bags with crayons or felt-tip markers. Punch a hole on the top side of each bag near the opening and tie a piece of yarn through the hole. (You may wish to reinforce the hole with tape.) Show your children how the kites will fill with air and fly up and down when the children run with them.

The Story of Purim

The Jewish holiday, Purim, usually falls on a day in mid-March. On Purim Eve in synagogues, the story of Purim is read aloud in Hebrew from a parchment scroll called a *Megillah*. The story, which is believed to have taken place around 400 B.C., tells about Haman and his plot to destroy all the Jews in Persia, and how they were saved by Queen Esther. On Purim, children often dress up in brightly colored costumes and go to the friends' and relatives' homes to deliver a *Shalach Manot*, a package filled with fruit, candy, and *Hamentashen* (a special three-cornered cake). Celebrate Purim with your children by dressing up in costumes, reading the Purim story, and doing the activities that follow.

Purim Masks

Make a mask for each of your children by cutting eye, nose, and mouth holes out of a paper plate. Let the children decorate their masks with felt-tip markers. Then let them glue on materials such as colored paper scraps, yarn, sequins, and glitter. When the glue has dried, attach the bottom part of each mask to a paper headband that fits around the child's forehead, making sure the chin of the mask is above the child's eyes. (Masks worn this way will not interfere with the children's vision or breathing.)

Noisy Fun

Fold a paper plate in half. Place a small amount of rice, gravel, or dried beans in the center of each plate. Securely fasten the edges together. Make one of these noisemakers for each of your children. Let the children decorate the plates with crayons, paint, felt-tip markers, or glued-on paper shapes. If desired, read the story of Purim to the children and have them follow the traditional custom of shaking their noisemakers whenever they hear Haman's name.

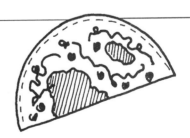

Extension: Have your children shake their noisemakers and wear their masks as they march in a Purim parade around the room.

Places People Live

Collage of Homes

Hang a piece of butcher paper on a wall at your children's eye level. Title the paper "Places People Live." Have the children look through magazines and newspapers to find pictures of different kinds of homes (houses, apartments, condominiums, trailers, houseboats, tents, etc.). Let them tear or cut out the pictures and glue them to the butcher paper any way they wish, to create a group collage. Encourage the children to talk about the different kinds of homes pictured in their collage as they are working.

Variation: Let younger children choose from precut pictures of homes that have been placed in a box.

Homes

Ask one child at a time to tell where he or she lives (in a house, an apartment, a mobile home, etc.). Then recite the following poem for the child, substituting his or her name for *Matthew* and a description of where he or she lives for *in a house.*

A squirrel lives in a tree,
  (*Make tree shape with hands.*)
A snail lives in a shell.
  (*Cover fist with opposite hand.*)
A bear lives in a cave,
  (*Make fist with thumb inside.*)
It suits her very well.

A fish lives in a fishbowl,
  (*Make circle with hands.*)
A bird lives in a nest.
  (*Cup hands together.*)
Matthew lives in a house,
  (*Make roof above head with arms.*)
He thinks his home is best.

Elizabeth McKinnon

Building a House

Sung to: "Twinkle, Twinkle, Little Star"

Building a house is lots of work.

First, you dig up lots of dirt.
    (Pretend to dig.)

Next, you pour a concrete floor,
    (Touch floor.)

Put up boards, and pound nails galore.
    (Pretend to hammer.)

Finally, the house is finished,
    (Clasp both hands together.)

And people are ready to live in it.

Diane Thom

I Know My Address

Encourage the children to learn their own addresses by doing the following activities.

- Play games in which the children must say their addresses. For example, have them pretend to order pizzas to be delivered to their homes. Or have them pretend to be lost and tell a "police officer" where they live.

- Write each child's address on a separate piece of paper and cover it with clear self-stick paper. Let the child trace over his or her address with a finger or a crayon while saying the address aloud. (Have the child erase the crayon marks by rubbing them with a dry facial tissue.)

- When a child has learned to say his or her address, write it on a plain postcard (or a large index card) that the child has decorated. Add a short note, if desired. Then mail the card so that the child will receive it at home as a special acknowledgment.

MOVEMENT · Windy Day Fun

Windy Scarves

Let each of your children experiment with a scarf. First ask the children to wrap their scarves around themselves like skirts and twirl across the room. Next have them run with their scarves tied around their shoulders like capes. Then tell the children that the scarves represent the wind. Have them use their scarves to show you gentle breezes, sudden gusts, gale winds, and tornadoes.

Storm Winds

Have your children pretend that a big wind-storm has hit in the play area. Tell them that they are getting tossed around in the wind, drenched in the rain, and knocked over by sudden gusts. Then tell them that an unexpected tornado is coming that will send them spinning far away. Have the children tell you where the tornado takes them.

Jack-in-the-Box

Show your children a jack-in-the-box. Play the music until the clown pops up. Then have the children pretend to be jack-in-the-boxes. Have them crouch down low while you recite the following rhyme. When they hear the word "Pop!" have them jump up.

Jack, Jack, down you go,
Down in your box, down so low.
Jack, Jack, there goes the top,
Quickly now, up you pop!

Author Unknown

Partner Switch

Help each of your children find a partner. Play some music and have the children perform an action, such as hopping, dancing, or skipping, with their partners. You might want to call out actions such as these: "Partners march! Partners spin! Partners tiptoe!" Or you can let the children choose their own actions. Each time you stop the music, help the children find new partners.

MUSIC • Songs for Windy Days

When I Look Into the Sky
Sung to: "Twinkle, Twinkle, Little Star"

When I look into the sky,
I can see the clouds go by.
They don't ever make a sound,
Letting wind push them around.
Some go fast and some go slow.
I wonder where the clouds all go.

Frank Dally

Come Fly a Kite
Sung to: "On Top of Old Smokey"

Oh, come fly a kite,
Way up in the sky.
Watch it climb so far
Up, up in the sky.

Oh, come fly a kite,
And just watch it sail.
Across the sky,
Waving its tail.

Jean Warren

I See the Wind
Sung to: "The Mulberry Bush"

I see the wind when the leaves dance by,
I see the wind when the clothes wave, "Hi!"
I see the wind when the trees bend low,
I see the wind when the flags all blow.

I see the wind when the kites fly high,
I see the wind when the clouds float by.
I see the wind when it blows my hair,
I see the wind most everywhere!

Jean Warren

Blow, Blow, Blow the Wind
Sung to: "Row, Row, Row Your Boat"

Blow, blow, blow the wind
Gently through the trees.
Blow, and blow, and blow, and blow.
How I like a breeze!

Blow, blow, blow the clouds,
Blow them through the sky.
Blow, and blow, and blow, and blow.
Watch the clouds roll by!

Diane Thom

March Winds Blow
Sung to: "Twinkle, Twinkle, Little Star"

March winds blow the kites around,
Blow them right up off the ground.
March means spring is almost here,
Sounds of birds you soon will hear.
Watch the leaves sprout on the trees,
Soon you'll see some honeybees.

Barbara B. Fleisher

Sing a Song of Springtime
Sung to: "Sing a Song of Sixpence"

Sing a song of springtime,
Sunshine fills the sky.
See the little bluebirds,
As they fly on by.
Look at all the flowers
Blooming pink and blue.
What a pretty time to sit
And watch things start anew.

Kathleen Cubley

Here Comes Spring
Sung to: "Three Blind Mice"

Here comes spring, here comes spring.
Bells will ring, children sing.
New plants are shooting from the ground,
Blossoms on the trees abound,
The earth awakens all around,
Here comes spring.

Jean Warren

Spring Colors
Sung to: "Happy Birthday"

The clouds are white.
  (Point up to the sky.)
The sky is blue.
The grass is green,
  (Pretend to touch grass.)
As spring comes anew.

The yellow daffodils
  (Crouch down and cover face with hands.)
Bloom from the earth.
  (Rise, uncover face, and lift arms.)
The little worm wiggles
  (Wiggle like a worm.)
Under the brown dirt.

The red ladybug
Will fly to and fro.
  (Flap elbows like ladybug's wings.)
She's happy to see
All the snow and frost go.
  (Smile and wave goodbye.)

Diane Thom

I'm a Little Shamrock
Sung to: "I'm a Little Teapot"

I'm a little shamrock, see my leaves.
Count my three petals, if you please.
If you give me water and lots of sun,
I'll bring you good luck and lots of fun!

Janice Bodenstedt

I'm a Little Leprechaun
Sung to: "I'm a Little Teapot"

I'm a little leprechaun,
Short and green.
I live under toadstools,
And I've never been seen!
If you follow a rainbow
To a pot of gold,
Your luck will change,
So I've been told.

Debbie Monts de Oca

Lucky the Leprechaun
Sung to: "Frosty the Snowman"

Lucky the leprechaun
Was the cutest elf I'd seen.
With a bright red hat
And two pointed ears
And a suit of velvet green.

Lucky the leprechaun
Found a pot one fine spring day.
It was filled with gold,
And so I'm told,
Lucky got his name that day.

There must have been real magic in
That old black pot he found,
For when he looked inside of it,
He began to dance around!

Lucky the leprechaun
Loved to dance and sing and play.
And he shared his gold
With the young and old,
For he knew his luck would stay.

Encourage your children to act out the song as you sing it.

Jean Warren

Worm Track Prints

Let your children dip 6-inch pieces of string into brown tempera paint and then pull the strings across sheets of construction paper to make "worm tracks." Encourage them to make their strings crawl and wiggle like real worms.

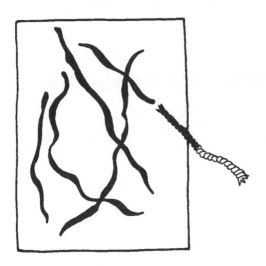

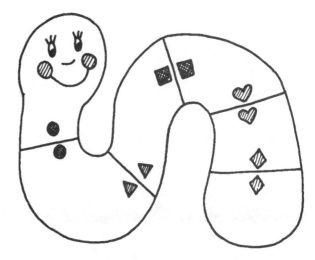

Worm Puzzle

Cut a large, curvy worm shape out of heavy paper. Cut the shape into six sections to make a Worm Puzzle. To help your children put the puzzle together, glue or draw matching shapes, colors, or numbers on either side of each cut line. Cover the puzzle pieces with clear self-stick paper for durability, if desired.

Worm Finger Puppets

Set out small paper cups and sheets of brown tissue paper or construction paper. Help each of your children make a finger-size hole in the bottom of one of the cups. Then let the children tear the brown paper into tiny pieces and fill their cup half full. To work their puppets, have the children hold their cup in one hand and stick the index fingers of their other hand up through the hole and brown paper "dirt." Have them wiggle their finger like a worm.

Observing Earthworms

Place an earthworm on top of some soil and let your children watch what it does. How does the earthworm move? What color is it? What does its skin look and feel like? What do you suppose the worm does in the soil? Explain that an earthworm hatches from an egg that is inside a cocoon in the soil. The worm is very tiny when it is born, and many worms hatch from one cocoon. The only facial feature an earthworm has is a mouth through which soil (an earthworm's food) enters. Little piles of an earthworm's used, or digested, soil can be found near the opening of the worm's tunnel. These are called castings.

Earthworm Hunt

Take your children on a nature walk to search for earthworms. Beforehand, locate a garden or compost pile where there are many worms, or "seed" a small prepared area with worms you have found in other places. (If necessary, check with a sporting goods store to find out where earthworms can be purchased in your area.) When you reach your selected site, use a spade to turn over the soil and let the children look for worms. Put the worms into a plastic container with enough damp soil to cover them. Then take them back to your room to observe earthworms in the Observing Earthworms activity on this page.

National Peanut Month

March is National Peanut Month, a time to honor the peanut and its most popular product, peanut butter. Besides celebrating with the following activities, you might want to plan a few peanut games. For example, why not have a peanut toss or a peanut hunt? Or have a peanut race and let your children push peanuts across the floor with their toes. Follow up by providing handfuls of peanuts for counting, shelling, and tasting.

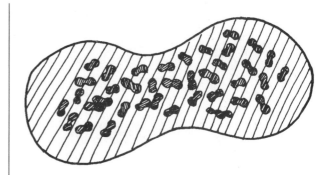

Peanut Shell Collages

Plan this activity at the end of your celebration to recycle the peanut shells saved from other activities. Cut peanut shapes out of heavy brown grocery bags or brown construction paper. Pour glue into shallow containers and set out bowls of peanut shells. Let your children dip the shells into the glue, rounded sides up, and place them all over their peanut shapes to create collages.

The Peanut Plant

Up through the ground the peanut plant grows,
  (Crouch down near floor.)

Peeking out its little, green nose.
  (Slowly start to rise.)

Reaching, reaching for the sky,
  (Raise arms above head.)

Growing, growing, growing high.
  (Stand on tiptoes.)

Then the flower starts to grow,
  (Make circle with arms.)

But it doesn't grow up, not it, oh no.
  (Shake head.)

Down it goes, sending shoots underground,
  (Bend over and touch floor with fingers.)

And there grow the peanuts, plump and round!
  (Kneel and pretend to dig up peanuts.)

Author Unknown

Peanut Number Game

Number five containers from 1 to 5. Place them on a table along with a basket containing 15 peanuts. Let your children take turns placing the appropriate number of peanuts in each container.

Peanut Butter

Let your children help shell a package of unsalted, roasted peanuts. Then help them grind the peanuts in a food grinder. Mix the ground nuts with some softened margarine or butter and add salt to taste. Serve on crackers, apple slices, or celery sticks. Or for a special treat, spread on slices of whole-wheat toast and top with warm applesauce.

Peanut Butter

Sung to: "Frère Jacques"

Peanut butter, peanut butter,
Good for you. Fun to chew.
Put peanuts in a blender,
Add a little oil.
Let it whirl. Let it swirl.

Peanut butter, peanut butter,
Now it's done. Oh, what fun!
Spread it on a sandwich.
Spread it on a cracker.
Good for you. Fun to chew.

Susan Peters

Mary Had a Little Lamb

Mary had a little lamb,
Its fleece was white as snow.
And everywhere that Mary went,
The lamb was sure to go.

It followed her to school one day,
Which was against the rule.
It made the children laugh and play
To see a lamb at school.

Traditional

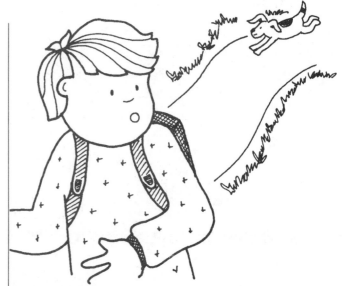

Pet Questions

Discuss with your children what they would do if their pets followed them to school. Ask them questions such as these: "Where would your pet wait for you? What would you do if your pet wanted to play? When would your pet eat?"

Cotton Ball Lambs

For each of your children, cut a lamb shape out of white posterboard or lightweight cardboard. Have your children use black felt-tip markers to draw facial features on their lamb shapes. Then let them glue cotton balls all over the bodies of the lambs to make "fleece as white as snow." When the glue has dried, clip two spring-type clothespins onto the bottom of each shape to make legs for the fluffy lambs to stand on.

Follow the Leader

Use the rhyme "Mary Had a Little Lamb" as a transitional song. Let your children take turns being Mary and have the rest of the children follow him or her out to play, to snack, or to circle time.

A Lamb at School

Sung to: "Little White Duck"

There's a little white lamb
Who goes to school each day.
A little white lamb
Who likes to work and play.
Watch him nibble all the books,
And in each lunch he will surely look.
There's a little white lamb
Who goes to school each day.
Baa, baa, baa.

Jean Warren

Salad Lambs

To make each Salad Lamb, place a mound of cottage cheese in the middle of a small plate. Flatten it with the back of a spoon and make a hollow in the center for the lamb's face. Let each of your children add two raisins for eyes and a red grape or a cherry tomato half for a nose to complete his or her salad.

"Wind Tricks" Flannelboard Patterns

Refer to page 81 for directions.

"Five Little Leprechauns" Patterns
Refer to page 81 for directions.

April

Rain Painting

On a rainy day, give each of your children a paper plate. Let the children sprinkle a few drops of food coloring on their plates. Have them put on their raincoats and walk outside, holding their plates in the rain for a few moments. After they bring their plates inside, talk about the designs created by the rain.

Umbrellas

Cut large umbrella shapes out of construction paper. Let your children paint the shapes as they wish. Hang the umbrella paintings on a wall or a bulletin board and attach construction paper handles.

Rain Collage

Let your children look through magazines to find pictures of rain. Have them tear or cut out the pictures. Let the children glue the pictures on a piece of butcher paper to make a Rain Collage. Encourage them to talk about the rain in each picture.

Egg Carton Caterpillars

Remove the lid from a cardboard egg carton and cut the bottom section in half, lengthwise, to make two "caterpillars." Cut one for each of your children. Let the children paint the egg cartons to resemble caterpillars. After the paint has dried, help each child make antennae for his or her caterpillar by bending a pipe cleaner in half and sticking it through the top of the first egg cup in the egg carton. Then let the children add eyes and mouths to their caterpillars with felt-tip markers.

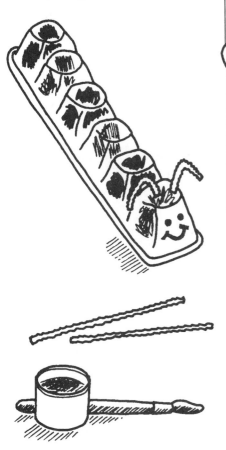

Collage Cartons

Prepare a Collage Carton for each of your children by filling the cups of an egg carton with materials such as dried beans, rice, popcorn kernels, pasta shapes, buttons, yarn, ribbon scraps, and cotton balls. Give each child one of the cartons and some glue. Help the children cut the lids off their cartons. Then let them glue their collage items on their lids.

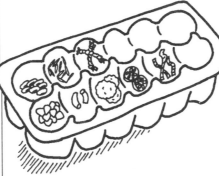

Egg Cup Bluebells

Cut the egg cups out of cardboard egg cartons. Then cut the cups into bluebell shapes as shown in the illustration. Let the children paint the bluebell shapes blue. When the paint has dried, make stems by inserting the ends of green pipe cleaners through the bottoms of the bluebells, bending the pipe cleaners into cane shapes. Let the children poke holes in the ends of precut leaf shapes and thread them on their bluebell stems.

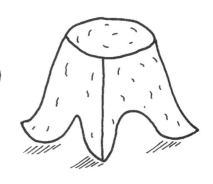

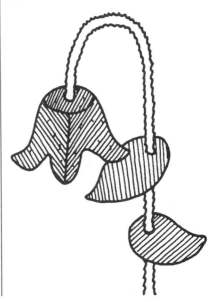

Sparkly Eggs

Squeeze the round ends of empty frozen juice cans to form oval shapes. Have your children dip the oval ends of the cans into glue and make prints on sheets of construction paper. Then let your children sprinkle glitter onto the glue.

Variation: Instead of juice cans, use egg-shaped cookie cutters.

Eggshell Mosaics

Rinse and crush broken eggshells and store them in a container. Prepare egg dye by combining 1 teaspoon vinegar with a few drops of food coloring and ½ cup warm water. Drop the crushed eggshells into the dye, stir, and remove when the eggshells are the desired color. Allow the colored eggshells to dry. Have your children glue the eggshells on sheets of construction paper to make colorful mosaics.

Swiss-Style Easter Eggs

Prepare different colored egg dyes by placing 1 teaspoon vinegar and a few drops of food coloring into each of several cups and adding ½ cup warm water. Have your children wrap leaves or grass around hard-cooked eggs. Help them secure the grass or leaves by putting the egg into a small square of nylon stocking. Tie the ends of the stocking together with a piece of string. Have the children hold their eggs by the strings and dip them into the dye for approximately 5 minutes. Place the eggs in an egg carton to dry before removing the nylon and grass or leaves.

Variation: Use pieces of masking tape instead of leaves or grass to make patterns on the eggs.

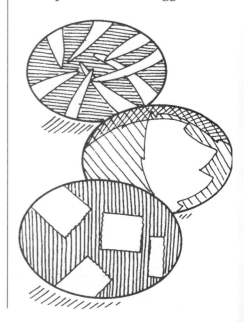

Eggs in a Basket

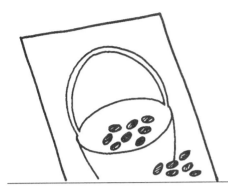

Give each of your children a sheet of construction paper with a simple Easter basket shape drawn on it. Pour small amounts of tempera paint into shallow containers. Have the children add egg shapes to their baskets by dipping their fingers, one at a time, into the paint and pressing them in and around their baskets.

Sack Baskets

Make an instant Easter basket for each of your children by folding a paper lunch sack in half lengthwise. Form a handle by rounding off the top corner and cutting out the middle of the sack as shown in the illustration. Give each child a basket. Let the children decorate their baskets with crayons, markers, or stickers. When the baskets are decorated, staple or glue the handles together.

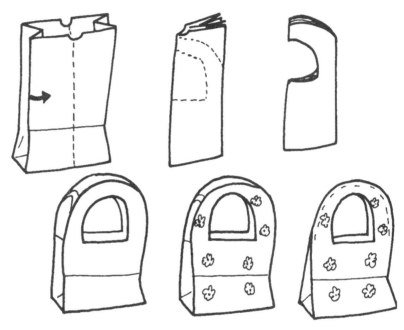

Woven Baskets

Cut margarine tubs as shown. Tape a piece of yarn to the bottom of each tub. Give each of your children one of the tubs. Show your children how to weave the yarn in and out of the plastic strips to form a basket. Help the children tie on additional pieces of yarn as necessary.

Bunny Estimations

Let your children bring in stuffed bunnies from home. Ask them to show their bunnies and to guess which bunny is the shortest, which is the tallest, and which bunnies have the longest and shortest ears. Use yarn to measure the bunnies' heights and ears. Compare the children's guesses with the actual answers.

Hopping Bunnies

Let your children pretend to be hopping bunnies. Then let one child be the leader and say, "Hopping bunnies jump _____ times," filling in the blank with a number from 1 to 10. Have the rest of the children hop that number of times. Let each child have a turn being the leader.

Bunny Classifying

Cut out several pictures of bunnies. Let the children classify them first by size then by color. Then mix up the pictures and have the children sort the pictures into categories they name.

Egg Patterns

Cut large egg shapes out of cardboard. Glue fabric or wallpaper on each egg and trim the edges. Cut each egg in half and mix up the egg halves. Let your children sort out the egg halves and match up the patterns to make whole eggs.

Easter Egg Match-Up

Collect 12 plastic eggs of various colors. Take the eggs apart and put the egg halves in a basket. Set out the basket and an egg carton. Let your children find egg halves of the same color, put them together, and place the whole eggs in the egg carton.

Number Eggs

Number the tops of 10 plastic eggs from 1 to 10 with a permanent felt-tip marker. Then number the bottom of each egg with a corresponding number of dots. Separate the tops and bottoms. Have your children try to match the correct tops and bottoms.

Variation: Have your children fill each egg with the corresponding number of dried beans.

Weather Chart

At the beginning of each week, make a chart to record the weather. Let your children add appropriate weather symbols to the chart each day. Weather symbols could include raindrops, clouds, sun, or lightning bolts.

Growth Chart

When your children are doing a gardening project such as planting seeds, let them help you create a pictorial growth chart. For example, your growth chart could include the following pictures: seed, seed and roots, seedling, and flowering plant.

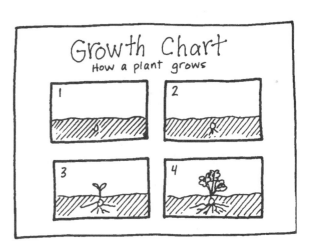

Length Graph

Help your children measure the lengths of different objects such as a box, a table, a jump rope, and a rug. Then record the lengths of the objects on a simple bar graph.

Math Miniatures

Number 10 pieces of heavy paper from 1 to 10. Below each numeral, draw a corresponding number of dots. Place 55 miniature objects in a basket. Have your child take a card and place one object on each dot. Then let the child choose another card and place one object on each dot. Continue until all the cards have been used. Have the child arrange the cards in numerical order.

Feelie Can

Remove the ends from a coffee can. Smooth out any rough edges. Cut the feet off two old socks, slip the socks over the ends of the can, and tape them securely in place. Place a small object through one of the socks and into the Feelie Can. Have one of your children place one or both hands through the socks. Have the child try to guess what object is inside the can just by touching it.

Playing Card Games

Remove and set aside the face cards from a deck of playing cards. Give the remaining number cards to one of your children. Ask the child to sort the cards by color, by suit, and by number.

Baby Chicks

Choose one of your children to be the Hen and have that child leave the room. Then select two or three other children to be Chicks. Instruct all the children to put their heads down so their faces cannot be seen. Have the Hen return to the room and call out "Cluck, cluck." The Chicks should then reply "Cheep, cheep." Have the Hen listen closely and try to locate the Chicks by the sounds they make. When the Hen finds a Chick, he or she should gently tap that child on the shoulder and have the Chick raise his or her head. When all of the Chicks are tapped, select a new Hen and begin the game again.

Sounds of Spring

Record the sounds of spring for your children. Use a tape recorder to record spring sounds such as birds singing, rain falling, children playing, and baby animals making sounds. Let the children listen to the sounds and describe what they hear.

Egg Sounds

Obtain plastic eggs and several small objects such as paper clips, macaroni, rice, pennies, marbles, and erasers. Place one type of object in each egg. Let your children shake the eggs and try to guess what's inside. You may wish to set out matching objects on a table and have the children place each egg next to the object they think is inside the egg.

Baby Bird

Traditional
Adapted by Jean Warren

Select a sheet of construction paper. While you read the following story, fold and cut the paper as indicated in the illustrations.

Once upon a time there was a mother bird who worked hard and built a beautiful nest. (*Fold paper in half and cut out a nest shape.*)

She sat on her nest one day and, after a while, she looked inside and saw a beautiful egg. (*Unfold nest to reveal egg shape.*)

She sat on her egg in the nest day and night. (*Fold egg back to nest shape.*)

One day two black beetles came to visit. (*Add a dot to both sides of nest shape to make two beetles.*)

The bird said, "I'm sorry, but I can't visit right now, for I fear that something is happening in my nest." (*Cut as indicated by dotted line. Add beak line.*)

"Oh, dear me," said the beetles, "we hear it too! It's getting louder and louder!" Just then, the mother bird peeked into her nest and cried, "Oh, no! My egg is all broken!" But she didn't cry long, because out popped her baby bird. (*Unfold paper to reveal baby bird.*)

The Funny Little Bunny Who Just Loved Honey

A European Folktale Adapted by Jean Warren

Once upon a time there was a funny little bunny who spent every day looking for honey. Oh, he liked carrots and spinach, too, but Funny Little Bunny just loved honey!

Sometimes he was lucky and found honey in old trees. But most of the time he had to figure out ways to sneak into Mrs. Bear's cave where he could help himself to a pawful of honey from her big honey jar.

Now, Mrs. Bear noticed that the honey in her big honey jar was going down and down. "Someone has been eating my honey, and I'm going to catch him," she said.

Mrs. Bear set up a trap. She put the honey jar up on the top shelf and tipped it just a little so it would fall when it was touched.

The next day when Mrs. Bear went out hunting, Funny Little Bunny hopped into her cave. He saw the honey jar on the top shelf and climbed up to help himself. But when he reached inside to get some honey the jar fell, Funny Little Bunny fell, and the honey fell all over Funny Little Bunny!

Oh dear! Funny Little Bunny tried and tried to move, but the honey was so thick, he stuck to whatever he touched.

When Mrs. Bear came home, Funny Little Bunny was stuck to the floor. "Well now, see what I've caught," laughed Mrs. Bear. "It looks like I'll be having bunny stew for dinner tonight."

Mrs. Bear filled a large black pot with water and set it in the fireplace. Then she lit a fire under the pot and went outside to get some turnips and potatoes to put in her stew.

Funny Little Bunny tried and tried to run, but he was stuck fast. "Oh, if only I could get away, I would never steal honey again!" he cried.

As the fire under the black pot grew hotter and hotter, the honey all over Funny Little Bunny grew thinner and thinner. It started running down his long ears, over his head, and down onto his little paws.

Soon Funny Little Bunny was able to move one foot, then another. Soon he was able to take one hop, then another. With a flip of his tail, Funny Little Bunny hopped right out of Mrs. Bear's cave and into the woods.

From that day on, Funny Little Bunny never ate honey. He just munched on carrots, spinach, and lettuce like other bunnies do.

Flannelboard Directions

Photocopy the story patterns on pages 132 and 133. Color and cut out the patterns. Cover them with clear self-stick paper for durability, if desired. Glue a felt strip to the back of each pattern. Place the patterns on a flannelboard. Use the patterns as you tell the story on this page. Or tell your children this story and let them use the patterns to retell it.

My Bunny

My bunny's ears are floppy.
(Place hands on each side of head and make them flop.)

My bunny's feet are hoppy.
(Hop.)

Her fur is soft,
(Stroke arm.)

And her nose is fluffy.
(Touch nose.)

Her tail is short and powder-puffy.
(Make tail with hands behind back.)

Author Unknown

The Rabbit

Can you make a rabbit,

With two ears so very long,
(Make rabbit ears with first two fingers.)

And let her hop, hop, hop about

On legs so small and strong?
(Move arm to make rabbit walk.)

She nibbles, nibbles carrots

For her dinner every day.
(Nibble with thumb and forefinger.)

As soon as she has had enough

She scampers far away.
(Hide arm behind back.)

Author Unknown

I Saw a Rabbit

I saw a rabbit.
(Wiggle two fingers behind head.)

I said, "Hello."
(Wave.)

He didn't stop.
(Shake head.)

He went down a hole.
(Swoop right hand through curved left arm.)

Now don't you fret—

You might see one, too.
(Wiggle two fingers behind ears.)

An Easter Rabbit

With some eggs for you!
(Cup hands together and hold out.)

Author Unknown

Earth Day Activities

April 22 is Earth Day. People across the country celebrate this day by wearing green, planting trees, and learning how to use resources wisely. As you discuss Earth Day with your children, have them name some activities they would like to do such as turning off the lights, planting flower seeds, wearing green, or recycling paper and aluminum cans. Then make a chart that lists those activities down the left side with the days of the week across the top. Have your children put an X by the activities they do each day.

Use Resources Wisely!

	Monday	Tuesday	Wednesday	Thursday	Friday
Turn off lights	X	X	X	X	X
Plant seeds			X		
Wear green	X			X	
Recycle	X	X	X	X	X

Earth Day Badges

Cut circles out of heavy paper. Set out the circles, green and blue paint, paintbrushes, and glitter. Let your children paint designs on the circles. Then have them sprinkle a small amount of glitter over the paint. Allow the paint to dry. Punch a hole in each circle and hang it from a piece of yarn. Let the children wear their Earth Day Badges as they sing the following song.

Sung to: "Yankee Doodle"

I'm proud to wear my Earth Day Badge—
I give the earth a hand.
I pick up litter, care for trees,
Recycle what I can.
I'm an Earth Day helper
Each and every day.
I take care of Mother Earth
In, oh, so many ways.

Gayle Bittinger

Planting Fun

Fill several dishpans or your sand table with potting soil. Set out small shovels, flowerpots, flower seeds, and squirt bottles filled with water. Let your children shovel the dirt into the flowerpots, plant some seeds, and squirt water on them. Have the children place their pots in a sunny window and check on them regularly. Encourage them to water their plants whenever the soil is dry.

Hint: Let your children collect rain water for watering their flower seeds.

Conserving Water

Talk with your children about conserving water. Explain that when we conserve water, we use less of it. Then show them one way they can conserve water. Place a bowl in the sink. Have one of the children wash his or her hands with the water running into the bowl. Take that bowl out of the sink and put another bowl in the sink. Have a second child wash his or her hands, turning off the water whenever possible. Ask the children to compare the two amounts of water. Which way of washing hands used the least amount of water? Then let the children use the water in the bowls to water plants.

Light Bulb Watcher

Let your children take turns being the Light Bulb Watcher. The Light Bulb Watcher turns off the lights whenever you leave the room and makes sure that no unnecessary lights are on. Make a necklace for the Light Bulb watcher by cutting a light bulb shape out of yellow construction paper and hanging it on a piece of yarn.

Variation: Make a light bulb necklace for each of your children and have all of them be Light Bulb Watchers. Let them wear their necklaces home to be Light Bulb Watchers there too.

Making Rain

Boil some water in a pot until steam forms above it. Fill a metal pie pan with ice cubes. Hold the pie pan above the pot in the steam "cloud." Have your children observe the drops of water that form and fall back into the pot like rain. (Close supervision is necessary when any appliance is used near children.)

Garden Hose Rainbow

On a sunny day, take your children outside. Stand with your back to the sun and spray water from the hose. Help your children look into the water spray to find the rainbow.

Indoor Rainbows

Place a small mirror in a clear glass of water. Put the glass on a sunny windowsill. Position the mirror in the glass so the sun will hit it and cause a rainbow to shine on a wall.

Individual Terrariums

Have each of your children fill a clear-plastic cup half full with dirt. Let the children plant small plants in the dirt, cover the dirt with wood chips or rocks, and sprinkle on a little water. Place another clear-plastic cup over each child's planted cup and glue or tape them together. Explain to the children that terrariums are self-watering. Encourage them to watch over the next few days how the water condenses on the tops of their terrariums and rains down on their plants.

The Miracle of Butterflies

Catch a caterpillar this spring. Fill a glass jar with twigs and bits of grass. Poke small air holes in the lid and place the caterpillar inside. Let your children watch the caterpillar spin a chrysalis or a cocoon and evolve into a butterfly or a moth. Open the jar and watch the butterfly or the moth flutter away outdoors.

Hint: You can purchase everything you need for this activity from a science supply store or a catalog where you are guaranteed a butterfly, not a moth.

Drumbeats

Play simple patterns on a hand drum to encourage walking, running, galloping, skipping, or jumping. Ask your children to determine what the drum is telling their feet to do. After they become proficient, change drumming patterns without stopping. See if the children can hear the differences and change their movements accordingly. If your space is limited, have the children just clap their hands to the drumbeats.

Line Walk

Place a line of masking tape on your floor or carpet. Let the children take turns walking in various ways on the tape such as on their toes, on their heels, backward, or sideways.

Walking Fun

Let your children demonstrate different kinds of walking as you ask questions such as these: "How lightly can you walk? How heavily? Can you walk tall? Can you walk close to the floor? How would you walk if you were feeling grouchy? Happy? Sad? Angry? Hot? Cold?"

Getting Started

Encourage your children's creative movement by providing them with a variety of streamers, such as the ones described below. Let them use the streamers while dancing and moving to different kinds of music.

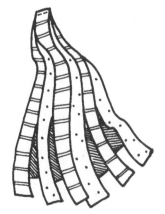

Simple Streamer

Cut 2-foot lengths of crepe paper, ribbon, plastic bag strips, or plastic surveyor's tape (available at hardware stores). Put 10 of the strips together and staple them at one end to make a streamer.

Ring Streamer

Cut the center out of a plastic lid to make a ring. Attach 2-foot lengths of crepe paper or ribbon to one side of the ring.

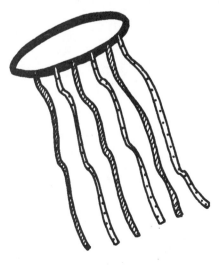

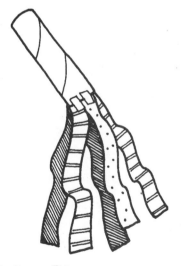

Tube Streamer

Attach lengths of crepe paper to the end of a cardboard paper towel tube to make a Tube Streamer.

Backward
Sung to: "Frère Jacques"

Sing it backward, sing it backward.

Backward it sing, backward it sing.

That sounds funny, that sounds funny.

Ho, ho, ho! He, he, he!

Substitute other three-word phrases such as *I love you, See you later,* or *April Fools' Day* for the words *Sing it backward.*" Be sure to sing the words backward on the second line.

Allison Lang

Giant, Giant Spider
Sung to: "Eensy Weensy Spider"

Giant, giant spider

Crawling up your back.

Here, let me help you

Give your back a whack.

It was very ugly,

So very mean and cruel.

Aren't you glad I saved you?

Happy April Fool!

Jean Warren

April Fools
Sung to: "Jingle Bells"

April Fools, April Fools,

What a lot of fun.

Everyone is playing tricks

On each and every one.

Men from Mars, falling stars,

Big black bugs, and more.

You trick me, I trick you,

That's what April Fools is for.

Jean Warren

Raindrops
Sung to: "Frère Jacques"

Raindrops falling, raindrops falling,
From the sky, from the sky.
Put up an umbrella,
Put up an umbrella,
Nice and dry, nice and dry.

Shower's over, shower's over,
Sun's aglow, sun's aglow.
See the pretty flowers,
See the pretty flowers,
In a row, in a row.

Jean Warren

Rainy Day
Sung to: "Twinkle, Twinkle, Little Star"

Rainy, rainy, rainy day,
Water puddles all for play.
The sky is cloudy, but I don't mind
Puddles, galoshes, and mud pies.
Rainy, rainy, rainy day,
In the rain I like to play.

Kristine Wagoner

Rain, Rain Falling Down
Sung to: "Row, Row, Row Your Boat"

Rain, rain falling down,
  (*Wiggle your fingers downward.*)
Falling on the ground.
Pitter, patter, pitter, patter,
What a lovely sound.

Substitute other words, such as *squishy*, *noisy*, or *silly*, for *lovely*.

Susan A. Miller

MUSIC • Songs About Bunnies

A Bunny

Sung to: "My Bonnie Lies Over the Ocean"

A bunny hops over the meadow,
  (Wiggle two fingers behind head.)

A bunny hops under a tree.
  (Look left.)

A bunny hops over the meadow,
  (Look right.)

I wish she'd hop over to me.

Hip, hop, hip, hop.
  (Hop in place with hands in front of chest.)

Hop over, hop over to me, to me.
  (Point to self.)

Hip, hop, hip, hop.
  (Hop in place with hands in front of chest.)

Hop over, hop over to me.
  (Point to self.)

Diane Thom

Flop, Flop, Flop

Sung to: "Row, Row, Row Your Boat"

Flop, flop, flop your ears,
Flop them up and down.
Flop, flop, flop your ears,
Flop them all around.

Peggy Wolf

I'm a Little Bunny

Sung to: "I'm a Little Teapot"

I'm a little bunny with a cotton tail.

See me hop down the trail.
  (Hop down a pretend lane.)

When I pass a carrot, my ears shake.
  (Put hands behind head and shake them.)

Then, of course, a bite I take. Crunch!
  (Pretend to bite a carrot.)

Joy Zomerdyke

Easter, Easter

Sung to: "Sailing, Sailing"

Easter, Easter, Easter time is here.
We'll decorate some pretty eggs
And hide them, yes, my dear.
Bunnies, baskets, new clothes everywhere,
We'll sing and dance and wear our hats
'Cause Easter time is here!

Colraine Hunley

Easter Parade

Sung to: "The Mulberry Bush"

Today we'll march in the Easter parade,
Easter parade, Easter parade.
Today we'll march in the Easter parade,
So early in the morning.

We'll play our drums in the Easter parade,
Easter parade, Easter parade.
We'll play our drums in the Easter parade,
So early in the morning.

We'll wear our best in the Easter parade,
Easter parade, Easter parade.
We'll wear out best in the Easter parade,
So early in the morning.

Karen Smith

Egg Hunt

Sung to: "The Mulberry Bush"

Here we go hunting all around,
All around, all around.
Here we go hunting all around,
To find our Easter eggs.

Additional verses: Here we go hopping all around; Here
we go skipping all around; Here we go jumping all around;
Here we go running all around.

Micki Nadort

Upside Down and Backward

Rearrange your room by turning things upside down and backward, including pictures, books, chairs, and tables. Let your children name all the things that are different.

Inside Out

Let your children eat cheese and crackers inside out. Instead of eating cheese between two crackers, let them eat a cracker between two slices of cheese.

Tops and Bottoms

Cut magazine pictures of people and animals in half and separate the tops and bottoms. Then have your children make funny pictures by combining mismatched tops and bottoms.

Riddles

Tell your children riddles about spring things and let the children guess what you are describing. For example, a riddle for a bird could be: "I live in a nest, I eat worms, and I can fly."

Striped Surprise

Cut an assortment of large and small shapes from corrugated cardboard. Have your children place thin pieces of paper over the corrugated side of the cardboard shapes and rub crayons over them. Stripes will appear like magic.

Stripe Jump

Place several equal lengths of masking tape on the floor parallel to one another, about 8 inches apart. Have your children practice jumping from stripe to stripe.

Striped Snacks

At snacktime, serve each of your children a stick of mozzarella string cheese on a plate. Demonstrate how to separate the cheese into strings. Let the children arrange the strings in stripes on their plates before eating the cheese.

Seeing Stripes

Go on a "stripe hunt" with your children. Have them search indoors and outdoors to find as many stripes as they can. Encourage them to be creative and look closely for stripes in places such as corduroy, chair slats, curtain pleats, blinds, lined writing paper, ladder rungs, or fence posts.

Exploring Baskets

Baskets offer a wonderful variety of year-round learning opportunities. Baskets may be made of straw, sticks, fabric, plastic, or other materials. They may hold food, wood, wastepaper, or even water. Invite your children and their families to bring baskets from home. Have the children examine the baskets and think about their uses. Include baskets in the housekeeping and block areas and let the children incorporate them into their play.

Big and Small Baskets

Display several baskets of different sizes. Talk with your children about the sizes and kinds of things that might fit in each one. Then mix up the baskets and have the children arrange them by size.

Basket Weaving

Give each of your children a plastic berry basket. Set out construction paper strips cut thinly enough to fit the spaces of the basket. Use several colors of construction paper so the finished products will be very colorful. Demonstrate for the children how to weave the paper through the basket. Have them start by putting the end of the first strip into one space and then pulling it through the next space. Tell them to continue until they have woven the first strip through to the end. Allow the children to add as many strips as they wish. As each child finishes, have him or her glue one strip across the top to make a handle.

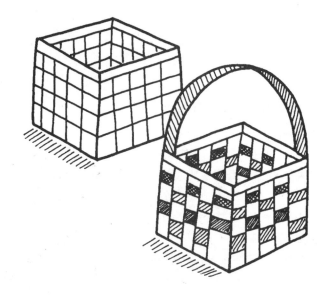

Basket Matching

Cut 10 basket shapes out of construction paper. Divide the basket shapes into pairs. Decorate each pair with flowers, stripes, or patterns. Mix up the shapes and let your children take turns finding the matching pairs of baskets.

In One Basket

Play a counting game with your children. You will need a basket and enough plastic eggs for each child to have at least one. Have the children sit in a circle. Show them the basket and have them guess how many eggs will fit in it. Then put an egg into it and say "One." Explain that you will pass the basket around the circle. As each child gets the basket, he or she should put one egg in and then say how many eggs are in the basket. Continue passing the basket around the circle until it is full. Count the eggs with your children. Help them compare their guesses to the actual number of eggs that fit in the basket.

Five Brown Baskets

Recite the following rhyme with your children. At the end of the rhyme, ask the children to tell you what they would like to hold if they were baskets.

Five brown baskets sitting in a row.
The first one said, "On a picnic I'll go."
The second one said, "Put flowers in me."
The third one said, "I'll hold shells from the sea."
The fourth one said, "Fill me with berries."
The fifth one said, "I'd like to hold cherries."

Margaret Timmons

Little Chick

As you recite the following poem, have your children act out the movements described.

Snuggled down inside
An egg that was white,
Was a tiny chick
With its head tucked tight.
Then it lifted its head,
Tapped the egg with its beak,
And quickly popped out—
Peep, peep, peep!

Colraine Hunley

Feathered Friends

For each of your children, cut a chick shape out of yellow construction paper. Give the children paintbrushes and glue. Have them use the brushes to spread glue all over their chick shapes. Then let them cover the glue with yellow feathers (available at craft stores). Have them complete their chicks by adding construction paper eyes and beaks.

Sequence Cards

Make simple sequence cards for your children that illustrate the different stages of a chick hatching. Have the cards show the egg in its nest, the egg cracking, the chick partly out of the egg, and the chick completely hatched.

Hatching Chicks

Use the poem "Little Chick" from the previous page to start a discussion of how chicks hatch. Talk about the mother hens who lay the eggs and sit on them to keep them warm, and about the baby chicks who begin tapping at the shells with their beaks until the shells crack and they are able to wiggle their way out. If you can, visit a farm that has baby chicks. Let your children watch the chicks eat, drink, and move around.

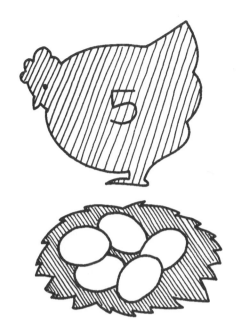

Whose Nest?

Cut five mother hen shapes, five nest shapes, and 15 egg shapes out of felt. Number the hens from 1 to 5. Glue different numbers of eggs, from 1 to 5, on the nest shapes. Place the nests on a flannelboard. Let the children help the mother hens find their nests by counting the eggs and matching each hen to the appropriate nest.

Deviled Egg "Chicks"

Remove the shell from a hard-cooked egg and cut the egg in half lengthwise. Scoop the yolk into a small bowl. Mix the egg yolk with mayonnaise and mustard to taste. Fill each egg white with half of the yolk mixture. Add two raisins and a small piece of carrot to each yolk mixture to make eyes and a beak. Makes 2 servings.

"The Funny Little Bunny Who Just Loved Honey" Flannelboard Patterns

Refer to page 114 for directions.

May

Paper Cup Flowers

Give each of your children several paper baking cups. Show the children how to cut the edges of the cups to make petals. Let the children glue the paper cups to sheets of construction paper. Have them use felt-tip markers to add stems, leaves, and grass to their flowers.

Window Flowers

Set out crayons with the papers removed, a cheese grater, and pieces of waxed paper. Help one of your children grate some of the crayons onto one of the pieces of waxed paper. Lay another piece of waxed paper on top of the shavings. Place the pieces of waxed paper between a folded damp cloth and carefully move an iron across the cloth to melt the crayons. (Close supervision is necessary when any appliance is used by or near children.) Repeat with each child. Encourage the children to notice how the crayon colors spread and mix together. Cut the children's papers into flower shapes and hang them in a window to let the light shine through.

Lovely Lilacs

Show your children some real lilacs. Let them touch and smell the fragrant flowers. Then have them make their own lilac art. Set out precut 2-inch squares of lavender, purple, or white tissue paper. Show the children how to twist one of the paper squares around a chopstick or the eraser end of a pencil to make a lilac blossom. Let the children make as many blossoms as they wish. After each child has made several blossoms, show the children how to glue their blossoms to craft sticks to make lilac branches. Use the lilac branches as springtime centerpieces, if desired.

Hint: It takes only a dab of glue to secure the blossoms to the craft sticks. Have your children apply the glue with cotton swabs for better control.

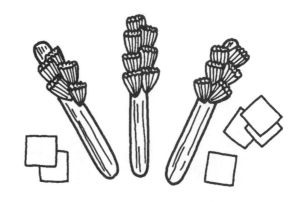

Tissue Paper Rainbows

Give each of your children a large piece of paper. Have each child brush an arc of liquid starch on his or her paper. Then let the children tear one color of tissue paper into small pieces and press the tissue pieces on top of the starch. When they finish the first arc, let them follow the same procedure to make other colored tissue paper arcs beneath the first one.

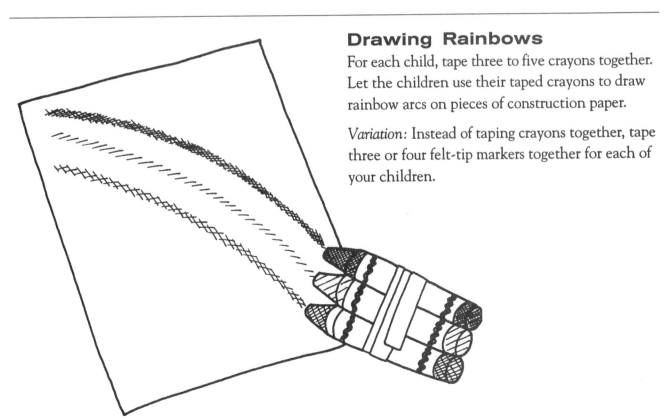

Drawing Rainbows

For each child, tape three to five crayons together. Let the children use their taped crayons to draw rainbow arcs on pieces of construction paper.

Variation: Instead of taping crayons together, tape three or four felt-tip markers together for each of your children.

Picture Frames

Set out buttons, pieces of old costume jewelry, beads, and glue. Give each of your children an old picture frame with the backing and glass removed. Have the children arrange the buttons, jewelry pieces, and beads on the frames and glue them in place. Allow the glue to dry before replacing the glass and backings. If desired, have the children draw pictures of themselves to put into their frames.

Fancy Tissue Boxes

Give each of your children an unopened facial tissue box. Have your children brush glue over small sections of their boxes. Let them place a variety of uncooked pasta shapes on the glue to create designs. Have them continue until the boxes are completely covered with pasta. Spray the boxes with gold spray paint in a well-ventilated area away from the children.

Spiced Tea Mix

To make the drink mix, combine three parts instant orange breakfast drink to one part instant tea. Have your children fill baby food jars with the drink mix. Screw the lids on tightly. To complete his or her gift, let each child select a precut fabric circle. Help the children place the circles over their lids and secure them with rubber bands. Attach a card with these directions: "Mix 1 heaping tablespoon drink mix with 1 cup hot or cold water for a delicious orange beverage."

Clay

1 cup salt
1 cup flour
½ cup water
Powdered tempera paint

Mix salt, flour, and water together in a bowl, adding more flour if necessary to make the mixture a doughy consistency. Sprinkle powdered tempera on and mix well. Objects made with the Clay will air dry in about 48 hours.

Crunchy Dough

1 shredded wheat biscuit
2 tablespoons glue
Food coloring, optional

Crumble the shredded wheat biscuit into a bowl. Add the glue and, if desired, several drops of food coloring. Mix the ingredients together until the cereal is completely coated. This recipe makes enough dough for one child. Objects made with the Crunchy Dough will air dry in about 12 hours.

Cornstarch Paint

1 cup water
2 tablespoons cornstarch
Food coloring

Mix the water, cornstarch, and several drops of food coloring together in a saucepan. Heat and stir the mixture until it thickens, about 5 minutes. Let it cool. Store in a covered container. Use the paint for fingerpainting or as an almost dripless easel paint. If the mixture becomes too thick, add water until it reaches the desired consistency.

Flower Pot

Make two photocopies of the flower patterns on page 164. Color and cut out the flower shapes. Attach each one to the top of a craft stick. Fill a flower pot with playdough. Let your children take turns "planting" the "flowers" in the flower pot. Ask them to plant the flowers in particular ways such as these: "Plant all the red flowers; Plant just the tulip flowers; Plant a blue and a yellow flower."

Spring Flower Sorting

Make four photocopies of the flower patterns on page 164. Color each page of flowers a different color. Cut out the cards and, if desired, cover them with clear self-stick paper for durability. Mix up the cards and let the children take turns sorting them by color.

Variation: Have your children sort the flower cards by kind rather than by color.

Counting Flowers

For each of your children, write a familiar number at the top of a sheet of construction paper and draw a matching number of stems at the bottom. Make several photocopies of the flower patterns on page 164. Cut out the flower shapes and place them in a pile. Have each child identify the number on his or her paper and take that number of flowers from the pile. Then let the children glue their flowers at the tops of the stems on their papers.

Variation: Instead of gluing on paper flower shapes, let your children attach flower stickers to the tops of their stems.

Clothesline Fun

Hang a length of clothesline between two chairs and clip spring-type clothespins on the line. Use the clothing patterns on page 165 as guides for cutting clothing shapes out of a variety of colors of fabric or paper. Place the shapes in a basket. Then let your children take turns "hanging up the wash" as they do the following activities.

Pattern Clothesline

Ask your children to hang up the wash in patterns (red-blue, red-blue; pants-shirt-sock, pants-shirt-sock; etc.).

Clothing Clothesline

Ask your children to hang up just the socks or just the shirts. Or ask them to hang the pants on one side of the line and the shirts on the other side.

Color Clothesline

Ask your children to hang up just the green clothes or just the yellow clothes. Or hang different-colored clothing shapes on the line and ask the children to hang matching colored shapes next to them.

Number Book

Number 10 sheets of construction paper from 1 to 10. Place a corresponding number of stickers on each page. Staple the pages together. Then let your children take turns identifying the numbers on the pages and counting the stickers.

Variation: Make a book for just one number, such as the numeral 4. Write the numeral on several sheets of construction paper. Then place a different set of four stickers on each page, such as four teddy bears, four rainbows, four flowers, or four stars.

Guessing Book

Punch three holes down the left-hand side of six sheets of plain paper and put them together with brass paper fasteners. Use a craft knife to cut a square through all six pages. Fold back the first page and cut a triangle through the remaining five pages. Repeat, cutting a circle through pages 3 to 6, a rectangle through pages 4 to 6, a heart through pages 5 and 6, and an oval through page 6. Attach a plastic page protector behind the pages. Cut several full-page pictures out of a magazine. Insert one of the pictures into the page protector. Let your children look through the shapes as they turn each page and have them try to guess what picture will be revealed when all the pages have been turned. Then put a new picture in the page protector and let them try again.

Sequence Cubes

Collect four plastic photo cubes and pictures of the four seasons. Insert a season picture in one side of each of the four cubes. Repeat with other events that can be shown in four steps such as a frog's growth, a tree shown in each season, a butterfly's life, a baby growing into an adult, and baking bread. Show the cubes to your children. Let them take turns finding the related pictures on each cube and arranging them in order.

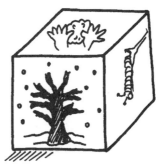

Classifying Toys

Show your children a basket of toys. Help them decide how to sort the toys. Offer them suggestions for categorizing such as small and large, hard and soft, or wood and plastic. Then have the children sort the toys into two piles. Mix up the toys and let them sort them in a different way. You may wish to let your children put the toys away according to one of these categories.

The Celebration

A Native American Folktale Adapted by Jean Warren

Tiny Flower pushed her head up through the ground. Was she too early for the party? No. For as she looked around, she saw many other flowers just arriving. During the long cold winter months, Tiny Flower had been waiting and preparing for her journey to the Land of the Light. She had dreamed about how tall she would grow and how beautiful and colorful her gown of soft petals would be. It had been a long wait and a tiring struggle up through the frozen ground. But it was worth it. Here she was, emerging into the promised light—surrounded by her friends and anxious for the party to begin.

Mother Nature was also anxious. The flowers kept arriving but not one had taken off its coat. Everyone knew that the celebration could not begin until the flowers shed their coats—filling the world with color.

"Oh, dear," sighed Mother Nature. "We can't have a party if everyone is all bundled up. Oh, what shall I do?" Then Mother Nature called for her children, the Wind, the Rain, and the Sun. "Help me children. Go and greet the flowers and see if you can persuade them to take off their coats."

"I will get the flowers to remove their coats," said the Wind, and out he went to greet the flowers. He blew and blew as hard as he could, hoping to trick them by blowing off their coats. But the harder he blew, the tighter they wrapped up. Finally the Wind gave up and went back to

tell his mother that they might as well call off the celebration this year.

"Don't worry, Mother," said the Rain, "we will have our celebration. I can get the flowers to remove their coats." So out went the Rain to greet the flowers. His plan was to rain so hard that the flowers would get their coats completely soaked and would have to take them off to dry. Down, down came the showers, but the flowers only wrapped up tighter and tighter. Seeing that his plan was not going to work, the Rain finally gave up and went back to his mother. He also suggested that they give up on their party plans.

"Let me try," said the Sun. "I will go out to greet the flowers and perhaps persuade them to take off their coats." So the Sun went out and welcomed the flowers with his warmth. Slowly the flowers warmed up. They peeked out their heads, stretched their arms, and smiled at the Sun. Soon the flowers grew warmer and warmer, and finally, they became so hot they tossed off their coats.

"Let the party begin," announced Mother Nature as the world gradually burst into color. All the animals rushed to greet the flowers. The birds sang songs of greeting and the bees did dances of welcome.

Tiny Flower was delighted with the Land of the Light. It was even more wonderful than she had imagined. She felt like a queen with so many new friends, a crown of gold, and a gown of green velvet. Tiny Flower even grew to love the Wind and the Rain. They soon found out that it was more fun being nice to the flowers than playing tricks on them. Tiny Flower enjoyed playing with the Wind, and she found the Rain refreshing. But most of all she loved the Sun for his warm and sunny smile!

Down in the Garden

Down in the garden, early in the morning,

See the yellow daffodils all in a row.
    (Bow heads.)

See them lift their heads and

Give their horns a blow.
    (Lift heads and pretend to blow horns.)

Toot, toot, toot, toot—off they go!

Jean Warren

My Flower Bed

See the purple and white blossoms

In the flower bed.

The daisy spreads its petals wide,
    (Hold palms outward with fingers open.)

The tulip bows its head.
    (Bend hands at wrist with fingers closed.)

Adapted Traditional

Pretending

I like to pretend that I am a rose
    (Cup hands.)

That grows and grows and grows and grows.
    (Open hands gradually.)

My hands are a rosebud closed up tight,
    (Close hands.)

With not a tiny speck of light.

Then slowly the petals open for me,
    (Open hands gradually.)

And here is a beautiful rose, you see!

Adapted Traditional

A Rainbow

Let your children take turns filling in the blanks to complete the following rainbow story.

I see a rainbow.

It is more colorful than _____.

My favorite rainbow color is _____.

If I look under the rainbow, I will find _____.

To catch a rainbow, I will _____.

I can use my rainbow to _____.

If I had two rainbows, I would give one to _____.

Jean Warren

Colors

Let your children take turns filling in the blanks to complete the colorful story that follows.

The world is full of colors.

The coldest color I can think of is _____.

The warmest color I can think of is _____.

The softest color I can think of is _____.

The scariest color I can think of is _____.

When I think of yellow, I think of _____.

When I think of red, I think of _____.

When I think of blue, I think of _____.

When I think of green, I think of _____.

My favorite color for a house is _____.

My favorite color for a flower is _____.

The funniest color I can think of is _____.

The color that makes me the happiest is _____.

Jean Warren

Trial Run

Planning is the key to successful field trips. Familiarize yourself with your field trip location ahead of time, if possible. Visiting the site will help you learn if there are potential hazards for young children and if drinking water and rest rooms are available.

Preparing Your Children

Tell your children when and where they will be going on a field trip, how they will get there, and what you expect to see. Show related photographs or pictures, if possible. Preparing your children ahead of time will relieve apprehension and make it easier for them to absorb new sights and sounds.

Stamp It On

Before leaving on a field trip, use your teaching center's rubber stamp and ink pad to print the name, address, and telephone number on each child's hand. Make sure that the children do not wear anything with their names printed on them, to prevent strangers from calling your children by their names.

Camera and Tape Recorder

Don't forget to take a camera and a tape recorder when you go on field trips. Later, the photos and recorded tapes can be used to review what your children learned.

Step Up to See

When you go on a field trip to a post office or other place that has high counters, take along a lightweight footstool. Your children can take turns standing on the footstool to see what is going on behind the counters.

Dramatic Play

Set up play situations that encourage your children to reenact field trips that you take. You'll find that children enjoy using the information they learn.

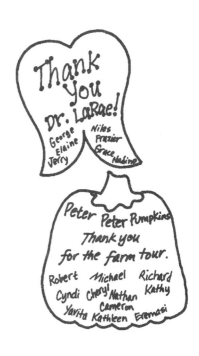

Keep Things Simple

On a field trip location, don't confuse your children by calling attention to every new thing in sight. Instead, help them concentrate on three or four things that are of interest.

Thank You Card

After a field trip, make a thank you card in an appropriate shape (a tooth shape for a trip to a dentist's office, a pumpkin shape for a visit to a pumpkin farm, etc.). If your children are unable to sign their own names, let them each make an inked fingerprint on the card. Then write each child's name under his or her fingerprint.

Alike and Different

Find two different kinds of dirt and put them in separate jars. Ask your children to compare the two kinds of dirt. How are they alike? How are they different? Which dirt would be best for growing plants? Why?

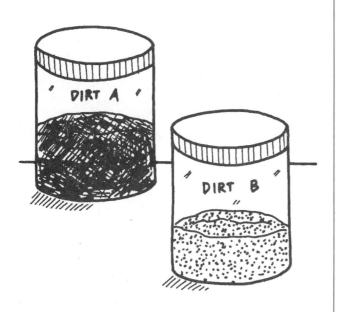

Dirt and Water

Partially fill a clear jar with dirt and water. Stir up the dirt and water and have your children observe what happens. Have them continue to watch the jar. What is happening now? Why is the dirt sinking to the bottom? What would happen if you stirred it up again?

Dirt Safari

Go outside with your children. Spread a newspaper out on the grass and put two or three scoops of dirt on it. Give the children small wire mesh strainers and magnifying glasses to use for examining the dirt. What does the dirt look like? What does it feel and smell like?

The Nose Knows

Challenge your children with a matching game. Collect several plastic margarine tubs. Poke several small holes in the lid of each tub. Place a different, scented item in each tub. (Peanut butter, lemons, cinnamon, and onions are just a few of the possibilities.) Cut out or draw a picture of each item and cover the pictures with clear self-stick paper for durability. Let your children smell the tubs and try to match them to the pictures of the items they contain.

Note: Remember to clean out the tubs at the end of the day.

Sweet Smelling Art

For a special sensory experience, add a few drops of peppermint, lemon, or vanilla extract to your children's playdough. Have your children draw pictures with scented markers. Encourage them to exchange pictures and compare scents.

The Smelling Song

Sung to: "It's Raining, It's Pouring"

I'm smelling, I'm smelling.
My nose is busy smelling.
This is the song I like to sing
When I smell most anything!

Kathy McCullough

Flowers Growing

By Jean Warren

Tell the following story to your children. Have them act out the movements as they listen.

Once upon a time there was a tiny flower seed buried deep in the cold, hard dirt. Gradually, as the spring came, the days grew longer, and the sun began to warm the earth. The little seed grew warmer and warmer and soon began to stretch and reach out for the warm earth above. As the seed stretched, he grew a stem and roots and became a plant. He worked hard pushing his roots down deep into the dirt to steady himself as he slowly climbed out of the dirt. He pushed and pushed and finally poked his head out of the ground.

With the help of the sun and the spring rains, the little plant grew straight and strong and soon developed a bud on the end of his stem. As the days grew warmer, his bud gradually unfolded, revealing a beautiful flower inside. All through the happy days of summer the little flower brightened the world, filling it with color and a delightful smell. The bees tickled his nose, and the wind helped him dance.

But as the summer wore on, the little flower soon began to grow tired. His color faded and he started to dry up. But we must not be sad for the little flower because he had been waiting all summer for this time. Now it was time for him to release the treasure pouch he had been storing up. With the help of the wind, the little flower scattered new seeds upon the earth, new seeds that would gradually work their way down into the soft warm earth, curl up, fall asleep, and wait to be awakened by the spring when it arrived once again.

Slithery Snake

Find one or more jump ropes long enough for your children to hold onto with about 3 feet between each child. Explain to the children that they are going to be a Slithery Snake. Have them hold on to the rope with their right hands and together move the long rope around the room, hissing and slithering. Play appropriate music, if desired.

Rope Leap

Choose two children to hold a long jump rope a few inches off the ground. Let the rest of the children take turns stepping over the rope with one foot and then the other, jumping over it with two feet, or hopping over it on one foot. Have the children take turns holding the rope so everyone gets a chance to jump over it.

MUSIC · Songs for May Day

May Day's Here
Sung to: "Three Blind Mice"

May Day's here, May Day's here.
Sun shines bright, sun shines bright.
Birds and butterflies are in flight,
Blooming flowers—such a sight!
Everything feels just right.
May Day's here!

Kristine Wagoner

May Basket
Sung to: "Did You Ever See a Lassie?"

Did you ever see a May basket,
May basket, May basket?
Did you ever see a May basket
That looked so good?
I worked for hours,
Then filled it with flowers.
Did you ever see a May basket
That looked so good?

Jean Warren

I Made a May Basket
Sung to: "A-Tisket, A-Tasket"

A-tisket, a-tasket,
I made a May basket.
I filled it up with flowers bright
And hung it on the door just right.

A-tisket, a-tasket,
I made a May basket.
Flowers are a sign of spring
And all the joy that it can bring.

Jean Warren

Flower Garden

Sung to: "The Farmer in the Dell"

The farmer plants the seeds,
The farmer plants the seeds.
Hi, ho, and cheery-oh,
The farmer plants the seeds.

Additional verses: The rain begins to fall; The sun begins to shine; The plants begin to grow; The buds all open up; The flowers are here at last.

Nancy H. Giles

Flowers Are Blooming

Sung to: "Frere Jacques"

Flowers are blooming,
Flowers are blooming,
All around, all around.
All the pretty colors,
All the pretty colors
Dot the ground,
Dot the ground.

Let's go see them,
Let's go see them,
Blooming bright,
Booming bright.
Use your nose to smell them.
Use your eyes to see them.
What a sight!
What a sight!

Sharon Clendenen

Out in My Garden

Sung to: "Down by the Station"

Out in my garden
Early in the morning,
See the little flowers
All in a row.
See the rows of daisies
And the rows of sweet peas.
Hoe-hoe, grow-grow,
In my garden, please.

Jean Warren

Rainbow Colors
Sung to: "Hush, Little Baby"

Rainbow purple, rainbow blue,
Rainbow green and yellow, too.
Rainbow orange, rainbow red,
Rainbow smiling overhead.

Come and count the colors with me.
How many colors can you see?
One, two, three, down to green,
Four, five, six colors can be seen.

Rainbow purple, rainbow blue,
Rainbow green and yellow, too.
Rainbow orange, rainbow red,
Rainbow smiling overhead.

Jean Warren

Rainbow
Sung to: "Mary Had a Little Lamb"

Rainbow over the waterfall,
Waterfall, waterfall,
Rainbow over the waterfall,
Rainbow over the tree.

Rainbow over the mountain,
Mountain, mountain,
Rainbow over the mountain,
Rainbow over the sea.

Rainbow over the flowers,
Flowers, flowers,
Rainbow over the flowers,
Rainbow over the bee.

Rainbow over the dancers,
Dancers, dancers,
Rainbow over the dancers,
Rainbow over me!

Jean Warren

We Love Mothers

Sung to: "Frère Jacques"

We love mothers. We love mothers.

Yes, we do. Yes, we do.

Mothers are for hugging,
  (Hug self.)

Mothers are for kissing.
  (Blow a kiss.)

We love you. Yes, we do.

Thank you, Mother. Thank you, Mother.

For your love, for your love.

Mothers are for hugging,
  (Hug self.)

Mothers are for kissing.
  (Blow a kiss.)

We love you. Yes, we do.

Additional verses: We love fathers;
grandmas; grandpas.

Barbara Fletcher

Mother Dear

Sung to: "Three Blind Mice"

Mother dear, Mother dear,
I love you. I love you.
For all the things that you do for me—
The songs, the care, and the love for me—
I'll thank you with a big hug from me,
Oh, Mother dear.

Nancy Nason Biddinger

I Love Mama

Sung to: "Mary Had a Little Lamb"

I love Mama, she loves me,
She loves me, she loves me.
We keep each other company,
Mama and me.

Stephanie Kidd Tyus

Celebrating Lei Day

May Day is Lei Day in Hawaii. On May 1, children and adults all wear colorful *leis* (garlands of flowers) draped over their shoulders. Leis express the "aloha spirit" of Hawaii, which is the spirit of friendship and love. Lei Day festivities include music, singing, and hula dancing. The hula dancers, wearing leis and grass skirts, gracefully move their hips while acting out the words of songs with their hands. There may be a *luau* (Hawaiian feast). The luau is held outdoors, and the main dish is a whole roast pig that has been cooked in a pit in the ground. Also included in the feast are yams, *poi* (mashed taro root) and platters of delicious tropical fruit, including bananas, mangoes, papayas, and fresh pineapple.

Hawaiian Words

Here are some Hawaiian words that you and your children might enjoy using.

- *Aloha* (ah-low-ha) is used to say both "hello" and "goodbye."

- *Wiki Wiki* (wee-kee wee-kee) means "hurry up."

- *Pau* (pow) means "finished." When you're all finished or all done with something, you can say "I'm all pau."

- *Humuhumunukunukuapua'a* (hoo-moo-hoo-moo-noo-koo-noo-koo-ah-poo-ah-ah) is the very long name for Hawaii's tiniest fish, the trigger fish. Once you have mastered the word, it's really fun to say!

Tissue Paper Leis

Cut 3-inch circles, squares, and triangles out of different colors of tissue paper and poke holes in the centers. Give each of your children a piece of yarn about 2 feet long with one end knotted and the other end wrapped with tape to make a "needle." Then let the children string the tissue paper "flowers" on their pieces of yarn to make leis. When they have finished, tie the leis around the children's necks.

Hula Hand Dancers

Use brown paper lunch sacks to make hula dancer hand puppets. Cut 5-inch fringes along the open ends of the sacks. Then pass out the flat sacks and help your children draw faces on the flaps. Let them attach small flower stickers or bits of colored tissue paper under their hula dancer faces to make leis. Then play recorded music of Hawaiian songs and let the children move their hand puppets to the music.

Hawaiian Luau

Celebrate Lei Day by turning snacktime into "luau time." Spread a sheet out on the floor and place paper or artificial flowers in the center for decorations. Let your children help peel and cube tropical fruits such as bananas, papayas, mangoes, and fresh pineapple. Arrange the fruits on paper plates and sprinkle on grated coconut, if desired. Let the children sit around the sheet on the floor and enjoy their snacks while listening to Hawaiian music.

Aloha Song

Sung to: "Happy Birthday"

Aloha to you,
Aloha to you,
Aloha, hello,
Aloha to you.

Aloha to you,
Aloha to you,
Aloha, goodbye,
Aloha to you.

Elizabeth McKinnon

Celebrating Cinco de Mayo

Cinco de Mayo, the Fifth of May, is one of Mexico's most important holidays. It commemorates the winning of a battle against the French on May 5, 1862, which eventually led to Mexico's independence. Cinco de Mayo is celebrated in Mexico and in many Mexican-American communities with parades, marching bands, and feasts that include music and dancing. In Mexico, the celebrations end at night with displays of colorful fireworks.

Mexican Serapes

To get into the spirit of your Mexican celebration, let your children make serapes to wear over their shoulders. For each child carefully tear off a four-piece section from a roll of heavy-duty white paper towels. On the back of each section tape over the perforated lines so that the towels will not come apart. Let the children snip fringes along the short ends of their towel sections (or cut the fringes yourself). Then let them use bright colors of fairly thick tempera paint to decorate their serapes with stripes, dots, or other designs. When the paint has dried, let the children wear their serapes draped over one shoulder or wrapped around both shoulders and fastened in front with a safety pin.

Paper Flowers

Let your children make large flower decorations for your Cinco de Mayo celebration. Have them fingerpaint with bright colors on pieces of white butcher paper or construction paper. When the paint has dried, cut each paper into a large flower shape. Let the children make centers for their flowers by gluing on crumpled pieces of colored tissue paper. Then display the flowers on a wall or a bulletin board.

Cinco de Mayo Parade

Make your celebration come alive by playing recorded music of Mexican songs and letting your children march around the room in a Cinco de Mayo Parade. Tie brightly colored sashes of crepe paper around the children's waists and let them use rhythm instruments to accompany the music.

Snacktime Fun

Let your children help make burritos for snacktime. Brown 1 pound ground beef and drain off the fat. Stir in 1 can (16 ounces) refried beans and heat until warm. Place a small flour tortilla on each child's plate and top it with a spoonful of the meat and bean mixture. Let the children sprinkle on grated cheese, if desired. Then roll up each tortilla and let the children enjoy eating their burritos with their fingers.

It's Cinco de Mayo Day

Sung to: "The Farmer in the Dell"

It's Cinco de Mayo Day,
It's Cinco de Mayo Day.
Let's clap our hands and shout "Olé!"
It's Cinco de Mayo Day.

Additional verses: Let's stomp our feet; twirl around; raise our arms; circle round.

Elizabeth McKinnon

Mary's Garden Mural

Place a long piece of butcher paper on a table or on the floor. Set out seed and flower catalogs. Have your children tear out pictures of flowers from the catalogs and glue them on the butcher paper to create a garden mural. Hang the completed mural on a wall or a bulletin board.

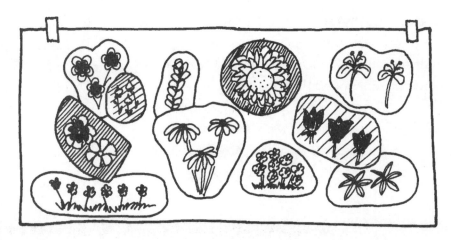

Gardening in Rows

Let your children plant seeds in their own garden "rows." Remove the lids from several cardboard egg cartons and save them for another use. Cut the bottoms of the egg cartons in half lengthwise to create rows. Give each child one row. Let the children fill the egg cups in their rows with potting soil. Have them plant fast-growing seeds, such as sunflower, radish, or marigold, in the dirt.

From time to time, ask your children to tell you how their gardens are growing.

Mary, Mary, Quite Contrary

Mary, Mary, quite contrary,
How does your garden grow?
With silver bells
And cockleshells,
And pretty maids all in a row.

Traditional

Mary Planted Her Garden

Sung to: "Mary Had a Little Lamb"

Mary planted her garden,
Her garden, her garden.
Mary planted her garden,
With rows of pretty bells.

Mary planted her garden,
Her garden, her garden.
Mary planted her garden,
With rows of cockleshells.

Let your children make up additional
verses as desired.

Gayle Bittinger

Such Pretty Flowers

For each of your children, make a paper plate "flower" and color it red, yellow, orange, blue, or pink. Add green construction paper stems and leaves. Have your children hold the flowers and sit in a circle. As you begin reading the following poem, have the children hunch over their flowers and pretend to be buds that have not opened yet. As you name each color of flower, have the children holding flowers of the same color uncurl themselves and stand up.

We are all such pretty flowers
Growing in Mary's garden bed.
When the rain comes down,
Up come the flowers of red.
  (*Red flowers stand up.*)

We are flowers that have grown
In the warmth of the sun.
Mary tends us gently—
Up come the yellow ones.
  (*Yellow flowers stand up.*)

We are flowers in the springtime,
We wear our petals bright.
Up come the orange flowers,
They are quite a pretty sight.
  (*Orange flowers stand up.*)

We are blossoms all in bloom,
Here are some in shades of blue.
  (*Blue flowers stand up.*)
And some of us are wearing pink
That glistens in the morning dew.
  (*Pink flowers stand up.*)

We are flowers in the garden
We are Mary's pride and joy.
But if you look more closely,
You'll see we're girls and boys!

Susan M. Paprocki

Spring Flower Sorting Patterns
Refer to page 140 for directions.

Clothesline Fun Patterns
Refer to page 141 for directions.

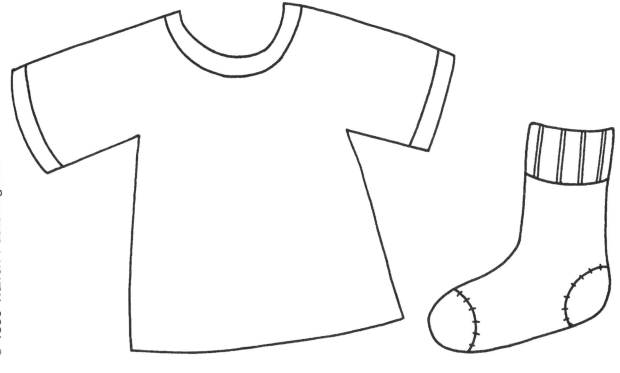

June

ART • Butterfly Ideas

Butterfly Feet

Have each of your children stand on a piece of paper with feet slightly apart. Trace around each child's feet to make "butterfly wings." Draw a butterfly body between each pair of wings and add antennae and smiling faces. Let the children decorate their butterflies with crayons. Then have them brush glue over their butterflies and sprinkle them with glitter.

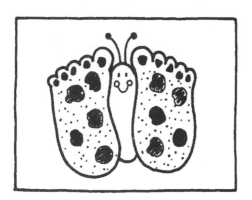

Mosaic Butterflies

Cut butterfly shapes from white construction paper. Set out assorted colors of 1-inch tissue paper squares, small containers of water, and paintbrushes. Have the children paint the butterfly shapes with water and place the tissue paper squares randomly on the shapes. Have them count to 10 and then remove the wet tissue paper to view their colorful creations.

Tissue Paper Butterflies

Cut various colors of tissue paper into 12-inch squares. Give each of your children a slot-type clothespin, a colored pipe cleaner, and one of the tissue paper squares. Have your children pinch their tissue squares together in the middle and then insert the tissue into the slots of their clothespins to make wings. Have them wind their pipe cleaners around the heads of their clothespins, leaving two small ends sticking up to form antennae. Let the children use felt-tip markers to color on eyes and to draw designs on the clothespin bodies of their butterflies. Then tie the butterflies to lengths of fishing line or string and hang them from the ceiling or in a window.

Tie Snakes

Collect a variety of old, wide neck ties. Let each of your children select a tie and stuff it with polyester fiberfill. Stitch the ends of the ties closed. Have the children glue on button eyes and yarn tongues to complete their snakes.

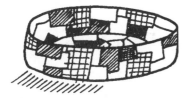

Pen Holders

Set out small blocks of wood and large wooden beads. (Make sure the hole in each bead is large enough to hold a ball point pen upright.) Have each of your children glue one of the wooden beads to one of the wooden blocks. Then let the children paint and decorate their wooden Pen Holders. Or let them glue on alphabet pasta to spell "Dad."

Change Holders

Gather large jar lids and remove their cardboard liners. Mix equal parts of liquid starch and glue. Have your children paint their lids, inside and out, with the starch and glue mixture. While the mixture is still wet, have them cover their lids with small pieces of colored tissue paper. Then have the children paint the lids with the starch and glue mixture one more time.

Nature Mural

Go on a walk with your children. Let them collect small nature objects such as feathers, flowers, leaves, and grass in small paper bags. When you return, let the children weave their objects through the holes in a fishing net. Encourage them to weave items horizontally, vertically, and diagonally. Hang the net on a wall or a bulletin board. Continue to add objects as the children find them.

Sidewalk Art

Set out several containers of chalk on a sidewalk or a driveway. Let your children use the chalk to draw designs on the concrete. Encourage them to work in small groups to create a large design. When everyone is finished, let the children clean off their designs with water from a hose.

Yarn Bubbles

Blow up a small balloon for each of your children. Mix equal parts of starch and glue together in shallow containers. Cut different colors of yarn into long pieces. Let the children dip the yarn pieces into the starch and glue mixture and wrap them around their balloons. Hang the balloons to dry. When the yarn has dried completely, pop the balloons and carefully remove them, leaving Yarn Bubbles.

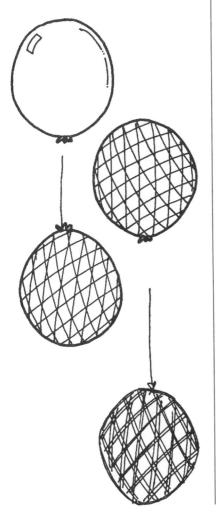

Wallpapered Box

Spread out newspapers on the floor and place a large appliance-size box on top. Set out a bucket of wallpaper paste, brushes or sponges, and leftover pieces of wallpaper. Let the children brush wallpaper paste on the backs of the wallpaper pieces and stick them all over the box.

Hint: Pieces of wrapping paper can be used in addition to the wallpaper. Or use prepasted wallpaper and water.

Printing With Gadgets

Pour small amounts of tempera paint into shallow containers. Set out a variety of kitchen gadgets such as a potato masher, a funnel, a spiral-type whisk, a cookie cutter, a tart pan, and a measuring cup. Give your children sheets of construction paper. Let them take turns dipping the various gadgets into the paint and pressing them onto their papers to make prints.

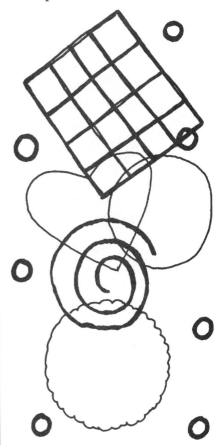

LEARNING GAMES • Parts and Wholes

Making Wholes

Collect magazine pictures of familiar objects such as houses, trees, and cars. Cut the pictures in half. If desired, cover the halves with clear self-stick paper for durability. Show your children half of an object and ask them if they can guess what it is. Then let the children find the other half that will make the object whole.

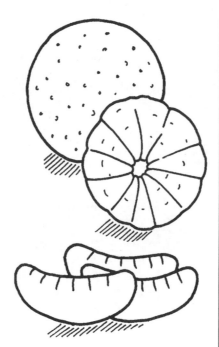

Orange Estimation

Ask your children to guess how many sections are in an unpeeled orange. Then peel the orange and count the sections with the children. Repeat for several days. The children's guesses will become more accurate each day.

Finding the Parts

Display some items that usually go together such as a key and a key chain, two halves of a bagel, a jar and a lid, and a felt-tip marker and its lid. Let your children look at the objects and decide how they can be matched to form new wholes.

Parts of Food

Cut apples into slices. Ask the children how many parts they want for snack. Or provide whole and half sandwiches. Let the children choose a whole or a half sandwich.

Cutting and Pasting

Collect a different color or pattern of paper for each of your children (construction paper, wallpaper, wrapping paper, etc.). Help the children cut their paper into strips. Have each child paste the ends of several strips of the same color together to make a short chain. Then put all of the children's chains together to make a long community chain. Help each child identify his or her part in the whole chain.

Catalog Parts

Give each of your children a catalog to look at. Have the children find different parts in their catalogs, such as toys, clothing, furniture, or jewelry. Ask the children to name different colors and items they see in each part.

Listening for Parts and Wholes

Have each of your children play an instrument into a tape recorder. Then tape the children marching around the room singing and playing their instruments together. Let the children listen to themselves playing their separate parts. Then let them hear the whole marching band.

Parts of Literature

Read a book to your children and then ask them questions such as these: "Which part did you like best? Which part made you happy? Which part was the longest? Which part made you scared? Which part made you laugh?"

Map Board

Draw a city map for your children on a piece of cardboard. Show houses, stores, and roads. Color each house and store as desired. Let your children drive miniature cars on the map. Encourage them to find a variety of ways to get from place to place. Give them directions such as these: "Drive from the gas station to the green house. Drive across the city. Drive to the grocery store. Pick up a friend at the yellow house."

Traveling Shoebox Game

Divide the inside of a shoebox lid into three sections. Draw a picture of land in one section, a picture of water in another section, and a picture of clouds in the last section. Glue pictures of different types of vehicles, such as cars, trucks, boats, airplanes, hot air balloons, and ferry boats on index cards. Have your children sort the cards according to where the vehicle travels—the ground, the water, or the air. Store the cards in the shoebox.

Ticket Game

Help your children create an airplane by arranging chairs, pillows, or benches in rows. Place index cards of various colors on a table for "tickets." Pretend to be the ticket agent. Before the children can ride on your airplane, call out which color of ticket you are accepting. As each child passes by the ticket table, have him or her select a ticket of that color to hand to you.

Variation: Instead of using colored tickets, make tickets with different shapes, sets of dots, or letters on them.

Fishing Game

Make fishing poles using wooden spoons or rolled up newspapers. Attach a short length of string to each pole. Tie a magnet to the end of each string. Cut colored construction paper into small fish shapes. Attach a paper clip to each fish. Give the fishing poles to your children. Let them use the poles to "catch" as many fish as they can. If desired, have them try to catch just the red fish, just the blue fish, etc.

Toothpick Patterns

Arrange toothpicks on large index cards in patterns. (See illustration.) Glue the toothpicks in place. Give each of your children one of the index cards and some toothpicks. Let the children try to copy the patterns shown on the cards.

Buzzy Bee's Rainy Day

By Donna Mullennix

Buzzy Bee was a hard worker. Every day he flew among the flowers, buzzing and singing,

> "I'm a buzzy little bee,
> I'm as busy as can be.
> I buzz to the flowers,
> One—two—three."

Buzzy flew on sunny days and on cloudy days. He buzzed on windy days and on still days. The only time he stopped buzzing was when it rained. On rainy days Buzzy Bee stayed inside the hive to keep dry.

One spring it rained and rained and rained. Buzzy Bee stayed inside his hive for five days. Then he said, "Bzzz. I'm tired of staying inside. I think I'll go out and buzz in the rain." Buzzy had never been in the rain before. He flew out of the hive singing,

> "I'm a buzzy little bee,
> I'm as busy as can be.
> I buzz to the flowers,
> One—two—three."

When he reached the garden, Buzzy was surprised to see that the flowers had shut their petals tight and were sleeping in the rain. "Wake up! Wake up!" he cried. But the flowers didn't hear him. So Buzzy decided to buzz around and see what else was in the spring besides flowers.

When he looked down, he saw a snail crawling slowly through the garden. "I love it when it rains," said the snail. "It's my favorite kind of weather. I love to crawl under the wet leaves and look for things to eat."

"Not me," said Buzzy. "I want it to stop raining so the flowers will wake up, for

I'm a buzzy little bee,
I'm as busy as can be.
I buzz to the flowers,
One—two—three."

Away flew Buzzy to a pond where he saw a frog hopping and croaking beside the water. "I love it when it rains," said the frog. "It's my favorite kind of weather. I love to get wet and hop in the mud."

"Not me," said Buzzy. "I want it to stop raining so the flowers will wake up, for

I'm a buzzy little bee,
I'm as busy as can be.
I buzz to the flowers,
One—two—three."

Buzzy flew to the middle of the pond where he saw a duck swimming and quacking in the water. "I love it when it rains," said the duck. "It's my favorite kind of weather. I love to swim and feel the rain running off my feathers."

"Not me," said Buzzy. "I want it to stop raining so the flowers will wake up, for

I'm a buzzy little bee,
I'm as busy as can be.
I buzz to the flowers,
One—two—three."

Buzzy suddenly felt something warm on his back. He looked up into a clear sky. The rain had stopped and now the sun was shining. "Bzzz," said Buzzy. "I love it when the sun shines. It's my favorite kind of weather!"

He flew back to the garden where the flowers were just waking up. When they saw Buzzy, they smiled and nodded their heads at him. Buzzy flapped his little wings and sang,

"I'm a HAPPY little bee,
"I'm as busy as can be.
I buzz to the flowers,
One—two—three."

Out in the Garden
By Jean Warren

Out in the garden,
Under the sun,
Grew some carrots—
Ryan picked one.

Out in the garden,
Under skies so blue,
Grew some carrots—
Tia picked two.

Out in the garden,
Near a big oak tree,
Grew some carrots—
Cameron picked three.

Out in the garden,
By the back door,
Grew some carrots—
Emily picked four.

Out in the garden,
Near a beehive,
Grew some carrots—
Max picked five.

We took those carrots
And washed the whole bunch,
Then we all sat down
And ate them for lunch.

Flannelboard Directions

Use the carrot pattern on page 196 as a guide to cut 15 carrot shapes out of orange and green felt. Place all the shapes on a flannelboard. Substitute the name of one of your children in each verse of the rhyme. As you say a child's name, have that child come up and take the appropriate number of carrot shapes off the flannelboard, one at a time, as you count out loud together.

Transportation Games • LANGUAGE

Making the Cards

Photocopy the transportation cards on page 197. If desired, color and cover them with clear self-stick paper. Cut out the cards and use them with the language activities on this page.

She'll Be Coming Round the Mountain

Have your children sing the first verse of the song "She'll Be Coming Round the Mountain." Then let them take turns drawing a transportation card, naming the vehicle on it, and making up a new verse to the song. For example, if a child draws the camper card and calls it a "big camper," have all the children sing the following song.

Sung to: "She'll be Coming Round the Mountain"

(He'll/She'll) be driving a big camper
When (he/she) comes.
(He'll/She'll) be driving a big camper
When (he/she) comes.
(He'll/She'll) be driving a big camper,
(He'll/She'll) be driving a big camper,
(He'll/She'll) be driving a big camper
When (he/she) comes.

Adapted Traditional

The Wheels on the Bus

Have your children sing several verses of the song "The Wheels on the Bus." Set out the transportation cards upside down in a pile. Have each child take a turn drawing a card and telling what part of the vehicle he or she wants to sing about and where the vehicle is traveling. For example, if a child draws the boat card; wants to sing about the boat's engine, and says the boat is traveling on a lake, have all the children sing the following song.

Sung to: "The Wheels on the Bus"

The motor on the boat goes vroom, vroom, vroom,
Vroom, vroom, vroom; vroom, vroom, vroom.
The motor on the boat goes vroom, vroom, vroom,
All around the lake.

Adapted Traditional

MY WORLD • Nature Walk

Be Prepared

A day or two before the outing, walk the trail yourself. Watch for hazards such as low hanging branches or prickly bushes. Make sure the planned route is not too difficult for your children. You may spot a bird's nest or an animal's burrow that you can point out to the children during the walk.

Color Comparisons

Cut small squares out of several different colors of construction paper. Hand them out to your children and have them try to find nature items of the same color. Leaves, wildflowers, bark, rocks, weeds, and feathers are some of the things the children could look for.

Nature Paint

If you are lucky enough to find a berry patch, collect some of the fruit to make Nature Paint. Crush the berries with a wooden spoon and add a drop or two of vinegar to prevent mold. Let the children use craft sticks to spread the Nature Paint on sheets of construction paper. (Be sure the children's clothing is covered when using a natural dye like this.)

Treasure Collectors

Before the walk, have your children make containers to hold the treasures they will find along the way. Let them decorate brown paper bags with nature stickers. Or have them add pipe cleaner handles to the bottom halves of cardboard milk cartons.

Nature Displays

To display the items your children collect, spread them out on a "nature table." Or let the children glue the items on cardboard to make nature collages. Or help each child make a see-through hanging display. Have the child arrange flat objects, such as leaves or flower petals, on the sticky side of a piece of clear self-stick paper. Place another piece of self-stick paper on top, sticky sides together, and smooth out any air bubbles. Cut the paper into a circle with pinking shears. Punch a hole at the top and add a yarn loop for hanging.

Our Job

Four-year-old Casey walks with crutches and leg braces. Three-year old Jennifer wears heavy glasses and is learning to "see" with the assistance of a dog. Five-year-old Jeremy hears with the help of a hearing aid. Mrs. Davis "speaks" with her hands. All of these people have special needs and special abilities. It is our job to help children accept and feel comfortable with all people, especially those whose abilities are different from theirs. The following activities can help young children better understand people with special needs.

In the Dramatic Play Area

Include tools used by people with special needs such as braces, canes, crutches, hearing aids, and child-size wheelchairs. Place the items in the area one at a time so your children can include these props in their everyday dramatic activities. You might also want to make special needs tools for some of your dolls.

In the Book Area

Provide books that show people with special needs as heroes and in leadership roles. (Ask your librarian for suggestions.) Offer your children some Braille books to explore. Then invite a person who can read Braille to come in and read them a story. Also, be sure that the posters, calendar pictures, and magazine photos you display depict people of all abilities engaged in active life styles.

Music and Movement

Use the activities on this page to increase sensitivity to people with different levels of ability. You will need a child-size wheelchair (many hospitals rent or lend wheelchairs), music with a heavy beat, soft instrumental music, and a speaker with the woofer exposed.

Feel the Music

Ask your children what they think it would be like if they could not hear music. Then ask if they think they can see or feel music. Put on the music with the heavy beat and show the children the speaker woofer pulsating from the beat. Help them feel the speaker with their hands.

Dancing on Wheels

Let your children take turns sitting in the wheelchair and trying to move about. Put on the soft instrumental music and encourage the children to dance while sitting in the chair. Have them move their arms, hands, and upper bodies, or move the wheels to slowly turn in circles. Let your children dance together.

Sign a Song

To help your children under-stand the concept of sign language, try doing a favorite fingerplay, such as "Eensy Weensy Spider," with actions only. Later, let your children make up their own signs for phrases such as "Good Job" or "Quiet, Please."

Exploring the Grass

On a warm and sunny summer day, take your children out to explore the grass. Let the children take off their shoes and socks and feel the grass with their bare feet. Ask the children, "How does the grass feel? Does it tickle your feet?" Let the children roll in the grass. Have them either roll separately or all together in the same direction.

Moving Like Insects

Encourage your children to explore the many insects who also like the grass in the summer. Have the children act like an army of ants marching across the grass. Then have them all hook together and pretend to be a large caterpillar crawling through the grass. Then let them scurry like beetles or hop like grasshoppers through the grass. Let them buzz and fly across the top of the grass like bees looking for flowers.

Bikes

Invite your children to join you on a pretend bike trip. To ride their pretend bikes, have the children lie on their backs and pedal their legs in the air. Ask the children where they would like to go on their trip.

Planes

Let your children pretend to be planes and fly around the play area, carefully avoiding other planes. When you wish to end this activity, have the children circle the airfield and take turns landing.

Trains

Have your children form a line. Ask each child to place his or her left hand on the shoulder of the person in front. Then have the children move their right hands in circles like the wheels of a train. To blow their "whistles," have them raise their right hand for a moment and pull imaginary handles. When the children tire of riding the train, toot your whistle and call out "All out for..." and have them decide on a destination.

Flutter, Flutter, Butterfly
Sung to: "Twinkle, Twinkle, Little Star"

Flutter, flutter, butterfly,
Floating in the summer sky.
Floating by for all to see,
Floating by so merrily.
Flutter, flutter, butterfly,
Floating in the summer sky.

Bonnie Woodard

Crickets Chirping
Sung to: "Frère Jacques"

Crickets chirping, crickets chirping.
Chirp, chirp, chirp,
Chirp, chirp, chirp.
Chirping in the tree tops,
Chirping that never stops.
Chirp, chirp, chirp,
Chirp, chirp, chirp.

Bonnie Woodard

Oh, the Ants Are Busy
Sung to: "She'll Be Coming Round the Mountain"

Oh, the ants are busy, busy as can be.
Oh, the ants are busy, busy as can be.
See them dig and dig and dig
Lots of tunnels, oh, so big.
Oh, the ants are busy, busy as can be.

Kristine Wagoner

Vegetables

Sung to: "Twinkle, Twinkle, Little Star"

Vegetables, vegetables, use a hoe,
Vegetables, vegetables, soon will grow.
Vegetables, vegetables, corn and potatoes,
Vegetables, vegetables, squash and tomatoes.
Vegetables, vegetables, washed and clean,
Vegetables, vegetables, red and green.

Vegetables, vegetables, what a treat,
Vegetables, vegetables, can't be beat.
Vegetables, vegetables, on a tray,
Vegetables, vegetables, every day.
Vegetables, vegetables, such good food,
Vegetables, vegetables, baked or stewed.

Vegetables, vegetables, on my plate,
Vegetables, vegetables, taste just great.
Vegetables, vegetables, are good for you.
Vegetables, vegetables, have a few.
Vegetables, vegetables, carrots and peas,
Vegetables, vegetables, have more, please.

Barbara B. Fleisher

Planting

Sung to: "Bingo"

There were some kids who wanted carrots
And this is what they did:
Plant, plant, plant the carrots,
Plant, plant, plant the carrots,
Plant, plant, plant the carrots,
And that is what they did.

Additional verses: Water the carrots; Weed the carrots; Pick the carrots; Cook the carrots; Eat the carrots.

Nancy Nason Biddinger

Mr. Crocodile
Sung to: "Twinkle, Twinkle, Little Star"

Mr. Croc, you look so mean!
Large and scaly, wet and green—
Your great big mouth has lots of teeth.
Your big, round belly's underneath.
You eat and eat all through the day,
Then it's time to swim away.

R. Hardy Garrison

The Tiger
Sung to: "Frere Jacques"

Orange and black, great big cat,
Four big paws, long sharp claws.
Through the jungle running.
Oh, I hear her coming.
Does she bite? What a sight!

Cynthia Walters

Monkeys Climb and Swing
Sung to: "London Bridge"

Monkeys screech and climb and swing,
Climb and swing, climb and swing.
Monkeys screech and climb and swing.
I love to watch them.

Betty Silkunas

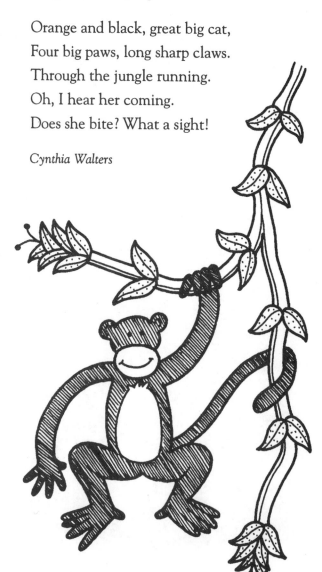

Father Dear
Sung to: "Jingle Bells"

Father's Day, Father's Day.
It is almost here.
It's the time when we say,
"Thank you, Father dear!"
Father's Day, Father's Day.
It is almost here.
Hugs and kisses to my dad.
I love you, Father dear!

Becky Valenick

It's Your Special Day
Sung to: "The Muffin Man"

Daddy, it's your special day,
And it's time for me to say,
I'm glad for all the things you do.
Thank you, Daddy. I love you!

Sue Brown

Oh, My Daddy
Sung to: "Clementine"

Oh, my daddy, oh, my daddy,
Oh, my very special dad,
I want to thank you very much
For being my special dad.

Patricia Coyne

Seed Mosaics

Show and discuss with your children various kinds of vegetable seeds. Then set out bowls of different kinds of seeds, glue, brushes, and pieces of paper. Have the children brush glue on the paper. Then let them arrange seeds on the glue to create Seed Mosaics.

Growing Garden Vegetables

Let your children grow their own garden vegetables to eat. Give each of the children a peat pot or a paper cup. Have the children fill their pots with dirt. Then let them plant several seeds in their pots. (Leaf lettuce and radishes are quick and easy to grow.) Have them place their pots in a warm, sunny spot and keep the soil moist. When the seeds become seedlings, let the children plant them outdoors in a garden. Have the children tend their garden until the vegetables are grown and ready to eat.

All in a Row

Use the vegetable patterns on page 196 as guides to cut out several of each vegetable shape from felt. Place the vegetables in a pile in front of a flannelboard. Let the children take turns sorting the vegetables and then arranging them in rows on the flannelboard.

Carrots and Peas

Carrots and peas,
Carrots and peas,
Where, oh, where
Are my carrots and peas?

I went to the garden
And what did I see?
Holes and vines,
But no carrots and peas.

I went to the kitchen
And what did I see?
Pods and tops,
But no carrots and peas.

I went to the stove
And what did I see?
A pan of water,
But no carrots and peas.

I went to the table
And what did I see?
A great big bowl
Full of carrots and peas.

Carrots and peas,
Carrots and peas,
Will somebody please pass
The carrots and peas?

Jean Warren

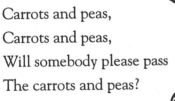

The Vegetable Man

Talk with your children about all the different kinds of vegetables you can grow in a garden. If desired, set out a display of vegetables or pictures of vegetables. Then read the following story out loud and let the children take turns filling in the blanks.

While I was walking down the street,

A vegetable man I happened to meet.

His head was a bumpy _____ .

His arms were long _____.

His body was a large _____.

His legs were two green _____.

His feet were round _____.

His fingers and toes were red _____.

He looked so good that on a hunch,

I invited the man home for lunch!

Jean Warren

Snacktime Fun

Set out a variety of salad vegetables such as lettuce, cucumbers, carrots, celery, tomatoes, radishes, zucchini, broccoli, and cauliflower. Let your children help wash and prepare the vegetables. Place each vegetable in a separate bowl. Set the bowls on a table to make a salad bar. Give the children plates. Show them how to spoon a small amount of each vegetable from the salad bar onto their plate. Then help each child add a small amount of salad dressing to their salad.

Musical Drawings

Provide large pieces of paper and crayons or felt-tip markers for your children. Play the classical piece "Flight of the Bumblebee" by Rimsky-Korsakov. Encourage the children to think of their crayons or markers as "bees" as they draw to the music.

Bees in a Honeycomb

Cut cardboard tubes into sections of equal length. Let your children make honeycombs by paper-clipping or gluing the sections together. Have your children make bee shapes using playdough for bodies and peppercorns for eyes. Bake the playdough bees at 250°F for about 1 hour, depending on their size. Let your children glue the bees to the honeycombs.

Matching Game

Cut five pairs of bee shapes out of construction paper. On each pair draw one, two, three, four, or five stripes. Cover the bees with clear self-stick paper for durability, if desired. Challenge your children to find each pair of bees by matching or counting the stripes.

Bee Stories

After talking about and looking at pictures of bees, have each of your children respond to the sentence, "If I were a bee I would...." Write down their stories on sheets of construction paper. Then let the children decorate them with yellow and black felt-tip markers.

Buzz

Select two of your children to be Searchers. Have them leave the room while you and the other children hide an object. When the Searchers return, have the other children start buzzing. The closer the Searchers get to the hidden object, the louder the others should buzz. The farther away the Searchers get from the hidden object, the softer the others should buzz. When the object is found, select two more children to be the Searchers.

Bees in the Beehives

Divide your children into groups of three. Have two of the children in each group hold hands to make a "beehive." Have the third child stand inside the beehive as a Bee. When a signal sounds, have all the Bees run to find a new hive. Repeat the action, letting the children take turns being hives and Bees.

Jungle Facts

Although these facts are provided for the teacher's information, older children may enjoy learning a little more about the jungle.

- Although many people use the word "jungle" to describe a tropical rain forest, a jungle is not the same. The floor of a jungle is covered with thick vines, while the floor of a tropical rain forest is clear.

- The biggest jungles are found in Central America, northern South America, and Central Africa.

- A jungle is home to many animals, including birds, monkeys, and reptiles. Grazing animals, such as zebras and giraffes, do not live in jungles but in open grasslands. Lions, who depend on grazing animals for prey, also live in grasslands. Other wild cats, such as jaguars and tigers, live in jungles and hunt in grasslands. Elephants can be found in both jungles and grasslands.

Animal Classification

Cut photographs of jungle animals, such as elephants, leopards, or parrots, out of nature magazines. Cover the photos with clear self-stick paper for durability. Let your children sort the pictures by characteristics such as body covering (fur, feathers, or skin), color, or number of legs.

Guess Who?

Place a piece of cardboard inside a large envelope. Use a craft knife to cut three or four large flaps in the front of the envelope. Place a picture of a jungle animal in the envelope. Raise one of the flaps and let your children guess what animal is shown in the picture. Continue raising flaps until someone guesses the animal's identity. Place a new picture in the envelope and continue playing as long as interest lasts.

Jungle Chant

At circle time, slowly say the name of a jungle animal. Clap once on each syllable. Repeat and have your children say the name of the animal and clap the rhythm. Include one-, two-, and three-syllable animal names such as frog, tiger, monkey, crocodile, and elephant.

Elephant Walk

Read the following poem to your children and have them act out the motions.

Right foot, left foot, down the street,
(Step with one foot, then the other, swaying from side to side.)

With my trunk and four big feet.
(Hold arms together in front and swing them like a trunk.)

I am gray and big and slow.
(Walk slowly around the room.)

Watch me as I come and go.

Adapted Traditional

Five Little Monkeys

Five little monkeys heard a tiger's roar,
(Hold up five fingers.)

One ran away, and then there were four.
(Hold up four fingers.)

Four little monkeys swinging through the trees,
(Swing four fingers back and forth.)

One swung away, and then there were three.
(Hold up three fingers.)

Three little monkeys heard someone shout, "Boo!"
(Look surprised.)

One went away, and then there were two.
(Hold up two fingers.)

Two little monkeys frolicked in the sun,
(Dance two fingers around.)

One went away, and then there was one.
(Hold up one finger.)

One little monkey, sad the day was done,
(Look sad.)

She went away, and then there were none.
(Hold up fist.)

R. Hardy Garrison

Vegetable Patterns
Refer to pages 178 and 190 for directions.

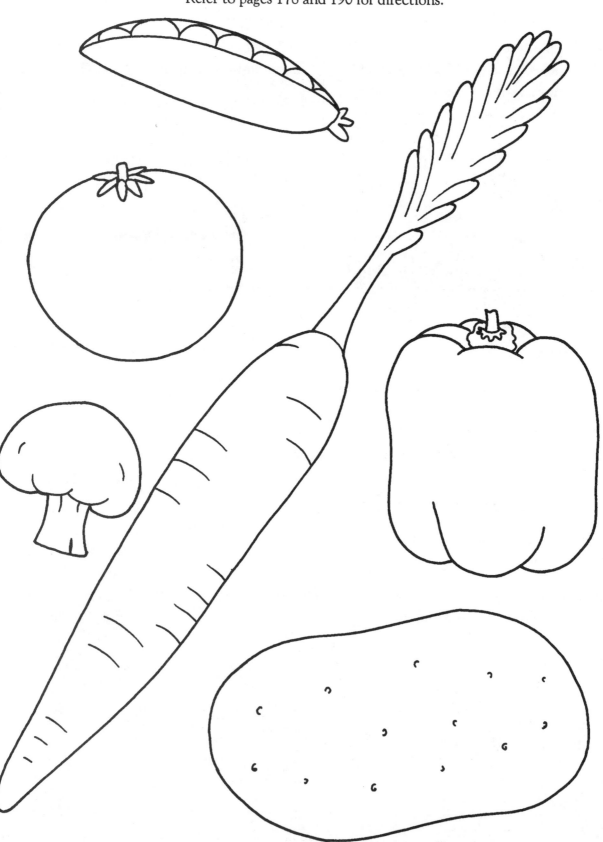

Transportation Cards

Refer to page 179 for directions.

July

Fireworks Mural

Collect plastic mesh dish scrubbers (available at grocery stores and variety stores). Pour small amounts of tempera paint into shallow containers. Place a piece of black butcher paper on a table. Have your children dip the dish scrubbers into the paint and lightly touch them to the butcher paper to make "fireworks" prints. Let the children continue until the black "sky" is filled with exploding fireworks. Then hang the mural on a wall or a bulletin board.

Variation: Let the children print fireworks on individual pieces of black construction paper.

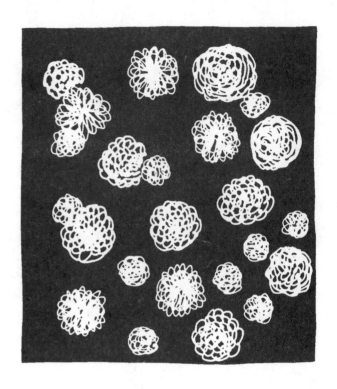

Ants at the Picnic Mural

Cut pictures of foods out of magazines. Give each of your children a paper plate. Have them glue their plates to a paper tablecloth. Then have the children glue the food pictures on the plates. Let them add "ants" to the mural by lightly touching their thumbs to washable black ink pads and pressing their thumbs on the tablecloth. Hang the tablecloth on a wall or a bulletin board.

Easy Octopus Art

For each of your children, draw seven 5½-inch lines along the length of a 9-by-12-inch piece of construction paper. Have the children cut along the lines on the papers to make octopus "arms." When they have finished, roll each paper into a tube and tape the uncut sides together to make the octopus body, leaving the arms free. Let the children attach self-stick circles for eyes. Then have them bend their octopus arms outward.

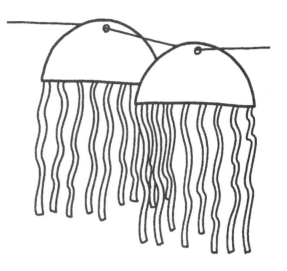

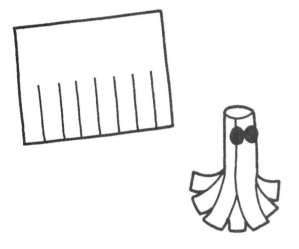

Jellyfish Art

Make a jellyfish body for each of your children by cutting a half-circle out of heavy white paper. Have the children cut thin strips out of white tissue paper and glue them to the backs of their jellyfish bodies to make tentacles. Hang the finished jellyfish on a string stretched across a window and watch them "swim" as air moves through the room.

Paper Plate Fish

Give each of your children a paper plate. Show the children how to cut a triangle shape out of one side of a paper plate. Then let each child cut a triangle out of his or her plate. Have the children glue their triangles to their plates to make tail fins. Let them decorate their fish plates with felt-tip markers.

Wagon Art

Cut paper to fit in a child's wagon. Put the paper into the wagon along with colored pencils. Place the wagon outside. Let one of your children take the wagon to a place in the yard. Encourage the child to create art on the paper in the wagon while bending over the side of the wagon or crawling into the wagon. Let the child move the wagon to as many places as he or she wants.

Window Painting

Mix powdered tempera paint with a small amount of liquid dishwashing soap to make a fingerpaint that is easy to clean up. Then put a small amount of the paint on the outside of a low window. Let your children take turns using fingers, cotton swabs, kitchen brushes, or plastic dish scrapers to make designs in the paint. To clean, spray with water and wipe with a rag.

Playdough Impressions

Have your children collect a variety of leaves and weeds. Give each of them a small lump of playdough or clay. Have the children make their playdough flat and smooth. Let them press the leaves and weeds into the playdough. Then help them carefully remove the leaves and weeds to leave impressions. Ask the children to match the impressions to the actual leaves and weeds.

Crazy T-Shirts

Have your children bring in old white T-shirts to tie-dye. Place large dishpans of several bright colors of cold water dye in an outside area. Help the children tightly wrap several rubber bands on their shirts in whatever patterns they choose. As each child directs you, dip sections of his or her shirt into different colors of dye. Allow the T-shirts to dry. Then have a Crazy T-Shirt fashion show and let the children describe their creations.

Hint: Avoid dipping the entire shirt into several colors of dye because it will turn out a brownish green color.

Variation: Have the children make Crazy T-Shirts by laying them on the ground and spatter-painting them with brushes and fabric paints.

Watermelon Fun

Cut a watermelon in half lengthwise. Let your children use plastic spoons or melon-ballers to scoop watermelon into paper bowls. Ask the children to guess how many seeds will be in their watermelon pieces. As they eat their watermelon, have them place the seeds on napkins. When the children finish eating, have them count their seeds. How did their guesses compare with the actual number of seeds? Lay the seeds out in the sun to dry. Then use them to make watermelon seed collages on pink paper.

Sun Visors

For each of your children, cut a hole in the middle of a large paper plate. Let the children decorate the rims of their paper plates with crayons and felt-tip markers. As they finish, help them slip their personally designed visors over their heads.

Shell Game

Hide an object under one of three shells lined up in a row. Then move the shells around and have your children guess which shell the object is hidden under.

Hint: Shells can often be purchased inexpensively at import stores or craft shops. Or check with local fish markets to see if they will let you have discarded shells or shell pieces.

Shell Hunt

Fill a pail or a dishpan half full with sand. Mix in some small shells. Invite one of your children to dig for shells. When the child is finished, help him or her count the shells. Then have the child place the shells on a piece of paper and draw a circle around each one. Write the corresponding numeral at the top of the page. Repeat with each child.

Shell Match-Ups

Collect pairs of different kinds of shells. Set out the shells in a random order. Let your children take turns finding the shells that match.

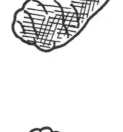

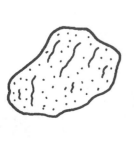

Puzzle Plates

Give each of your children a paper plate with a solid color painted around the rim. Let the children use felt-tip markers to draw pictures on their plates. Then cut each plate into three to six puzzle pieces (depending on the age of the child). Give the children their puzzle pieces and plain paper plates to use as bases. Let the children put their own puzzles together. Then have them exchange puzzles with friends.

Color Match

Paint paper plates a variety of colors (one colored paper plate for each pair of children). Cut the plates in half and give each of your children one piece. Have the children sit in a circle and select a child to begin by holding up his or her colored plate half. Then have the child with the matching colored plate half hold it up too. Put the plates together. Continue until all the plates are matched up.

Counting Game

With a felt-tip marker, divide a paper plate into four to eight wedges (depending on the age of the child). Number the wedges, starting with 1. Give each of your children a numbered plate and some small counting objects such as dried beans or buttons. Have the child identify each numeral and count out the corresponding number of beans to place on each wedge.

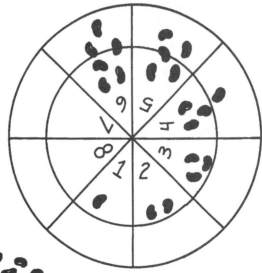

Hard or Soft

Collect several hard items such as a block, a pan, a toy car, a bowl, and a box. Then collect several soft items such as a stuffed animal, a velvet ribbon, a piece of fake fur, a chenille pipe cleaner, and a cotton ball. Draw a picture of a block on a large sheet of paper and print the word "hard" under it. Draw a picture of a stuffed animal on another sheet of paper and print the word "soft" under it. Place the items and the papers on the floor. Let each child choose an item and place it on the appropriate paper.

Opposites Matching Game

Cut out magazine pictures of things that are opposite such as a big house and a small house or a young person and an old person. Mount the pictures on index cards and, if desired, cover them with clear self-stick paper for durability. Mix up the cards and let the children take turns finding the pairs of opposites.

Long and Short

Prepare a tray using pairs of real objects to introduce the concept of long and short. Choose objects that come in long and short lengths such as candles, spoons, plastic drinking straws, and nails. Set out the pairs. Let each of your children choose and describe a pair of objects, telling which one is long and which one is short.

Variation: Apply the same idea to the concept of big and little.

Flag Time

Show your children the American flag or a picture of one. Discuss with your children where they see the flag. Ask them to name the colors on the flag. Together, count the red stripes, the white stripes, and the stars.

Stars and Stripes

Cut star shapes and stripes out of red, white, and blue felt. Place the stars and stripes in front of a flannelboard. Begin by playing a simple matching game. Put one of the stars on the flannelboard. Have one of your children place a matching colored star below it. Then place a star and a stripe on the flannelboard. Ask another child to place matching shapes below those. Continue placing more stars and stripes on the flannelboard, making patterns with them as you do. Help the children discover the patterns as they put on the matching shapes.

Fourth of July Sorting Game

Cut small, medium-sized, and large star shapes and bell shapes out of red, white, and blue construction paper. Mix up the shapes. Let your children sort the shapes according to color, shape, or size.

Five Little Fish

Five little fish swimming by the shore.
One got caught, and then there were four.

Four little fish swimming in the sea.
One got caught, and then there were three.

Three little fish swimming in the blue.
One got caught, and then there were two.

Two little fish swimming in the sun.
One got caught, and then there was one.

One little fish swimming for home.
Decided it was best never to roam.

Jean Warren

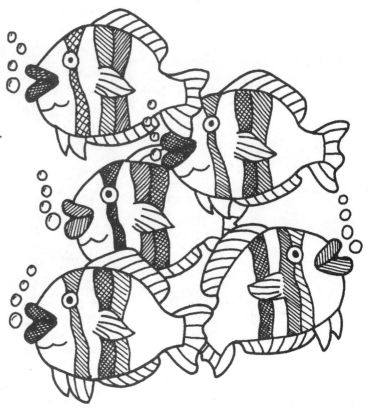

At the Beach

I dig holes in the sand with my fingers.
  (Wiggle fingers.)

I dig holes in the sand with my toes.
  (Wiggle toes.)

Then I pour some water in the holes,
  (Pretend to pour water.)

I wonder where it goes?
  (Move hands out to sides, palms up.)

Elizabeth McKinnon

Little Sad Clown
By Jean Warren

Once there was a little clown
Who looked so very sad,
No matter what trick she did,
It always turned out bad.

She tried juggling balls
And running up the aisles,
But no matter what she did
The crowd would never smile.

Everybody liked her
But she always looked so sad,
Everyone would start to cry,
And, for a clown, that's bad.

Then one day she tried a trick
Of walking upside down.
Soon everyone was laughing
At this funny little clown.

She wondered why they all would laugh
When she was upside down.
She didn't know that turned this way
Her face was not a frown.

For when she stood upon her hands
And walked around a while,
The frown that was upon her face
Turned right into a smile.

Rhyme Directions
Photocopy the sad clown pattern on page 228. Show the clown to your children as you read the rhyme on this page. At the end of the rhyme, turn the sad clown upside down to make a happy clown. If desired, make a copy of the clown for each child. Repeat the rhyme, letting the children fill in as many words as they can.

Rubber Glove Puppet

Wash and dry an old rubber glove. Draw facial features on each finger with a permanent felt-tip marker. Use the Rubber Glove Puppet while telling a multi-character story.

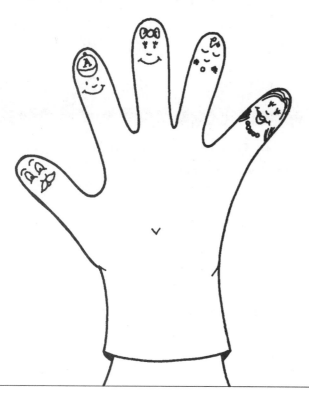

Bottle Puppet

Rinse and dry an empty liquid dishwashing detergent bottle and discard the cap. Hold the bottle upside down. Glue or tape a piece of fabric around the bottom two-thirds of the bottle, leaving the top third of the bottle uncovered for a face. Use permanent felt-tip markers to draw eyes, a nose, and a mouth on the face part of the bottle. Glue pieces of yarn to the top of the bottle for hair.

Envelope Puppet

Tuck in the flap of a business-size envelope. Place your hand inside the envelope with your fingers at one end and your thumb at the other end. Bend the middle of the envelope and bring your fingers and thumb together to make the puppet. Use felt-tip markers to draw on facial features. Open and close your hand to make the puppet talk.

Fruit and Veggie Puppets

Fresh fruits and vegetables make great spur of the moment puppets. Hold the fruit or vegetable by the bottom and use straight pins to attach a scrap of cloth around it so your hand is hidden. Carve or draw on facial features or pin on facial features cut from felt or construction paper. Almost any kind of firm fruit or vegetable has great puppet potential. Try using unpeeled apples, bananas, potatoes, zucchini, or carrots. These puppets are a fun way to discuss good eating habits with your children.

Puppet Stage

Collect a rectangular pop-up facial tissue box. Cut out one of the long sides of the box. Hold the box so that the cutout opening is at the bottom and the oval opening is toward the audience. Insert any small puppets, such as the Wooden Spoon Puppets on this page, through the bottom of the box so they show through the oval opening.

Wooden Spoon Puppets

Use felt-tip markers to draw faces on wooden ice cream spoons. Glue on felt or construction paper clothing. Add yarn hair for a finishing touch. If desired, use the puppets with the Puppet Stage activity described on this page.

MY WORLD • Things That Fly

Making a Parachute

Cut four 12-inch pieces of string. Tie the strings to the four corners of an old handkerchief or fabric square. Then thread the ends of the strings through the hole in an empty spool. Tie the ends into a knot too big to slip back out through the hole. Use the parachute outside. Let the children take turns tossing the parachute up into the air and watching it float down to the ground.

Airplane

Use the patterns on page 229 as guides for cutting an airplane body shape, a wing shape, and a tail shape out of a plastic-foam food tray. Make slits in the airplane body as indicated by the dotted lines. Insert the wing shape through the wide slit in the airplane body and the tail shape into the notched slit at the end. Let your children take turns flying the plane outside in an open area.

Rocket

Thread a long length of string through a plastic drinking straw. Have two of your children hold the string tight between them. Blow up a balloon and have another child hold the end closed while you tape the straw to the side of the balloon as shown. When you say "Go," have the child let go of the balloon to make it "rocket" along the string.

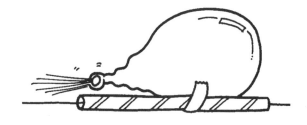

Facts About Jellyfish

Share these jellyfish facts with your children.

- Jellyfish live in the sea, usually along the coast.

- There are various colors of jellyfish, including clear, pale orange, pink, and blue.

- Jellyfish swim by taking water inside their bodies and pushing it out to propel themselves upward.

- Jellyfish sting fish with their tentacles to catch them for food.

Jellyfish Game

Attach crepe paper streamers to a length of yarn. Select one child to be the Jellyfish and tie the streamer-covered yarn around his or her waist for tentacles. Let the other children pretend to be fish. Have the Jellyfish chase the fish and try to touch them with his or her "tentacles." When a fish is caught by the Jellyfish it must stand still. The last fish touched is the next Jellyfish.

Jellyfish Colors

Cut out jellyfish shapes in orange, pink, blue, and clear (use clear self-stick paper). Attach a wooden craft stick to each shape to make a puppet. Hold up the pink jellyfish while you sing the following song. Repeat, holding up the other puppets and substituting the names of their colors for *pink*.

Sung to: "My Bonnie Lies Over the Ocean"

This jellyfish lives in the ocean,
This jellyfish lives in the sea.
This jellyfish lives in the ocean,
Oh, pink jellyfish, swim by me.

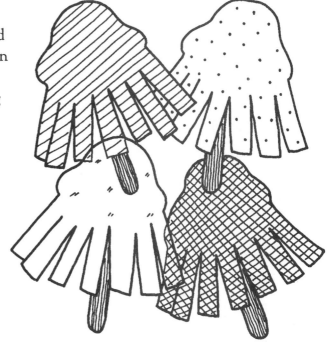

Susan Peters

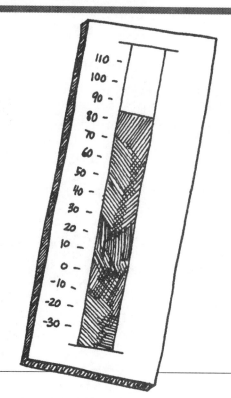

Thermometer

Summertime is a good time to help children learn how to read a thermometer. Obtain a large outdoor thermometer and place it where your children can see it. Then make a play thermometer for your children. Cut a small slit at the top and bottom of a rectangular piece of cardboard. Color half of a white ribbon red. Thread the ribbon through the slits and tie it in the back. Mark the front of the cardboard with the degrees found on your thermometer. As the temperature changes during the day, have the children change their play thermometer by moving the red part of the ribbon up or down.

Underwater Exploration

Make a simple underwater viewer for your children by cutting off and discarding the top and bottom of a 2-liter plastic bottle. Cover one end of the remaining middle section with plastic wrap. Secure the wrap with a large rubber band. Have the children view underwater scenes in a wading pool or a tub of water.

Sand

See if your children can tell you where sand comes from. Show them rocks and shells and a handful of sand. Explain that over time, powerful waves smash the rocks and shells into tiny pieces. The water keeps the pieces clean. These pieces are sand. Then explain that when rocks break down into tiny pieces and mix with decayed plants, they become dirt. Have your children compare sand and dirt. Have them look at wet and dry sand. See if the children can think of things to do with wet and dry sand.

What Is Biodegradable?

Let your children dig four small holes outside in the dirt. Have them place a lettuce leaf in the first hole, a piece of paper in the second one, a plastic bag in the third one, and a piece of plastic foam in the fourth one. Have the children fill the holes up with dirt and mark them with sticks or rocks. In two or three months go back out to the holes. Explain to your children that things that decay in the earth are called *biodegradable*. Let the children dig up the items. What did they find? Which item was the most biodegradable? Which was the least? What happens when things like plastic-foam cups are thrown away? What happens when lettuce leaves are thrown away? Which is better for our earth?

Rummage Sale

Have a Rummage Sale to promote reusing items and reducing waste. Ask your children and their parents to bring in things they no longer use. Let the children help you sort the items by type, set up displays, make signs, and sell the items. Donate leftover items to a local charity.

Worm Composting

Line a sturdy cardboard box with plastic. Make 10 small holes in the bottom of the box for drainage. Fill the box with a bedding material such as grass, peat moss, or straw. Add some red worms (available at bait or garden shops). Keep the bedding material moist. Let the children feed the worms any leftover food scraps except meat, fat, and bones. Then have them observe what happens. How do worms help us? When the original bedding material is no longer recognizable, push it over to one side of the box and add new bedding material. In about a week, after the worms have moved to the new material, carefully scoop out the composted material and let the children use it to fertilize a flower or vegetable garden.

Space Adventure

Invite your children to go on a Space Adventure. Have the children put on imaginary space helmets and large moon boots before continuing on with the following activities.

Count Down

Count down from 10 to 1 and let your children "blast off" in their individual spaceships. Be sure that the children use their "radar" to prevent collisions with the other spaceships.

Orbiting

When your children reach outer space, have them slow down and begin to orbit the moon (which could be a rubber ball placed in the center of the room).

Moon Landing

Encourage your children to land on the moon. Have them climb out of their spaceships and walk around in their moon boots. Ask them to pick up rock samples from the moon surface and plant a flag in the ground. Finally, have your children take imaginary photographs of their adventure and come home for a landing.

Can Stilts

Gather two cans of the same size for each of your children. For each can, use a hammer and a nail to punch two holes opposite each other about 1 inch below the top rim. Thread a rope through each can by bringing the rope through one hole and out the other. Tie the ends together, leaving enough rope to reach a child's waist. Give each child two of the cans. Have them put their feet on top of their cans, grasp the rope loops, and pull up on the cans to take steps.

Water Painting

Let your children have fun with outdoor water painting. Give them large paint brushes and let them "paint" the house, garage, or side of a building with water. Encourage them to paint in patterns or designs as well as straight up and down.

Bottle Scoops

Make scoops by diagonally cutting off the bottoms of plastic laundry detergent bottles. Make a yarn ball by wrapping yarn around a piece of cardboard, sliding the cardboard out, and tying the yarn together in the middle. Let the children use the scoops to toss and catch the yarn ball.

Variation: Let your children use the scoops to toss and catch small sponges or crumpled newspaper balls.

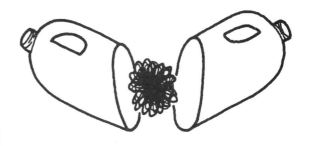

MUSIC • Fourth of July Songs

This Is July
Sung to: "Frère Jacques"

Fourth of July, Fourth of July,
Independence Day, Independence Day.
Hear the bands playing,
See our flag waving.
Fourth of July, Fourth of July.

Gayle Bittinger

Fireworks in the Sky
Sung to: "Row, Row, Row Your Boat"

Boom, crack, whistle, pop!
Fireworks in the sky.
See them lighting up the night,
On the Fourth of July.

Red, blue, gold, and green,
With fireworks we say,
"Happy Birthday, America,
It's Independence Day!"

Elizabeth McKinnon

Beat a Drum
Sung to: "Clementine"

Beat a drum, march along,
Give a cheer, "Hip, hip, hurray!"
Wave a flag, sing a song.
Happy Independence Day!

See the fireworks in the sky,
Give a cheer, "Hip, hip, hurray!"
Happy Birthday to America.
How we love the U.S.A.!"

Lois Putnam

Colors of Our Flag

Sung to: "Three Blind Mice"

Red, white, and blue. Red, white, and blue.
Colors of our flag. Colors of our flag.
Soon it will be the Fourth of July,
And that, you know, is the reason why
We sing about our country's flag,
Red, white, and blue.

Barbara B. Fleisher

Wave a Flag

Sung to: "Did You Ever See a Lassie?"

Did you ever wave a flag,
A flag, a flag?
Did you ever wave a flag,
For your country?
Wave this way and that way,
And this way and that way.
Did you ever wave a flag,
For your country?

Barbara Paxson

Statue of Liberty

Sung to: "I'm a Little Teapot"

I'm a giant statue, see my torch,
Symbol of freedom and peace for all.
See me in the harbor
So straight and tall,
Welcoming the people, one and all.

Betty Loew White

Summer's Here!

Sung to: "Frère Jacques"

Days are longer, sunshine's stronger.
Summer's here! Summer's here!
Let's jump through the sprinkler,
Let's make lemonade,
Summer's here! Summer's here!

Diane Thom

Sand Castle

Sung to: "Pop! Goes the Weasel"

Sand castle on the beach,
I built you nice and strong.
The tide washed in upon the sand—
Whoops! You were gone.

Saundra Winnett

Fish, Fish

Sung to: "Skip to My Lou"

Fish, fish, swim up high,
Fish, fish, swim down low,
Fish, fish, swim so fast,
Fish, fish, swim so slow.

Have your children pretend to be fish and act out
the motions described in the song.

Betty Silkunas

Did You Ever See an Airplane?

Sung to: "Did You Ever See a Lassie?"

Did you ever see an airplane,
An airplane, an airplane?
Did you ever see an airplane
Way up in the sky?
There are big ones and small ones
And short ones and tall ones.
Did you ever see an airplane
Way up in the sky?

Judith Taylor Burtchet

Rockets and Airplanes

Sung to: "Twinkle, Twinkle, Little Star"

Rockets and airplanes flying high,
  (Spread out arms, twist at waist.)
Flying fast up in the sky.
The Concorde makes a sonic BOOM!
  (Clap.)
A spaceship flies up to the moon.
Maybe someday I'll ride a jet,
Or be a pilot, better yet.
  (Pretend to fly jet.)

Diane Thom

Helicopter

Sung to: "Frère Jacques"

Helicopter, helicopter
In the sky, in the sky.
Flying all around,
Going up and down,
In the sky, in the sky.

Judith Taylor Burtchet

Paint Washes

Have your children use crayons to draw pictures on sheets of construction paper. Make a wash by diluting tempera paint with water. Let the children brush the paint wash over their papers to make the crayon drawings stand out.

Droplet Designs

Fill several cups with water and add a few drops of food coloring to each cup. Give each of your children an eyedropper and a piece of fabric or absorbent paper such as a coffee filter or a paper towel. Let the children use the eyedroppers to drop colored water on their fabric or papers. Have them observe as the water evaporates, leaving only the color on the absorbent material.

Sound

Fill four glasses with different levels of water. Carefully strike each glass with a spoon. Each glass will make a different sound. Ask your children questions such as these: "Which sound is the highest? Which sound is the lowest? How could we make even higher or lower sounds?"

Water Charades

Make cards with pictures of different activities you can do in or with water such as swimming, brushing teeth, watering plants, or taking a bath. Sitting in a group, ask one of your children to draw a card and, without showing it to anyone, act out the movement pictured on the card. Once the other children have guessed the activity, let another child draw a card. Continue until each child has had a turn.

I Live in the Water

Discuss with your children animals that live in the water and animals that do not. Then say the name of an animal. If the animal lives in water, have the children clap their hands. If the animal does not, have them remain quiet.

Variation: Instead of clapping, have your children make swimming motions whenever they hear the name of an animal that lives in water.

Water Table Tips

Add variety to your water table with the following ideas.

- Add liquid dishwashing detergent to the water for bubble-making with eggbeaters or plastic drinking straws.

- Set out plastic drinking straws to use for blowing toy boats across the water.

- Add one or two drops of food coloring to the water.

- Vary the temperature of the water.

- Set out measuring cups, funnels, strainers, and basters.

- Provide objects that sink and objects that float.

The Three Little Pigs

Read or tell the story "The Three Little Pigs" to your children. Let them act out the parts of the pigs and the wolf. Encourage them to retell the story to you and to one another.

Paper Plate Pigs

Let your children paint paper plates light pink to use for pig faces. Cut ear shapes and circles for noses out of a darker shade of pink construction paper. When the plates have dried, let the children glue on the ear and nose shapes. Have them each glue two circles punched out of black construction paper onto their pig noses. Then let them glue on larger black circles for eyes.

House Pictures

Set out pieces of dried grass for straw; wooden toothpicks for sticks; and small, red construction paper rectangles for bricks. Let your children glue the materials on pieces of light blue construction paper to create straw houses, stick houses, and brick houses. When the glue has dried, display the House Pictures on a wall or a bulletin board.

Pig Finger Puppets

Make three Pig Finger Puppets, like the one shown in the illustration, to use when telling "The Three Little Pigs." To make each puppet, select a cardboard egg carton. Cut out, in a single piece, one egg cup and two adjacent cones. Trim the cones to look like pig ears. Hold the egg cup so that the ears are on top and carefully cut an X in the bottom side of the cup for a finger opening. Paint the puppet pink and add facial features with a felt-tip marker.

Three Little Pigs
Sung to: "Three Blind Mice"

Three little pigs, three little pigs,
Each built a house, each built a house.
The wolf came by, and he huffed and puffed.
The straw and stick houses were not so tough.
Thank goodness, the brick house was strong enough
For three little pigs!

Kathy McCullough

Paper Plate Clowns

Give each of your children a paper plate to use for a clown face. Have the children glue large construction paper triangles to their plates for clown hats. Then give them small construction paper squares, circles, and triangles to glue on their plates for facial features. Let the children decorate their clown hats with circle stickers and cotton balls. Let them also glue yarn "hair" on the sides of their plates, if desired.

Circus Train

Let your children work together to make a Circus Train. Have them decorate cardboard boxes with paints, crepe paper streamers, and colorful paper scraps. Join the boxes together with heavy yarn and add a yarn handle. Have the children place stuffed animals in the decorated boxes. Then let them take turns pulling their Circus Train around the room.

Clown Beanbag Toss

Draw a large clown face on a piece of butcher paper, cardboard, or fabric. Collect several beanbags. Tape the clown face to the floor and put a line of masking tape on the floor a few feet away from the clown. Have your children stand behind the line and take turns trying to toss a beanbag onto the clown's nose.

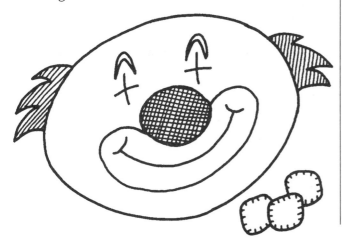

Circus Snacks

Let your children decorate paper lunch bags with crayon designs. At snacktime, place pretzels or popcorn inside the bags. Serve with small cups of lemonade, if desired.

Variation: For a special treat, purchase boxes of "Barnum's Animals" animal crackers. Provide one box for each child or divide up the crakers from several boxes and place them in individual sandwich bags. Let the children use the boxes to make a miniature circus train.

Did You Ever See a Clown?

Have your children form a circle. Each time you sing the song, let a different child stand in the middle and act out clown movements for the other children to imitate.

Sung to: "Did You Ever See a Lassie?"

Did you ever see a clown,
A clown, a clown?
Did you ever see a clown
Move this way and that?
Move this way and that way,
Move this way and that way.
Did you ever see a clown
Move this way and that?

Paula C. Foreman

Little Sad Clown Pattern

Refer to page 209 for directions.

© 1995 Warren Publishing House

Reproducible Teaching-Aid Patterns

Airplane Pattern

Refer to page 212 for directions.

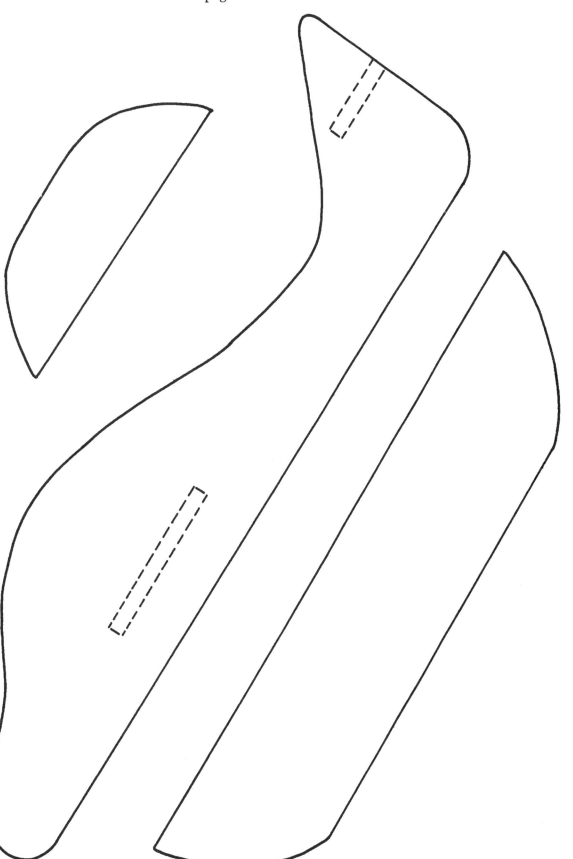

August

ART • Sunny Day Fun

Sunshine Art

Set out shallow containers of yellow, red, and orange tempera paint. Let your children dip round-shaped objects into the paint to make sun prints on blue construction paper. Have them try using the end of a washed and dried corncob, the head of a daisy or dandelion flower (use the stem as a handle), a wooden spoon, or a plastic drinking glass.

Sunshine Collage

Tape two pieces of white or yellow butcher paper together to make a large square. Cut a sun shape out of the square and hang it on a wall or a bulletin board at your children's eye level. Set out a variety of magazines that have pictures of summer activities and foods. Let the children look through the magazines and have them cut or tear out pictures of things that remind them of summer. Then have them paste or tape their pictures to the sun shape.

Sun Prints

Take your children outside to collect leaves, small rocks, and twigs. Have them arrange their items on pieces of dark-colored construction paper. Then help your children find a sunny spot where the wind will not blow the items away. (A spot near a window works well for this activity.) Have them set their papers in the sunny spot. After several hours, have your children lift their items and observe the color of the paper underneath. The sun faded all the areas that were not covered by the objects.

Colored Sand

Fill a large coffee can half full with fine-grain sand. Add enough liquid tempera paint to dampen the sand. Close the lid securely and shake the can until the sand and paint are thoroughly mixed. Let the sand stand uncovered for several days until dry. Use the Colored Sand with the Sand Paintings and Sand Jars activities on this page.

Sand Paintings

Pour Colored Sand into large Parmesan cheese or sugar shakers. Have your children brush glue on cardboard or construction paper and sprinkle Colored Sand on the glue. Help them shake off any excess sand before letting their Sand Paintings dry.

Sand Jars

Make several colors of Colored Sand. Give each of your children a spoon and a baby food jar with a lid. Have the children spoon different layers of Colored Sand into their jars to create designs. Be sure they fill their jars to the top. Secure the lids tightly and set the jars on their lids for display.

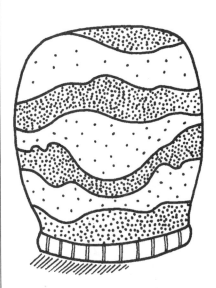

Sand Playdough

Mix together 2 cups all-purpose flour, 1 cup salt, 1 cup water, and a few drops vegetable oil. Add ½ to ¾ cup sand until the dough is the desired texture. Let your children play with the Sand Playdough and encourage them to describe how it feels.

Nature Collages

Go on a nature walk with your children. Give the children bags for collecting wild flowers, leaves, grasses, twigs, and other finds. After the walk, give each child a plastic-foam tray filled with Goop (see following recipe). Let the children arrange their treasures in the Goop to create Nature Collages. Allow the collages to dry before displaying them.

Goop—Mix 1 cup warm water with 1 cup salt. Add 2 teaspoons vegetable oil and enough flour to make the mixture sticky.

Textured Rubbings

Give each of your children a piece of plain paper and crayons with the papers removed. Let the children experiment with making rubbings of things they find outside such as sidewalks, brick walls, wooden benches, and fences. If your play area does not have a variety of textured surfaces, visit a park or other areas in your neighborhood.

Dandelion Seed Art

Take your children outside to a place where dandelions have gone to seed. Give each of the children a piece of dark construction paper and a paintbrush. Set out several shallow containers of glue. Let the children paint glue all over their papers. Then help the children hold their papers behind the dandelions while they blow the seeds onto their papers.

Rock Sculptures

Go on a rock hunt with your children. Give the children small paper bags to hold their rocks. When the hunt is over, have the children sort their rocks by size. Set out bottles of glue and let the children glue their rocks together to make sculptures. Help them discover that if they put the larger rocks on the bottom, their sculptures will stand up better.

Nature Sculptures

Have each of your children spread a layer of wet sand on a paper plate and press objects such as shells, twigs, and pebbles into the center of it. Mix plaster of Paris with water and carefully pour the mixture over the sand. Allow the sculptures to dry overnight. Then turn them over, remove the paper plates, and brush off the excess sand.

Hint: Insert paper clips to use as hangers while the plaster is still wet.

LEARNING GAMES • Picnic Fun

What's Inside?

Secretly place an object in a picnic basket.
Have your children guess what the object is from
the clues that you give them. For example, if
you have hidden a ball in the basket, give your
children clues such as these: "It is round. It
bounces. You play catch with it."

What Is Missing?

Take your children on an imaginary picnic.
Spread out a blanket and place picnic items on
the blanket. Then have the children pretend
to take a nap and close their eyes. While they
are "asleep," take away one of the items. Have
the children wake up and guess which item is
missing. To make the game more challenging,
take more than one object each time.

Setting the Picnic Table

Set out four placemats on a picnic tablecloth.
Place plates on three of the placemats. Ask your
children if you have enough plates for all the
placemats. Ask them how many more you need.
Then place five napkins on the tablecloth. Ask
the children if you have the right number of
napkins. Encourage them to tell you what you
should do. Continue the game with utensils
and glasses.

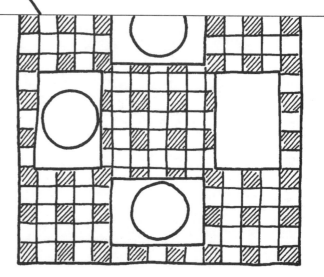

Planes in Their Hangars

On a sheet of butcher paper, draw three large rectangles to represent airplane hangars. Draw one rectangle with a red felt-tip marker, one with a yellow marker, and one with a blue marker. Cut out six airplane shapes each from red, yellow, and blue construction paper. Mix up the shapes. Then let the children place the airplanes in the matching colored hangars. Encourage them to line up the planes from front to back and from left to right.

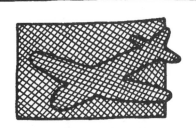 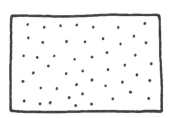 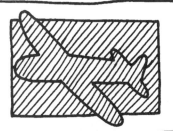

Paper Plate Match-Up

Use a felt-tip marker to divide a paper plate in half. Divide each half into five sections. Color each section on one half of the plate a different color. Color the sections on the other half of the plate the same colors but in a different order. Fasten two paper arrows to the center of the paper plate with a brass paper fastener. Have your children take turns pointing the two arrows at matching colors.

Clipping Colors

Set up a clothesline for your children. Purchase colored clothespins or paint wooden spring-type clothespins various colors. Mix up the different colors and have the children sort them by color and clip them to the line.

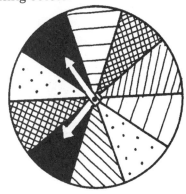

Poker Chip Patterns

Place red, white, and blue poker chips in a bowl. Use the chips to create a simple pattern such as red-blue-white, red-blue-white. Let one of your children copy the pattern by placing matching poker chips below yours. As your children become more experienced, encourage them to copy and then continue the pattern.

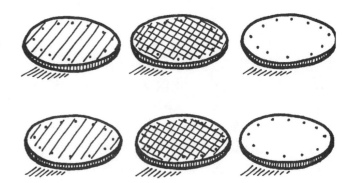

Number Strips

Use the Number Strip Patterns on page 260 as guides for cutting strips out of cardboard or felt. Or photocopy the pattern page, cover it with clear self-stick paper for durability, and cut out the strips. Make a set of strips for each of your children. Let them experiment with arranging the strips to make steps, a pyramid, or other shapes. Set out a long strip and ask them to find two smaller strips that can be put together to make a strip the same size.

Number Cards

Number 10 index cards from 1 to 10 with numerals or sets of dots. Mix up the cards and have your children place the cards in the proper sequence. When the cards are in the correct order, have the children count down while pointing to each card. Let the children yell "Blast Off" at the end.

Which Is Bigger?

Name two objects and have your children tell you which object is bigger. Try naming objects such as a house and a car, an apple and a basketball, a table and a toothbrush, or a flower and a tree. Then play the game again, this time asking which item is smaller.

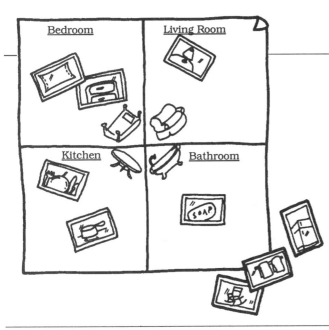

All Around the House

Divide a large piece of paper into four sections to make a simple floor plan. Label each section a different room in a house such as a kitchen, a bedroom, a living room, and a bathroom. Cut out magazine pictures of objects you would find in each of the four rooms. Set out the floor plan and the magazine pictures. Have your children sort the pictures by placing them in the appropriate rooms.

Rock Collections

Encourage your children to collect rocks. Then have them sort the rocks by color, markings, or size. Shells, leaves, and other natural objects can be sorted in similar ways.

The Dinosaur Who Couldn't Roar

Adapted by Jean Warren from a Song by Diane Thom

Once there was a dinosaur
Who tried and tried, but couldn't roar.

He would open his mouth real wide,
But all he found were giggles inside.

He couldn't be mean, he couldn't be gruff,
He couldn't roar, he couldn't be tough.

"I wish I could roar," the dinosaur said,
Every night as he went off to bed.

And, what do you know, one day he could roar.
He roared all day till his throat was sore.

But when he looked, he was all alone
No one had liked his roaring tone.

Being tough wasn't much fun,
If it meant you were the only one.

So the next time the dinosaur went out to play,
He took his roar and threw it away.

Then he opened up his mouth real wide
And shared again the giggles inside.

So, if you think you need to roar,
Just remember the dinosaur.

It's better to have lots of fun,
Than be the only roaring one.

Flannelboard Directions
Use the pattern on page 261 as a guide for cutting a dinosaur shape out of felt. Add details with felt-tip markers as desired. Place the dinosaur on a flannelboard when you tell the story on this page.

Nursery Rhyme Pantomimes

Set out illustrations of familiar nursery rhymes. Choose two of your children to select one of the pictures and act out the rhyme shown on it. Let the other children try to guess which rhyme it is. Repeat until everyone has had a turn.

Nursery Rhyme Names

Print the names of nursery rhyme characters on self-stick labels. Give each of your children a label to wear at circle time. Address each child by his or her character name.

Nursery Rhyme Sequence Cards

Select a nursery rhyme that tells a story such as "Jack and Jill" or "Humpty Dumpty." Choose four or five events from the rhyme and draw a simple picture representing each event on a separate index card. For example, if you chose "Jack and Jill," you could draw Jack and Jill walking up a hill, Jack and Jill with a pail of water, Jack falling down, and Jill falling down. Then mix up the cards and let your children take turns placing them in order.

Hint: Look for appropriate illustrations in old nursery rhyme books, cut them out, and cover them with clear self-stick paper.

How the Sun Got in the Sky

A Native American Legend Adapted by Jean Warren

Long, long ago, half of the earth was dark and half of the earth was light.

The animals who lived on the light side were happy and strong because they had the sun. But the animals who lived on the dark side were cold and hungry. "If only we had the sun," they said, "then we would be warm and plants would grow, and we would have food."

One day, the animals who lived on the dark side got together and marched over to the light side of the earth. There they found the animals who lived on the light side playing catch with the sun.

"We have come to ask if we may borrow the sun," said the animals from the dark side.

"No! No!" cried the animals from the light side. "We need the sun for ourselves."

The animals from the dark side didn't know what to do. They knew they were not strong enough to capture the sun. Then they thought of a way to trick the animals from the light side into sharing the sun with them.

"Let's have a contest to see who is strongest," they said. "Whichever side wins will get to keep the sun."

Now the animals from the light side loved contests because they always won. So they happily agreed.

Each side picked its strongest animal. The animals from the light side chose Black Bear.

He was 10 feet tall and stronger than all the other animals put together. The animals from the dark side chose Gray Fox.

First, Gray Fox picked up a rock and threw it as far as he could. Black Bear picked up a rock and threw it ten times farther. The animals from the light side all clapped. There was no way they could lose this contest.

Next, Gray Fox picked up a tree trunk and threw it as far as he could. Black Bear laughed. Then he picked up a tree trunk and threw it clear across the river. The animals from the light side danced up and down. No animal from the dark side was as strong as Black Bear.

Finally, Gray Fox picked up the sun and threw it as high as he could. It sailed up over treetops, then fell back down to the ground. Then Black Bear picked up the sun. "I'll show these animals just how strong I really am," he said. He threw back his arm and tossed the sun up, up, as far as he could. The animals from the light side clapped and cheered as the sun went higher and higher into the sky.

"We won! We won!" they cried. "Black Bear is the strongest!"

The animals from the dark side started back home. But when they got there, they found that it was no longer dark. Black Bear had thrown the sun so high in the sky that it stayed there, sending warmth and light to both sides of the earth.

The animals from the dark side were so happy that they joined hands and danced around in a big circle. "Our trick worked!" they laughed. "Black Bear won the contest, but he helped us to win the sun!"

Buckle Up

Purchase used seat belts from an auto wrecking yard. Shorten them as necessary with scissors. Then use a hot glue gun to attach the seat belts to several child-size chairs in your room. (Make sure that each seatbelt is just large enough to fit across a child's lap when fastened.) Let your children line up the chairs to make cars. Set out road maps and a cardboard pizza round for a "steering wheel." Remind your children to buckle up before they start to "drive."

The Car Song

Sung to: "When Johnny Comes Marching Home"

We like to travel in our car,
Hurrah, hurrah.
A car can take us near or far,
Hurrah, hurrah.
We buckle up before we go,
Whether we're going fast or slow,
So we'll all be safer while riding in our car!

Vicki Swanning

Safe Drivers

Let your children practice the rules of the road as they play with their outdoor riding toys. Draw lines on the sidewalk with chalk or use rope to make a highway divider. Set up different traffic patterns and post traffic signs. Set up a gas station by the side of the road so "drivers" can get gas, oil, water, and air. Provide props such as an oil can, a bicycle tire pump, and a tool box.

Kaleidoscope

Gather two identical rectangular travel-size mirrors. Place one of the mirrors on a piece of cardboard and trace around it. Cut out the cardboard shape. Arrange the mirrors, face down, on a flat surface with the piece of cardboard between them. Fasten the sides together with masking tape. Stand the mirrors and cardboard up so they form a triangle with the mirrors facing inside. Tape the remaining sides together. Tape a piece of waxed paper over one end. The Kaleidoscope is now ready to use. Let your children take turns placing small nature items such as a flower petal, a tiny pebble and a piece of grass inside the Kaleidoscope on the waxed paper. Have the children hold the Kaleidoscope and look down into it to see six reflections of the items. Let the children gently shake the items to change the reflections.

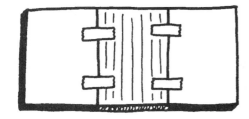

Periscope

Use a craft knife to cut a small slit across one side of a small rectangular cracker box, 2 inches from the top. On the same side, cut out a 2-inch square near the bottom. On the opposite side, cut a slit 2 inches from the bottom of the box and a 2-inch square near the top. Insert a rectangular travel-size mirror through the top slit so that it extends from the slit to the top of the box. Insert an identical mirror through the bottom slit so that it extends from the slit to the bottom of the box. (The reflective sides of the mirrors should face each other.) Tape the mirrors securely in place. The Periscope is now ready to use. Let your children take turns looking through one of the square openings to see the view from the other opening. Encourage the children to try hiding behind a chair and slowly raising the Periscope until they can see over the chair. Or have them use it to look around corners.

Exploring Science

Explore the magic and wonder of science with your children by sharing the following activities with them. Encourage the children to observe and discuss what happens. Ask them to make hypotheses about what they have observed. It is not necessary for them to guess correctly. Just ask them to think about possible causes. Explanations are provided for you, however. Share them with the children, if you wish.

Racing Talcum Powder

Put water into a shallow container. Gently sprinkle talcum powder on top of the water. Have your children note that the powder is floating on the water. Then, as the children watch, add a drop of liquid soap to the water. The talcum powder will "race" to the sides of the container. Repeat as many times as desired, using fresh water each time.

Explanation: Water has a surface tension, allowing the talcum powder to float on top of it. The soap breaks the surface tension, pushing the powder to the sides of the container as it spreads across the water.

The Magic Bottle

Cover a glass soft-drink bottle with aluminum foil. Find a cork that just fits into the opening of the bottle. Push the cork into the bottle. Cut a 1-foot length of thick rope. Show your children the bottle. (Do not tell them about the cork inside.) Put the rope into the bottle and try to suspend the bottle from it. (The bottle will drop.) Then put the rope into the bottle, turn the bottle upside down, and gently tug on the rope to secure the rope between the side of the bottle's neck and the cork. Turn the bottle right side up and suspend the bottle from the rope.

Explanation: When you turn the bottle upside down and tug on the rope, it becomes lodged between the cork and the side of the bottle. Because the bottle is covered with foil, it appears to be suspended from the rope alone.

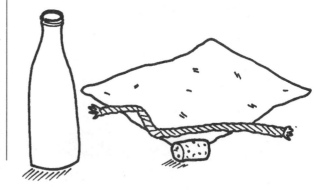

Magnet Magic

Fill a jar with water and place a paper clip in it. (Be sure the paper clip you use is magnetic—some are not.) Make the paper clip dance up and down in the water by moving a magnet up and down outside the jar.

Explanation: The paper clip moves because the magnetic force from the magnet can pass through the glass and water to the paper clip.

Balloon Blow-Up

Put ½ to 1 inch of hot water in the bottom of a glass soft-drink bottle. Place a balloon over the opening of the bottle so that the balloon hangs down into the bottle. Then put the bottle into a bowl of cold water and let your children watch the balloon inflate inside the bottle.

Explanation: The hot water heats the air inside the bottle. When the bottle is put into cold water, the air cools. This creates a vacuum that pulls at the balloon and causes it to inflate.

Impossible Leg Lifts

Have one of your children stand sideways to a wall with his or her right foot, hip, and shoulder pressed against it. Then have the child try lifting his or her left leg.

Explanation: Your child cannot lift his or her leg because leaning against the wall changes the child's center of gravity.

Follow the Leader

When you first arrive at the playground, play a version of Follow the Leader to help your children become familiar with the equipment and its layout. Have the children follow you as you lead them through and name the equipment. Find new ways to move over, under, and through the equipment.

Merry-Go-Round Walk

Have your children sit on the edge of the merry-go-round with their feet on the ground. Let them experiment with different ways to "walk" it around in a circle such as slowly, quickly, or with everyone using only one foot.

Playground Imagination

Encourage your children to imagine that pieces of playground equipment are other things. For example, the slide could become a spacecraft or a skyscraper; the merry-go-round might be a carousel at a fair; the climbing structure could be a castle, a cave, or a ship.

Counting Game

Play this game while you are pushing one of your children in a swing. After the child is seated in the swing, ask him or her to choose a number between 1 and 20. Then push the child that many times. Encourage the child, and any other children waiting for their turn, to count along with you.

Sneaky Snakes

Have your children lie on their stomachs with their hands in the "push-up" position. Have them slowly "sneak" their heads toward the ceiling by straightening their arms while leaving their lower bodies on the floor.

Cat Stretches

Have your children get on their hands and knees. Tell them to slowly "walk" their arms out in front of them, one after the other, until arms and upper body are fully extended. Then have them stretch like cats by leaning each shoulder first one way, then the other.

Wet and Dry Noodles

Have your children lie on their backs. Ask them to be "wet noodles." Check their arms and legs to see if they are limp and relaxed. Then tell the children to be "dry noodles." Check for straight, stiff arms and legs.

Summer, Summer

Sung to: "Old MacDonald Had a Farm"

Summer, summer is such fun,
Yes, oh, yes, it is.
There's so much that you can do,
Yes, oh, yes, there is.
You can go to the pool and keep real cool,
Jump right in and take a swim.
Summer, summer is such fun,
Yes, oh, yes, it is.

Summer, summer is such fun,
Yes, oh, yes, it is.
There's so much that you can do,
Yes, oh, yes, there is.
You can hear a band or sit on the sand,
Play in the sea or play catch with me.
Summer, summer is such fun,
Yes, oh, yes, it is.

Barbara B. Fleisher

Sing a Song of Sunshine

Sung to: "Sing a Song of Sixpence"

Sing a song of sunshine,
Be happy every day.
Sing a song of sunshine,
You'll chase the clouds away.
Be happy every moment,
No matter what you do.
Just sing and sing and sing and sing,
And let the sun shine through.

Jean Warren

Playground Fun
Sung to: "Take Me Out to the Ball Game"

Let's go out to the playground,
Take me out to the swings.
Seesaws and sliding boards,
Climbers, too,
I like the jungle gym,
How about you?
For it's fun to run, jump, and slide.
If you don't have fun, it's a shame.
Oh, let's sing, play, have a good day,
At the old playground.

Betty Silkunas

Playground Song
Sung to: "Mary Had a Little Lamb"

I like to climb on the jungle gym,
Jungle gym, jungle gym.
I like to climb on the jungle gym
On the big playground.

Additional verses: I like to go up in the swing; down the
steep slide.

Barbara B. Fleisher

Go Out and Play
Sung to: "The Bear Went Over the Mountain"

It's time to go out and play,
It's time to go out and play,
It's time to go out and play,
With all your friends today.

Judy Hall

Picnic in the Park

Sung to: "She'll Be Coming Round the Mountain"

Yes, we'll all go on a picnic in the park.
Yes, we'll all go on a picnic in the park.
Bring some lunch and bring a ball,
There will be such fun for all.
Yes, we'll all go on a picnic in the park.

Barbara Paxson

The Picnic Basket

Sung to: "Pop! Goes the Weasel"

Put salad, soda, and sandwiches in,
Forks and plates and cups.
Our picnic basket is filled to the top.
But I can't pick it up!

I'll eat some salad and sandwiches, too,
I'll drink some soda pop.
Now my basket's not so full,
And I can pick it up!

Deborah Zumbar

Ants at the Picnic

Sung to: "Skip to My Lou"

Ants at the picnic, what'll I do?
Ants at the picnic, what'll I do?
Ants at the picnic, what'll I do?
Guess I will eat real quickly!

Betty Silkunas

All Around the Swamp

Sung to: "The Wheels on the Bus"

The pteranodon's wings went flap, flap, flap,
Flap, flap, flap; flap, flap, flap.
The pteranodon's wings went flap, flap, flap,
All around the swamp.

Additional verses: The tyrannosaurus rex went grr; The triceratops' horns went poke; The apatosaurus went munch; The stegosaurus' tail went spike.

Yosie Yoshimura

Dinosaurs

Sung to: "Row, Row, Row Your Boat"

Great big dinosaurs
Lived so long ago.
Some liked land, and some liked water.
Some flew in the air.

Great big dinosaurs
Lived so long ago.
Some had horns, and some had spikes.
Some had wings like bats.

Great big dinosaurs
Lived so long ago.
Some ate plants, and some ate meat,
But now there are no more.

Allane and Jennifer Eastberg

Tyrannosaurus Rex

Sung to: "Mary Had a Little Lamb"

Dinosaurs walked on this earth,
On this earth, on this earth.
Dinosaurs walked on this earth,
A long, long time ago.

Tyrannosaurus rex was the king,
Was the king, was the king.
Tyrannosaurus rex was the king,
A long, long time ago.

Rosemary Giordano

Giant Anthill

Cut a giant anthill shape out of brown wrapping paper or butcher paper and place it on the floor. Help the children draw rooms and tunnels all across the anthill. Let them add Fingerprint Ants as described in the activity on this page.

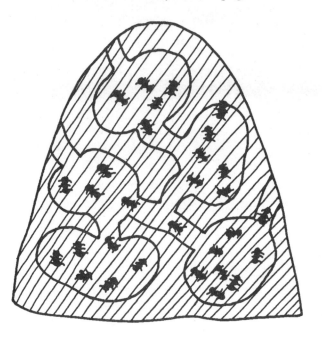

Fingerprint Ants

To add "ants" to the Giant Anthill activity on this page, make an ink pad by folding a paper towel in half and placing it in a plastic-foam tray. Pour a little black tempera paint on top of the paper towel. Give each of your children a new, unsharpened pencil. To make an ant print, have each child press the eraser end of his or her pencil in the ink pad and make three prints in a row on the anthill shape. Let the children make as many ants prints as they like. Help the children use black fine-tip markers to add six legs to each ant.

Ants in the Nest

Number the bottoms of paper baking cups from 1 to 6 and place them in a 6-cup muffin tin. Give the children 21 raisins or small black buttons for ants. Let them place the appropriate number of "ants" into each paper baking cup "nest."

Ant Search

Take your children on an ant search so they can observe ants in their natural habitat. Ants tend to make nests under boards, rocks, or leaves. They also build anthills on sidewalks and in grass. Be sure not to disturb the nests. (Children are less likely to destroy a nest after watching how diligently the ants work to build it.) If you cannot go to the ants, have them come to you by placing a juicy piece of fruit outside as bait. Return to the fruit an hour later to observe the ants that have found it. Place a tiny piece of the fruit away from the rest, and you may observe how two ants will work together to carry a piece of fruit to their nest.

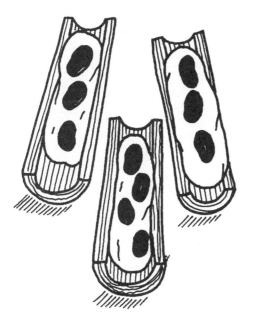

Ants on a Log

Let your children make "logs" by filling celery sticks with peanut butter. Then give them each three or four raisin "ants" to place on top of their logs.

Variation: For a different kind of stuffing have the children mix together equal portions of peanut butter, grated carrots, and crushed shredded wheat. Let them press the mixture into the celery sticks and then place the raisins on top.

Coconut Discovery

Show your children a coconut. Let them hold it and shake it. See if they can guess what makes the sloshing sound inside. Point out the three shiny black spots called *eyes* at one end of the coconut. Some people think the eyes make a "monkey face."

Coconut Clappers

Have an adult hold a coconut on a towel while you use a saw to cut it in half. Pour out the liquid. If desired, bake the coconut halves at 200°F for 20 minutes to make the meat easier to remove. Use a table knife to scrape out all of the meat. Let the children taste the coconut meat. Give the coconut halves to one of the children and show him or her how to clap the cut ends together. Let each child have a chance to beat out rhythms with the Coconut Clappers.

Coconut Milk

Use the coconut meat from your coconuts to make coconut milk. Whirl together 1 cup fresh, ½-inch coconut chunks and 1 cup hot water in a blender or food processor. Allow the mixture to steep for 30 minutes before straining it through two thicknesses of cheesecloth. Squeeze out the Coconut Milk and throw away the meat. Makes 1 cup.

Basic Bubbles

Gently mix together 1 cup Joy liquid dishwashing detergent, 2 cups water, and 1 tablespoon sugar. For best results, store this solution in a covered container for a few days before using it.

Bubble Blowers

Many common household items can be used as bubble blowers. Let your children try blowing bubbles with funnels, cookie cutters with open centers, juice cans with both ends removed, or plastic hangers.

The Bubble Game

Join hands with your children in a circle. Have everyone walk forward while holding hands, forming as small a circle as possible. Then sing the following song and move as directed.

Sung to: "Ring Around the Rosie"

Blow air in our bubble.
  (Move one step backward while holding hands.)
Blow air in our bubble.
  (Move one step backward while holding hands.)
Bigger, bigger,
  (Move one step backward while holding hands.)
We stop and pop!
  (Drop hands and fall to the ground.)

Lois E. Putnam

Pasta-Saurus

Set out a variety of uncooked pasta shapes such as elbows, wheels, shells, and tubes. Give each of your children a piece of construction paper. Let your children glue the pasta shapes to the paper to create dinosaurs.

Variation: For younger children, you may wish to draw outlines of dinosaurs on the papers.

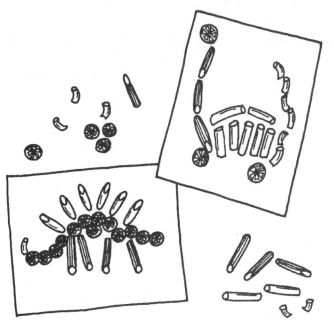

Fossil Hunt

Bury several plastic dinosaur "fossils" in a large pan of cornmeal or sand and place the pan on a table. Let your children take turns going on a Fossil Hunt. Give one of the children a spoon for digging in the cornmeal. When a fossil is discovered, ask the child to identify it by looking carefully at its characteristics.

Playdough Fossils

Make gray playdough by adding a small amount of powdered black tempera paint to your regular recipe. Place the playdough and some plastic dinosaurs on a table. Let the children make "fossils" by pressing the dinosaurs into the playdough and then carefully removing them to see the imprint left behind.

Tyrannosaurus Toss

Draw a picture of a large tyrannosaurus head on a piece of sturdy cardboard. Use a craft knife to cut out the dinosaur's mouth, including lots of teeth. Then prop the cardboard tyrannosaurus head against a chair or secure it with tape across a doorway. Give your children beanbags and let them take turns "feeding" the dinosaur by tossing beanbags into its mouth.

Snacktime Fun

To turn an ordinary sandwich into a delicious treat, slice the sandwich in half diagonally. Place each sandwich half on a plate. (The long side should be at the bottom of the plate.) On each half, arrange triangular tortilla chips along the two short sides of the sandwich. Place a banana half on one side for the dinosaur's neck and head. Add a raisin for an eye.

Dino Stompers

Clean and disinfect a few pairs of oversized rubber boots. Spray the boots with green or purple paint and let them dry thoroughly. Add green or red sticker dots for toes, if desired. Let your children wear the boots and walk like dinosaurs.

Number Strips Pattern
Refer to page 238 for directions.

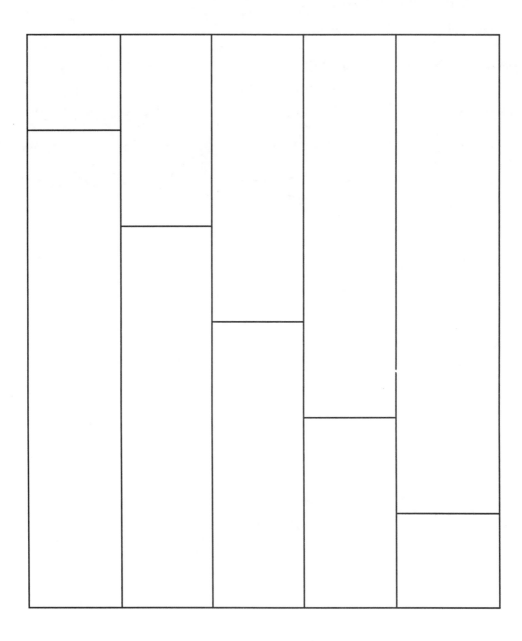

Dinosaur Pattern

Refer to page 240 for directions.

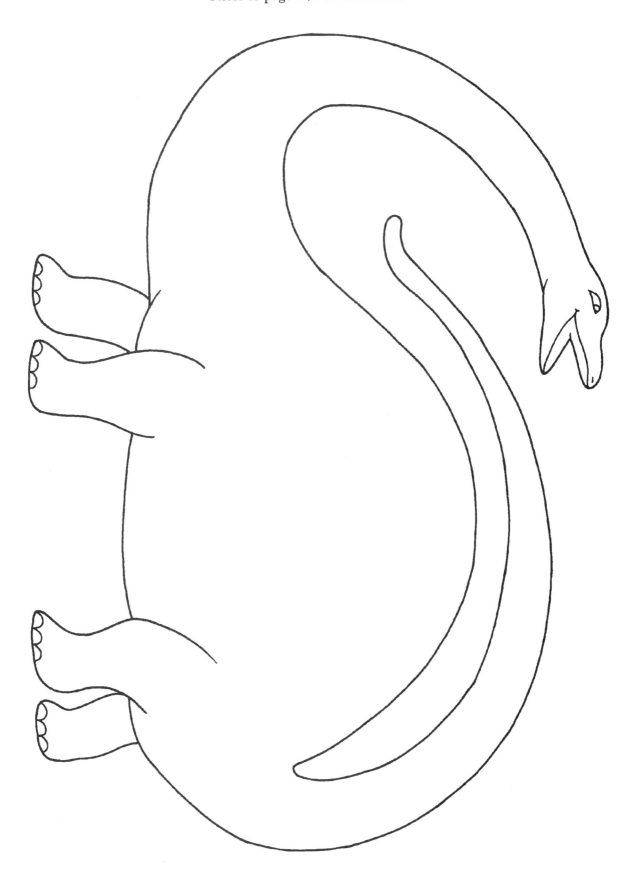

September

ART • Leaf Fun

Leaf Paintbrushes

Have each of your children collect one small- to medium-sized leaf with a long stem. Let the children paint with their leaves, using the leaves as brushes and the stems as handles.

Leaf Rubbings

Have your children gather different kinds of fall leaves. Show the children how to arrange the leaves on a table, place sheets of thin paper over them, and rub across them with the sides of crayons or chalk to make rubbings.

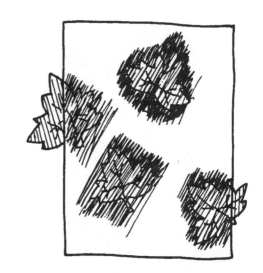

Leaf Creatures

Give your children an assortment of pretty fall leaves, construction paper, glue, and felt-tip markers. Have the children choose leaves and glue them to their papers. Let them use the felt-tip markers to add arms, legs, hands, feet, hair, eyes, and any other features to make Leaf Creatures.

Aluminum Foil Leaves

Set out pieces of aluminum foil and a variety of fall leaves. Let each child select a leaf, place it under a piece of foil, and gently press and rub the foil with his or her hand to get a leaf print. Then have the children glue their leaf prints to pieces of construction paper.

Leaf Prints

Set out fall leaves; newpaper; red, yellow, and orange tempera paint; paintbrushes; and black construction paper. Have your children select one or two leaves and place them on a piece of newspaper. Let them paint their leaves red, yellow, and orange. Then help each child place a sheet of black construction paper over the painted leaves and gently press down to make a print.

Fall Faces

Cut 4½-inch circles out of construction paper. Collect a variety of fall leaves. Give each of your children one of the circles and a piece of construction paper. Have the children glue their circles on their papers. Then let them glue leaves around their circles as desired for hair. Have them complete their faces by adding facial features with felt-tip markers.

Glitter Bag

Put some glitter into a resealable plastic bag. Set out small items to be decorated such as pine cones, spools, wooden clothespins, or craft sticks. Have each child choose an item and brush it with thin white glue. Then have the child drop his or her item in the glitter bag and seal the top. Let the child shake the bag to cover the item with glitter and open it to discover the sparkly item inside.

Silvery Pictures

Tear off a square of aluminum foil for each of your children. Have the children use water-based felt-tip markers to make designs on the foil squares. Write each child's name on his or her picture with a permanent marker, then set the pictures out to dry for several hours. The foil will resist the ink slightly, so you may want to blot these pictures with a tissue before sending them home with your children.

Gold Collage

Collect gold items such as gift wrap, a Christmas tree garland, stars, glitter, sequins, or ribbon. Set out dark-colored construction paper and glue. Let your children glue the gold items to the dark paper to make shiny collages.

School Bus Mural

Cut a large school bus shape from white butcher paper. (Make the bus long enough to cut a window for each child's photo.) Collect a photo of each of your children. Have the children work together to paint the school bus shape yellow. Set aside to dry. Outline the wheels, windows, and other details on the bus shape with a black felt-tip marker or crayon. Cut out one window shape in the bus for each child. Attach the school bus to a wall at your children's eye level. Glue one photo in each window opening.

Variation: Instead of photos, use pictures your children have drawn of themselves.

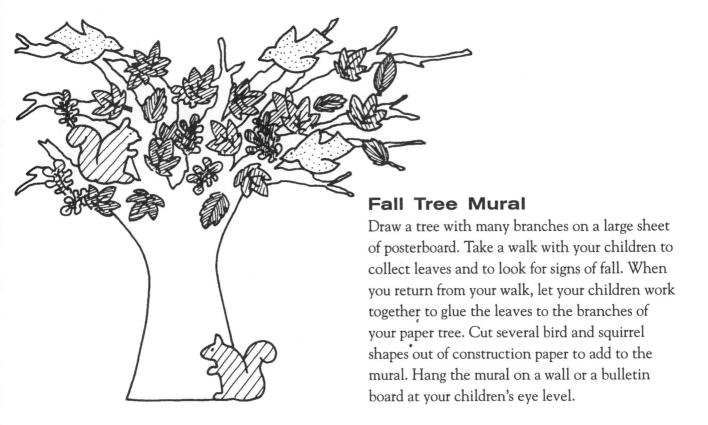

Fall Tree Mural

Draw a tree with many branches on a large sheet of posterboard. Take a walk with your children to collect leaves and to look for signs of fall. When you return from your walk, let your children work together to glue the leaves to the branches of your paper tree. Cut several bird and squirrel shapes out of construction paper to add to the mural. Hang the mural on a wall or a bulletin board at your children's eye level.

Shape Sorting

Collect a variety of fall leaves. Show the leaves to your children. Point out the different shapes and colors of the leaves. Let the children take turns sorting the leaves by shape or by color.

Matching

Collect five medium-sized fall leaves. Trace each of their outlines on a separate piece of paper. Challenge your children to match each leaf to its outline. This activity must be used the same day it is prepared because the leaves will curl and shrink as they dry out.

Autumn Leaf Express

Use colorful fall leaves to teach and reinforce color skills. Take your children outside to an area with lots of autumn leaves on the ground. Tell the children that you are the conductor of a train. In order to ride on your train, they must find a leaf the color that you announce. When you say, "All aboard the Yellow Leaf Express," have the children find yellow leaves, hop aboard the "train," and chug around the area. Stop the train, announce a new color, have the children collect new leaves, and begin the fun again.

Leaf Pairs

Collect six pairs of fall leaves. Press the leaves between heavy books for several days. Mount each leaf on an index card and cover with clear self-stick paper for durability. Let your children match the pairs of leaves. If many leaves are available in your area, let the children make their own leaf pairs.

Number Leaves

Cut five large leaves of different shapes out of heavy paper, and then cut each leaf into three sections. Label each section of the first leaf with the numeral 1, each section of the second leaf with the numeral 2, and so on. Scramble all the leaf pieces in a large box. Have your children put the leaves together by first matching the numerals and then assembling the leaf shapes.

Texture Tree

Cut a large tree trunk shape out of brown butcher paper and hang it up at your children's eye level. Collect a variety of different textured materials such as sandpaper, burlap, nylon netting, velvet, flannel, corduroy, fake fur, and aluminum foil. Cut a leaf shape out of each type of material. Attach the leaf shapes to the tree. Let the children touch the different textured leaves. Encourage them to describe how each leaf feels.

Sorting Shapes

Fill a laundry basket with familiar items that have definite shapes such as a rubber ball, a softball, a wooden block, a book, a plastic egg, a cookie cutter, a box, a postcard, a scarf, and a baking pan. Let your children look through the items and sort them by their shapes.

Guessing Game

Cut four different shapes out of construction paper. Have your children sit in a circle. Put the shapes in the middle and ask one child to close his or her eyes. Have the next child take one of the construction paper shapes and hide it behind his or her back. Then ask the first child to open his or her eyes and guess which shape is missing. Continue playing the game until each child has had a chance to hide a shape and to guess which shape is missing.

Shape Book

Fill the pages of a magnetic-page photo album with a variety of construction paper shapes in different colors and sizes. Set out the book along with a water-based felt-tip marker. Show your children how to use the marker on the plastic pages to trace around the shapes. Clean the pages of the book with a damp cloth after each child's turn.

Our Shapes

Cut several circles, rectangles, triangles, squares, and ovals, out of construction paper. Give each of your children one of the shapes. While you sing each verse in the following song, have the children with the appropriate shapes hold them up.

Sung to: "Did You Ever See a Lassie?"

Did you ever see a circle,
A circle, a circle?
Did you ever see a circle?
It looks like a ball.

Did you ever see a rectangle,
Rectangle, rectangle?
Did you ever see a rectangle?
It looks like a door.

Did you ever see a triangle,
Triangle, triangle?
Did you ever see a triangle?
It looks like a sail.

Did you ever see a square,
A square, a square?
Did you ever see a square?
It looks like a box.

Did you ever see an oval,
An oval, an oval?
Did you ever see an oval?
It looks like an egg.

Priscilla M. Starrett

Shape Pegboard

Set a piece of pegboard on a table. Use a black felt-tip marker to draw a line between the holes in the pegboard to make large shape outlines. Let the children follow the outlines and insert golf tees in the holes to make shapes.

Amelia's Autumn Day

By Mary A. Barich

It was a cool, crisp morning. Amelia's two brothers were at school, and she had the whole day ahead to explore.

A few months earlier all the children had been at home, and they had played barefoot in the hot sun. That was summer. But now it was autumn, and a light frost covered the cars and the rooftops.

Amelia put on her warm sweater. She gave her mother a hug and a kiss and went out in her backyard to play. The yard was big, and there were always fun things to do in it. If it had been a spring day, Amelia might have picked some flowers to give to her mother. If it had been a winter day, she might have had fun making a snowpal. But today was an autumn day, so she chased some red and gold leaves that a gusty wind had scattered across the grass.

Amelia looked straight up into the giant sky. She remembered watching pretty orange and yellow butterflies fly across the sky in summer. But today there were no butterflies. They were all gone. Most of the birds, too, had flown away to warmer places. Now the sky was filled with fluffy gray clouds that sailed by overhead. Amelia saw one cloud that was shaped like a kitten. Another looked just like a castle.

Amelia skipped over to a corner of the yard where she found an old wooden bucket under the apple tree. One by one, she picked some apples from the tree. Then carefully she put them into the bucket. Amelia remembered how small and green the apples had been in summer. But now they were big and red and just right for making pies.

When Amelia's bucket was almost full, she heard her mother's call for lunch. She hurried inside, eager to tell her mother about her fun morning.

During lunch, Amelia and her mother talked about the different seasons of the year. Amelia decided that winter was fun because there was snow on the ground. Spring was fun, too, because the flowers were in bloom, the birds came back, and everything was such a pretty green. And summer was fun because the days were hot and sunny, and there was lots to do with the other children who were out of school.

But autumn! Amelia exclaimed. Autumn was now! And in autumn there were colorful leaves, fluffy gray clouds, and bright red apples to enjoy!

With lunch finished, Amelia put on her sweater again and skipped back out the door. Autumn was really a fun time of year, and she didn't want to miss a minute of it!

Why the Animals Don't Talk

A Native American Folktale Adapted by Jean Warren

Many years ago, when people came to this great land, the animals of the forest talked. The people learned many things from the friendly animals.

The horse taught them how to run fast.

The bear showed them how to follow a trail.

The racoon taught them how to climb trees.

The beaver taught them how to catch fish and build houses.

The dog taught them how to be patient.

The people and the animals lived happily together for many years. The people practiced all that the animals had taught them and became very skilled at living in the woods. So skilled, in fact, that they began to feel they were better than the animals.

Soon the people started taking more than their share. They robbed the forests of timber for their boats and took animal furs to make their clothes. They even stole honey from the bees.

The animals got worried and called a meeting. They were mad because the people had taken what they had taught them and were now using that knowledge to outwit, outrun, and outthink them.

"Well, I for one will not tell them any more secrets," said the beaver.

"Neither will we," said the horse and the dog.

"My mouth will be sealed," said the bear.

"So will ours," said the raccoon and the beaver.

And that is why to this day the animals don't talk.

Flannelboard Directions
Photocopy the story patterns on pages 292 and 293 and cut them out. If desired, color the patterns and cover them with clear self-stick paper. Attach strips of felt to the backs of the patterns. Use the patterns on a flannelboard as you read the story on this page to your children.

Friends

Friends are big,
Friends are small.
Friends will help you
If you fall.

Friends are happy,
Friends are sad.
Friends can make
Each other glad.

Friends are short,
Friends are tall.
Friends are happy
When you call.

Friends are young,
Friends are old.
Friends are worth
Much more than gold.

Friends are near,
Friends are far.
Friends will like you
As you are.

Friends are dark,
Friends are light.
Friends will bring you
Much delight!

Jean Warren

Friends Old and New

Making friends is fun to do—
You like me and I like you.
   (Point to others, then self, then others.)
Friends are great, let's make a few.
Then we'll have friends old and new.
   (Nod head.)

Tami Hall

We Play Together

I have a friend who lives near me.
   (Point to other person.)
We play together happily.
We ride our bikes and throw a ball
   (Pretend to ride bike, then toss ball.)
In winter, summer, spring, and fall.

Karen Vollmer

Fostering Language Skills at Show-and-Tell

Make show-and-tell a more creative and productive language experience by using themes for this special time. Themes provide the structure needed to make show-and-tell a more interesting language experience while still allowing your children the freedom to choose their own items to share and talk about.

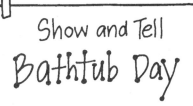

Tips for Using Themes

Keep the following tips in mind when incorporating themes into your show-and-tell time.

- Provide several weeks of "free" show-and-tell before using themes.

- Keep parents informed of your show-and-tell themes so they can help their children prepare for the activity. This can be done by posting the theme on a bulletin board each week.

- Choose a specific day for show-and-tell and consistently schedule the activity each week.

- If a child brings in an item not related to the theme of the week, accept it willingly.

Show-and-Tell Themes

Use the following theme suggestions to get started. As the weeks go by, you will discover additional themes that will foster your children's creativity and language skills.

Color or Shape Day—Have your children bring in items that are a particular color or shape.

Food Day—Ask your children to bring in foods to eat. Discuss the colors, shapes, smells, and tastes of the foods brought in.

Signs of Fall Day—Celebrate the beginning of fall by asking your children to bring in signs of fall such as leaves or acorns.

Bathtub Day—Have your children bring in items they use in the bathtub.

Material Day—Have your children bring in items that are made from the same material such as items made from wood, plastic, metal, or cloth.

Moving Day—Ask each of your children to bring in something that moves such as a toy car, a yo-yo, or a music box.

Who Am I?

Give each of your children a doll shape cut out of heavy paper. Place several mirrors around the room. Let the children look in the mirrors to discover their hair and eye color and other special features. Then have them color their dolls to look just like themselves. Tell them to make their dolls as special as they are. Hang the dolls in a long row around your room, touching hands. Discuss each child's similarities and differences while pointing out how each child is special. Do this activity at the beginning of the year and again at the end of they year to show the children and their parents how much the children's self-concept changed during the year.

Picture Me

Collect a photograph of each of your children. (Make photocopies of the photos so your children can do this activity more than once.) Have the children draw pictures of things that interest them such as a bus, a person on a horse, a flower, or a swimming pool. When the children are finished, cut a hole in an appropriate place in each child's picture and tape in its place a photocopy of the child's photograph. This makes for fun and occasionally humorous pictures.

Invite Table

A fun way to encourage your children to mingle and make new friends at the beginning of a school year is to have an Invite Table. Each day, tape a different child's name to the Invite Table. For that day, that child may invite any one child at a time to share the table's activities with him or her. At the beginning of the school year, you select the table's activities such as blocks or playdough. As the year progresses, the child in charge of the Invite Table may choose the activity to share.

All About Me

Try this year-long project with your children. Make a poster for each child and attach his or her photograph to it. Let the children add their handprints to their posters in the colors of their choice. Throughout the year, add additional items about the children that coordinate with stories, units, or special occasions. You could include such events and items as birthdays, families, favorite foods, heights, favorite activities, and special interests. These posters become very popular in the classroom and are well received by parents. But most of all, they make the children feel special.

Tape a Voice

Set out a tape recorder and several blank tapes. Show your children how to use the tape recorder to record their voices. Then let the children take turns recording and listening to their voices. Provide time for them to experiment with their voices without others present.

Make a Mood

Find recordings of music with different moods. Play the music for your children. Have them talk about the mood in each piece of music. Then ask them to talk about times when they were in those moods. Then let the children dance, move, or draw to the different types of music.

A Day for Grandparents

Grandparents' Day is celebrated on the first Sunday in September following Labor Day. On this day, people express love and appreciation for their grandparents by giving cards and presents and by holding family gatherings. Talk with your children about the roles that grandparents play. Encourage them to describe some of the special times they have spent with their grandparents by sharing stories from your own childhood.

Flannelboard Families

Cut figures of older men and women and of young boys and girls out of store catalogs or magazines to make sets of "grandparents" and "grandchildren." Cover the figures with clear self-stick paper and glue strips of felt on the backs. At circle time, let each child choose grandparents and a number of grandchildren and place the figures on a flannelboard. Then let the child tell several sentences about his or her flannelboard family.

Decorated Bookmarks

Let your children make bookmarks to give as presents for Grandparent's Day. Cut construction paper into 2½-by-7½-inch strips. Have the children decorate a strip for each of their grandparents by dribbling on glue and sprinkling with glitter, gluing on pressed leaves or wildflowers, or by attaching colorful stickers. Write the children's names on the backs of their bookmarks and let them stamp on their thumbprints. Then cover both sides of the bookmarks with clear self-stick paper.

The Jewish New Year

Rosh Hashanah, the Jewish New Year, is celebrated during the first two days of the month of *Tishri*, usually in mid-September. Rosh Hashanah is a holy time devoted to prayer and self-reflection. It is also a time to look ahead to the coming year, and to wish friends and family *Shanah Tovah*, a good year.

A Sweet Year

Apples dipped in honey are one of the traditional foods eaten during Rosh Hashanah to symbolize a sweet year. Have your children dip apple wedges in honey for a sweet treat.

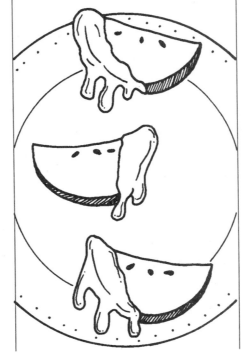

New Year's Cards

For each of your children, make a folded paper card with the words "Shanah Tovah" written inside. Have the children decorate the fronts of their cards with felt-tip markers, stickers, and glued-on scraps of paper.

Shanah Tovah

Sung to: "Clementine"

Shanah Tovah, a good year,
A good year to you!
Shanah Tovah, a good year,
A good year to you!

Susan Hodges

MOVEMENT • Fall Fun

Harvest Time

Let your children act out ways to help harvest fruits and vegetables. Have them pretend to climb up ladders to pick fruit. Let them imagine they are digging for potatoes in the dirt. Give each child the opportunity to name a fruit or vegetable and have everyone act out how it is gathered.

Autumn Leaves

Have your children imagine they are colorful fall leaves on a tree, swaying in the autumn breeze. Then have them pretend a strong wind comes by and sends them twirling and swirling to the ground. Let the children experiment with different ways to fall to the ground. Next, have all the children pretend they are raking up the fallen leaves into a big pile. When the pile is completed, let the children decide how to end this movement activity. For example, they could play in the leaves, the wind could scatter their leaves, or the children could hide under leaves.

Tricky Jumping

Use pieces of masking tape to make a path on the floor as shown in the illustration. Show the tape to your children and explain that when there are two pieces of tape, they should jump with both feet inside the tape and when there is one piece of tape, they should jump with both feet outside the tape. Then let the children take turns jumping along the path. Make the pattern as easy or as difficult as desired.

It's Amazing

Use masking tape to make a crazy maze on the floor. Encourage your children to move through the maze in a variety of different ways. Have them move sideways, walk backward, skip, tiptoe, hop, or crawl.

Kick-Off Game

Outside or in a large open room, place a foam ball on a spray can lid. Let your children take turns kicking the ball off the lid. Vary the game by using different shaped balls or by using heavier and heavier balls.

Jumping Game

Kneel on the floor holding a rope "snake." Have your children stand all around you. Wiggle the snake back and forth across the floor and have the children jump to get out of its way.

MUSIC · Songs About Leaves

Falling, Falling
Sung to: "Twinkle, Twinkle, Little Star"

Falling, falling, falling leaves,
Mother Nature, did you sneeze?
Red ones, yellow ones, orange and brown,
Big ones, little ones on the ground.
Falling, falling, falling leaves,
Mother Nature, did you sneeze?

Pat Cook

Fall Is Here
Sung to: "Frère Jacques"

Fall is here. Fall is here.
Yes, it is. Yes, it is.
All the leaves are falling.
All the leaves are falling.
Crunch, crunch, crunch.
Crunch, crunch, crunch.

Melinda Perry

Down by the Oak Tree
Sung to: "Down by the Station"

Down by the oak tree
On an autumn morning,
See all the yellow leaves
Whirling to and fro.
See how they twist and turn,
Whirling, whirling, whirling.
Down, down, down, down,
Off they blow.

Repeat, substituting the names of other colors for *yellow*.

Lois E. Putnam

Look at the Apples
Sung to: "The Mulberry Bush"

Look at the apple I have found,
So fat and rosy on the ground.
Mother will wash it and cut it in two,
Half for me and half for you.

Martha T. Lyon

Ten Apples
Sung to: "Ten Little Indians"

One red, two red, three red apples,
Four red, five red, six red apples,
Seven red, eight red, nine red apples,
Ten red apples.

Additional verses: yellow; green; big; little.

Betty Ruth Baker

Applesauce
Sung to: "Yankee Doodle"

Peel an apple,
Cut it up,
Cook it in a pot.
When you taste it
You will find
It's applesauce you've got!

Martha T. Lyon

I Am an Apple
Sung to: "The Farmer in the Dell"

I am an apple,
Growing on a tree.
If you want some applesauce,
Just cook me.

Polly Reedy

Welcome to Our Group

Sung to: "Row, Row, Row Your Boat"

Welcome to our group.
We're glad you're here today!
We know you'll have a lot of fun,
While you learn and play!

Kathy McCullough

Who Is Here Today?

Sung to: "Twinkle, Twinkle, Little Star"

Let's see who is here today.
Who has come to join our play?
Everyone sit close at hand,
Say your name, then you can stand.
Let's see who is here today.
Who has come to join our play?

Ellen Bedford

I'm Glad You Came to School

Sung to: "The Farmer in the Dell"

I'm glad you came to school,
I'm glad you came to school.
I've planned lots of fun for you,
I'm glad you came to school.

It's time for you to go,
It's time for you to go.
I'll see you tomorrow,
But now, it's time to go.

Sing the first verse to greet your children and the second verse as they go home, replacing *tomorrow* with the word or phrase that describes your group's next meeting time.

Sue Brown

We Share

Sung to: "Twinkle, Twinkle, Little Star"

We share all our blocks and toys
With the other girls and boys.
Crayons, scissors, paint, and glue,
Puzzles, books, the easel, too.
We take turns because it's fair,
And we're happy when we share.

Sue Brown

If You're Ready

Sung to: "If You're Happy and You Know It"

If you're ready for a story find a seat.
If you're ready for a story find a seat.
If you're ready for a story,
Check your hands and then your feet.
If you're ready for a story find a seat.

Sue Brown

It's Time

Sung to: "The Farmer in the Dell"

It's time to come to group,
It's time to come to group.
Come on over, find a seat,
It's time to come to group.

Sue Brown

Bouncy, Bouncy, Bouncy

Have your children stand or sit in a circle. Bounce or roll a ball to a child and say the first verse of the following rhyme. When the child catches the ball, have him or her bounce or roll the ball back to you while you help him or her respond with the second verse. Continue playing until each child has had a chance to say his or her name.

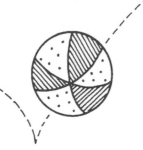

Bouncy, bouncy, bouncy,
Will you play my game?
Bouncy, bouncy, bouncy,
What is your name?

Bouncy, bouncy, bouncy,
I'll play your game.
Bouncy, bouncy, bouncy,
_____ is my name.

Jean Warren

This Letter

Collect an envelope for each of your children. Write a child's name on each envelope. Put the envelopes into a box. Select a child to be the letter carrier. Have the child choose an envelope from the box. Read the name out loud. Have the letter carrier deliver the envelope to that child while you sing the song below, substituting the name on the envelope for *Rhiannon*. At the end of the song, have that child be the next letter carrier to choose an envelope from the box and deliver it.

Sung to: "Did You Ever See a Lassie?"

This letter's for Rhiannon,
For Rhiannon, for Rhiannon.
This letter's for Rhiannon,
Please stand up right now.

Jane Woods

What Are You Wearing?

Have your children sit in a circle. Sing the song below, substituting one of the children's names for *Cormac* and an article of clothing that the child is wearing for *blue pants*. If you wish, have the child stand up as you sing the song. Sing a verse of the song for each child.

Sung to: "Mary Had a Little Lamb"

Cormac wore his blue pants,
His blue pants, his blue pants.
Cormac wore his blue pants
To preschool today.

Jane Woods

Friends Hold Hands

Ask your children how they know when people are friends. Maybe they see people smile at each other, hug, play together, talk, kiss, or hold hands. Tell them that they will have a chance to show everyone they are friends by making "hand holding" handprints. Tape a piece of butcher paper to the floor. Set out several shallow containers with flesh-toned paint (brown, tan, beige, peach, etc.) near the paper. Invite your children to cooperate as they dip their hands in the paint and print adjoining handprints along the paper. Hang the banner at your children's eye level where they might notice that everyone has hands and skin but the color of their skin and the size of their hands might differ.

Wiggly Friends

Make finger gelatin (see recipe below). Spray a child-shaped cookie cutter with nonstick cooking spray and help each of your children cut two shapes from the finger gelatin. Encourage each child to share one of his or her shapes with a friend. Discuss how friends share food. Ask the children to name other things friends might share.

Finger Gelatin—Empty 4 envelopes plain gelatin into a large bowl. Pour 1 cup cold apple juice on top of the gelatin and let stand 1 minute. Heat 3 more cups apple juice to boiling and stir the hot juice into the gelatin mixture. Pour the gelatin mixture into a 9-by-13-inch pan sprayed with nonstick cooking spray and chill at least 3 hours or until gelatin is firm.

Cork Printing

Set out corks and red tempera paint for your children to use to print "apples" on trees that have been cut out of construction paper. Later, use the prints for counting practice.

Observing Changes

Observe and discuss with your children what raw apples look like. Ask them to predict what will happen when apples are cooked. Bake one apple whole. Slice and simmer another one. Have your children compare the results to the raw apples. What changes occured in color, texture, and taste?

Apple Collages

Give each of your children a small paper plate and a piece of red paper. Have the children tear their papers into small pieces and glue the pieces on their plates. Add green paper stem shapes. Hang the finished collages as room decorations.

Comparing Seeds

Have your children use a magnifying glass to look at seeds in and out of an apple. Ask them to compare the apple seeds with other fruit seeds, such as orange or grape seeds, that you have set out.

Number Recognition Game

Glue a felt tree on each of five cardboard squares. Number the squares from 1 to 5. Cut out 15 felt apple shapes. To play the game, have one of your children identify the number on one of the squares and place that number of apples on the tree.

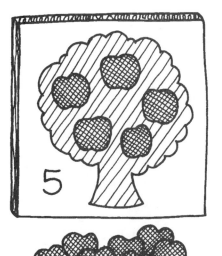

Sorting Apples

Have your children sort different colored real or cardboard apples into baskets. Let them count how many red, green, and yellow apples there are. Then ask your children to arrange each group of apples by size, from large to small.

Apple Game

Place five to eight apples in front of your children. Have them count the apples. Ask them to close their eyes while you remove some of the apples. Help the children figure out how many apples are gone.

Apple Coleslaw

Let your children help you make this apple snack. In a large bowl, mix together ¼ cup mayonnaise, ¼ cup milk, and 1 teaspoon lemon juice. Grate 1 large apple and 1 small cabbage. Add to mayonnaise mixture. Stir until apple and cabbage are moistened. Serve in small bowls.

The Moon

Show your children pictures of the moon. Talk about the craters and ridges found on the surface of the moon. Show the children pictures of the different phases of the moon, from a crescent moon to a full moon. Encourage the children to tell about a time when they have seen the moon at night. What did it look like? How did the moonlight make the world around them look? In what ways is moonlight different from sunlight?

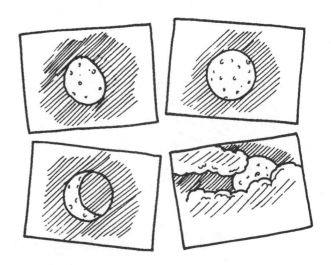

Man in the Moon Plates

Explain to your children that some people imagine that they see a face on the moon because of the positions of its darker-colored spots. They call this face "the man in the moon." Then give each child a white paper plate. Cut a variety of shapes out of black or gray construction paper. Have your children glue the shapes on their paper plates to make man in the moon faces.

Playdough Moons

Give each of your children a piece of white playdough and have them form balls to create "moons." Encourage them to create bumpy surfaces on their moons by making holes for craters and pinching the playdough together to make ridges.

Moonbeam Game

Have your children form a circle. Choose one child to be the Moon who stands in the middle, holding a flashlight. As everyone says the rhyme below, let the Moon shine the light on one child. Then let that child be the Moon. Continue until every child has had a turn.

Moonbeam, moonbeam,
Who do you see?
Moonbeam, moonbeam,
Shine on me!

Margaret Timmons

Moon Cakes

Give each of your children a rice cake. Talk about its texture. Is it smooth or bumpy? Explain that the moon is bumpy too. It is covered with craters and ridges. Let the children spread peanut butter on their rice cakes. (Stir a little apple juice into the peanut butter to make it easier to spread.) Have the children top their rice cakes with grape halves, sunflower seeds, and raisins.

Moon Glow, Moon Glow

Sung to: "Twinkle, Twinkle, Little Star"

Moon glow, moon glow, in the night.

Moon glow, moon glow, gentle light.

How I love to see you there,

Softly shining everywhere!

Moon glow, moon glow, in the night.

Moon glow, moon glow, gentle light.

Margaret Timmons

"Why the Animals Don't Talk" Story Patterns
Refer to page 273 for directions.

October

ART • Spider Fun

Spider Printing

Collect one toilet-tissue tube for each of your children. Cut eight 1-inch slits around one end of each tube. Give a tube and a sheet of construction paper to each child. Show the children how to bend the slit ends of their rolls outward to create "spider legs." Pour small amounts of black tempera paint into shallow containers. Let the children dip their spider legs into the black paint and press them onto their papers to make spider prints.

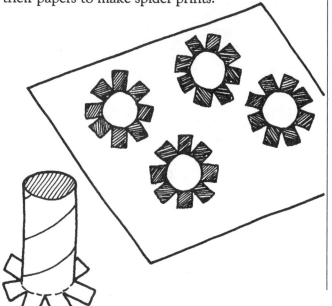

Spider Webs

Cut a piece of black construction paper to fit the bottom of a round baking pan. Put the paper in the pan and pour a small amount of white tempera paint in the middle of the paper. Give the pan to one of your children. Have the child place a marble in the pan. Show the child how to tilt the pan back and forth to make the marble roll through the paint. As the marble passes through the paint it will leave trails of white across the paper, resembling a spider's web.

Egg Carton Spiders

Cut the egg cups out of a cardboard egg carton. Cut pipe cleaners into 3-inch sections. To make each spider, poke four pipe cleaners through each cup sideways as shown in the illustration. Bend the ends to resemble eight spider legs. Give each of your children one of the spiders. Have the children paint their spiders black. After the paint dries, attach a length of elastic thread to the middle of each spider. Let the children hold onto their threads and bounce their spiders up and down as they take them for a walk.

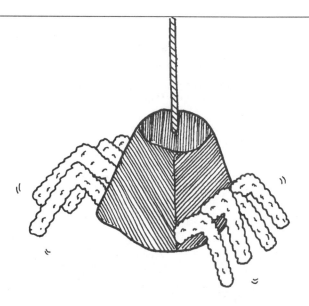

Pumpkin Patch

Give each of your children a small paper sack. Have the children make their sacks look like small pumpkins by stuffing them with crumpled pieces of newpaper. Then help the children close their sacks by twisting the tops together and securing them with pieces of tape or twist ties. Let the children paint their pumpkin shapes orange. Allow the paint to dry. Make a giant Pumpkin Patch by stringing the children's pumpkins together with a long piece of green yarn. Arrange the pumpkins and yarn around the room or on a bulletin board. Tape green construction paper leaves near the pumpkins.

Sponge Pumpkins

Cut sponges into small shapes. Pour small amounts of orange tempera paint into shallow containers. Give each of your children a small paper plate. Let the children use the sponges to sponge-paint their plates orange. After the orange paint dries, set out shallow containers of black tempera paint. Have the children dip the sponges into the black paint and press them on their orange plates to make faces.

Hint: Attach clothespins to the small sponge shapes to make them easier to handle.

Playdough Pumpkins

Collect a plastic lid for each of your children. Give each child one of the lids, some orange playdough, and some popcorn kernels. Have the children press the orange playdough into the lids. Then let them press the popcorn kernels into the playdough to make jack-o'-lantern faces. Allow the playdough to dry. The Playdough Pumpkins can be left in their lids or taken out for display.

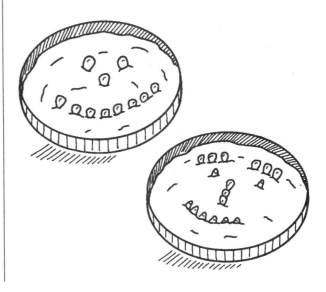

Gallery

Create an art gallery for your room. Collect inexpensive frames at flea markets and sales. Place artwork in the frames, using mats made out of construction paper. Hang the pictures on a wall at your children's eye level. Rotate the art frequently.

Art Clips

Make personalized Art Clips for each of your children's artwork. Attach large metal clips to a wall at the children's eye level. Use a permanent felt-tip marker to write each child's name on a different clip. Have the children choose the pictures they want to display from their clips. Let the children decide when to change their artwork.

Display Backgrounds

Display your children's artwork on backgrounds of contrasting colors and textures to draw more attention to the children's masterpieces. To cover large display areas easily, use disposable plastic or paper tablecloths, colored butcher paper, seasonal wrapping paper, or colored tissue paper. Grass cloth, burlap, or nylon net provide different textures for your display area.

Jump Rope Display

Purchase an inexpensive multi-colored jump rope (or use a jump rope you already have). Attach the rope between two poles, along a wall, or across a door opening. Use clothespins to hang paintings or other artwork from the jump rope to create a colorful display.

Banner-Style Display

Turn long, narrow pieces of your children's art into banners. Cut a wooden dowel a few inches longer than the width of one of the children's pieces of art. Attach the top edge of the artwork to the dowel. Tie a piece of yarn to both ends of the dowel for hanging.

Stationery Art

Small artwork can be made into stationery or notecards. Glue the pictures to pieces of folded construction paper.

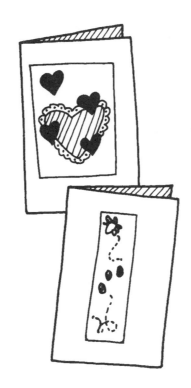

Art Collections

Designate one of your children to be the "artist of the week." Display the child's artwork in a special area. At the end of the week, photograph the collection and the artist. Take the artwork down and begin again with another child. Keep the photos in an album or frame them and hang them on a wall.

LEARNING GAMES • Pumpkin Fun

All in a Row

Draw simple cards showing the stages of a pumpkin's growth (a small pumpkin plant, a plant with a blossom, a plant with a green pumpkin, and a plant with an orange pumpkin). Show the cards to your children. Talk about the stages of a pumpkin's growth. Then mix up the cards and let the children take turns putting them in order.

Pumpkin Teeth Counting Game

Cut pumpkin shapes out of orange felt. On each pumpkin, draw a simple jack-o'-lantern face with a large smile but no teeth. Number the pumpkins from 1 to 5. Cut 15 tooth shapes out of white felt. Place the pumpkins on a flannelboard. Have your children take turns identifying the numbers on the pumpkins and placing the appropriate number of teeth in each pumpkin's mouth.

Pumpkin Matching

Draw the outline of a pumpkin on each of 12 index cards. Divide the cards into six pairs. Draw different jack-o'-lantern faces on each pair of pumpkin cards. Mix up the cards. Let your children take turns finding the pumpkins with matching faces.

Teaching Lotto

Cut posterboard into 9-inch squares to make gameboards. Divide each gameboard into nine squares and draw pictures, shapes, numbers, etc., in the squares. For each gameboard, make a set of nine matching game cards on 3-inch squares cut from posterboard. Tape a 6-inch posterboard square to the back of each gameboard to make an envelope for holding that board's game cards. Then let your children play matching games by placing the game cards on top of the corresponding squares on the gameboards.

Teaching Wheel

Cut a 12-inch circle out of posterboard. Divide the circle into eight sections and draw shapes, letters, numbers, etc., in the sections. Draw matching shapes, letters, numbers, etc., on eight spring-type clothespins. Then let your children clip the clothespins around the edge of the wheel on the matching sections.

Teaching Dominoes

Cut heavy paper into 21 small cards about 2 by 4 inches each. Divide each card in half with a line and draw a shape, a set of dots, a colored circle, etc., in each half. Give each of your children an equal number of cards and place the remaining cards face down in a pile. Let the children play dominoes with the cards until all the cards have been played.

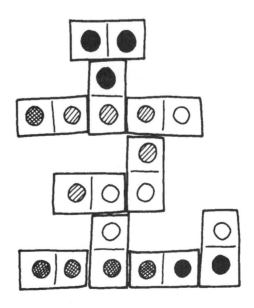

Hearing

Find the Timer—Let your children try to find a hidden kitchen timer by listening for its ticking.

Following Directions—Record simple one-, two-, or three-step directions on a tape recorder. For example, a two-step direction could be, "Find a crayon and put it on the table." Have your children play back the directions and follow them.

Patterns—Ask your children to listen with their eyes closed while you clap in a pattern (one slow-two fast, one slow-two fast, etc.). Then have them echo your claps.

Touch

Touch Table—Set up a Touch Table. Put out a variety of objects that are interesting to touch such as a smooth rock, a rough shell, a soft feather, and a prickly pine cone.

Sensory Beanbags—Make beanbags and fill each one with a different stuffing such as sawdust, foam pieces, gravel, rice, or plastic-foam peanuts.

Fingerpainting—Let your children fingerpaint using liquid starch or shaving cream. Add cornmeal to change the texture of the fingerpaint.

Sight

Memory Game—Show your children three or four common objects as you count, "One, two, three." Cover the objects and ask the children, "What did you see?"

Sight Walk—Go on a Sight Walk with your children. Take along binoculars and magnifying glasses.

Smell

Spicy Scents—Have your children smell spices and extracts from the kitchen. Which ones do they like the best?

Smelling Trips—Take your children on field trips to places that have distinctive smells such as a bakery, a florist shop, a farm, or a zoo.

Taste

Taste Test—Ask your children to close their eyes while they try to identify familiar foods by taste only.

Comparing Tastes—Let your children compare the taste of different varieties of the same foods such as red and green seedless grapes, Golden Delicious and Granny Smith apples, and Cheddar and mozzarella cheeses.

LANGUAGE • Storytime

The Wise Old Owl

Adapted by Jean Warren

Once upon a time, there were two little mice who lived in a big, old farmhouse.

The farmer didn't mind having the mice around. But the farmer's wife said they made too much mess, and she wanted to get rid of them.

So she went to the wise old owl and asked him what she could do. "Simple," said the owl, "get a cat."

So the farmer's wife brought home a cat. Soon the mice were gone, but the cat often broke things when it jumped up on the furniture. This made the wife mad, so she went back to the wise old owl.

"Please, Mr. Owl," said the woman, "tell me how can I get rid of the cat?"

"Simple," said the owl, "get a dog."

So the woman got a dog and took it home. Soon the cat was gone, but the woman wasn't happy. The dog barked too much and chewed up her slippers. Back went the woman to the owl.

"Mr. Owl, please tell me how I can get rid of the dog."

"Simple," said the owl, "get a tiger."

So the farmer's wife bought a tiger and took it home. The dog left quickly, but much to her

dismay, the woman watched the tiger run through her house smashing everything in sight.

Back went the woman to the owl. "Mr. Owl, please tell me how I can get rid of the tiger."

"Simple," said the owl, "get an elephant."

Off the woman went to buy an elephant and take it home. When the tiger saw the elephant, he left in a hurry. But the woman watched in horror as the elephant broke windows and put holes through her walls.

"Oh, no," cried the woman, "what can I do?"

So back she went to the owl. "Please, Mr. Owl, tell me how I can get rid of the elephant."

"Simple," said the owl, "get two small mice."

So the woman went in search of two small mice and took them home.

When the elephant saw the mice he ran quickly out of the house. And the farmer and his wife and the two mice lived happily every after in the big, old farmhouse.

Flannelboard Directions
Photocopy the patterns on pages 324 and 325. Color the patterns and cover them with clear self-stick paper for durability, if desired. Attach a piece of felt to the back of each pattern. Place the patterns on a flannelboard as you tell the story on this page. Then let your children use the patterns to retell the story.

The Pumpkin Story

By Jean Warren

Early one morning as the sun popped out,
A little white seed began to sprout.

It pushed its head up through the ground,
Waved its arms, and looked around.

The little plant seemed so very low,
But then the plant began to grow.

It grew up the hill, to the very top,
And there at last it decided to stop.

Out popped a flower, a great big one,
As gold as the color of the setting sun.

The plant was happy until one day
The beautiful flower fell away.

Then the plant grew sad, it felt real low,
Until a green ball started to grow.

The green ball grew to a great big size,
Then turned all orange, a big surprise!

Way up high at the top of the hill,
That giant pumpkin sat very still.

It saw some children playing down below
And wished that down the hill it could go.

It leaned to the left. It leaned to the right.
It pushed and pushed with all its might.

And soon enough, it reached its goal,
And down the hill it started to roll.

It rolled and rolled, slow, then fast,
Until the children it reached at last.

The children took the pumpkin to the county fair,
Where it won a blue ribbon that it could wear.

They said it was the biggest of all the rest.
They said that, for a pumpkin, it was the best.

The pumpkin was so happy, it wanted to grin.
It isn't every day a ribbon you win.

The children felt sorry for the pumpkin with
   no grin,
So they carved out a smile and set a candle in.

Now that pumpkin's as happy as can be,
For it's a jack-o'-lantern for all to see.

Movement Fun
Encourage your children to act out the
pumpkin's movements as your read the story
to them.

Knock, Knock Rhymes • LANGUAGE

Who's That Knocking at My Door?

Tell your children about a friendly family of mice who like to come visiting. Explain that when Father Mouse comes visiting, he knocks twice very loudly. When Mother Mouse comes visiting, she knocks four times very fast. And when Baby Mouse comes visiting, she knocks three times very softly. Have the children hide their eyes and listen while you pretend to be one of the visiting mice and knock on a wall or a table in the appropriate way. Let the children guess which mouse has come to visit. Repeat as long as interest lasts.

Trick-or-Treaters

Say the following rhyme with your children. Pause at the blank and ask one child to fill it in. Repeat with the additional verses until each child has had a turn.

Knock, knock, sounds like more

Trick-or-treaters at my door.

I open the door and what do I see?

Two green _____ smiling at me!

Additional verses: A great, big _____; A tiny, tiny _____; An ugly old _____; A funny brown _____; A beautiful _____; A big, white _____; Ten little _____.

Jean Warren

Hand Bones

Our hands are made up of many bones. Explain to your children that each finger is made up of three bones that are held together by stretchy bands called ligaments. Cut plastic drinking straws into ¾-inch lengths. Help each child trace his or her hands on bright paper. Have the children glue three straw sections to each finger to represent finger bones.

Rib Vests

Discuss with your children how every person has 22 ribs, 11 on each side. Our ribs protect our heart and lungs. Let them try to feel their ribs. Then have the children decorate Rib Vests. Cut large brown grocery bags into vests, as shown in the illustration. Let each child use white paint or crayons to draw 11 ribs on each front side of his or her vest.

All Thumbs

Tell your children about the way our thumbs help us hold things firmly. Have them try to pick up things without their thumbs. Let them try to eat snack or lunch without using their thumbs.

Back to Back

Explain to your children that our backs are made up of lots of little bones that help us stand and sit straight, and they also help us bend, twist, and turn. Have your children pair up. Help them stand back to back and link their arms. Let the pairs of children try walking across the room with their arms linked. Challenge them to keep their arms linked while they sit down and stand up.

Leggy Lengths

Discuss legs with your children. Show them magazine pictures of people using their legs to do a variety of activities. Point out that legs come in many lengths and are made of three bones: the femur (thigh bone), the tibia (shin bone), and the fibula (found behind the tibia). Then make a bar graph on a large sheet of paper. Measure the length of each child's leg from hip to heel. Record the measurement on the bar graph, drawing the bar as the child's leg and copying the child's shoes and socks. Repeat for each child. Your children will enjoy interpreting the results and comparing leg lengths.

Joints Song

Sung to: "Frère Jacques"

Find your elbows, find your elbows.
Bend them now, this is how.
Elbows bend your arm bones,
Elbows bend your arm bones.
Bend them now, bend them now.

Find your knees, find your knees.
Bend them now, this is how.
Knees bend your leg bones,
Knees bend your leg bones.
Bend them now, bend
    them now.

Have your children bend the appropriate joints while singing this song.

Betty Silkunas

MY WORLD · Recycling Fun

Save a Tree

Explain to your children that recycling a 3-foot stack of newspaper will save one tree from being cut down and turned into paper. Then put a piece of masking tape 3 feet up on a wall in your room. Have the children bring in newspapers and stack them in a pile under the tape. Each time a 3-foot stack is collected, take the stack to a recycling center and put a mark on a tree-shaped chart. At the end of the month or another specified time, count how many trees your children have saved. Then celebrate by going outside and having a picnic under a tree!

Clean Up Earth

Sung to: "Frère Jacques"

Let's recycle, let's recycle.
Do it now, you know how.
Save your glass and cans,
Newspapers and pie pans,
Clean up earth, clean up earth.

Martha Thomas

Recycling Station

Set out brightly painted boxes that are clearly labeled as containers for collecting recyclable items such as glass, cans, paper, and plastic. Encourage your children to bring these items and put them into the appropriate boxes. Also encourage them to use these boxes throughout the day. Talk about how recycling helps the earth by reducing the amount of garbage and conserving natural resources. Take the boxes to a recycling center and use the money received to purchase materials for your program.

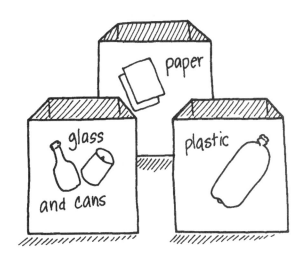

Recycling Baskets

Set out two wastebaskets in your room. Tape a piece of construction paper and other examples of paper that can be recycled to one of the wastebaskets. To the other basket, tape a napkin, a facial tissue, and other samples of nonrecyclable garbage. Then talk with your children about recycling and its benefits. Discuss the two wastebaskets with your children. Set out several examples of recyclable paper and nonrecyclable garbage and let the children put them into the appropriate cans. Encourage the children to ask you if they have any questions about what is recyclable and what is not.

Stomp and Pitch

Collect three to five empty, uncrushed aluminum cans for each of your children. Set out the cans in a row and place several boxes about 3 feet away. Have the children smash the cans as flat as possible and pitch the flattened cans into the boxes. Stomping and pitching are great ways for children to exercise their strength and large motor skills. Recycle the cans when you are finished.

Pumpkin Patch

Select two or three of your children to be Farmers. Have the remaining children join hands to form a long, winding pumpkin vine. Ask every second or third child on the vine to become a Pumpkin. Have the Pumpkins crouch down and hug their knees. At your signal, have the Farmers "pull" the Pumpkins off the vine by gently rolling them over onto their sides. Then have the Pumpkins roll away. Repeat until every child has had a turn being a Pumpkin and a Farmer.

Black Cat Warm-Up

Have your children imitate cat movements. Ask them to show you how cats walk, play with balls of string, curl up in front of warm fires, or drink bowls of milk. Have the children pretend to be cats that are happy, afraid, angry, or hungry.

Moving to Music

Play Halloween music and let your children try out different "Halloween moves." For example, have them fly like bats or owls, roll like pumpkins, crawl like spiders, or prowl like black cats. If desired, let the children take turns leading the others as they move around the room.

Parachute Fun • MOVEMENT

Fun With a Parachute

Parachute games are wonderful indoor or outdoor movement activities. They give children a chance to work cooperatively, and they reinforce concepts such as opposites and following directions. Best of all, children love these activities. If you don't have access to a parachute, use a blanket, a shower curtain, or a large sheet for these activities.

Name Game

Have your children hold a parachute by the edges. As you sing the following song, have them raise the parachute above their heads so it billows like a big tent. When a child is named, have him or her run under the parachute and grab it on the other side. Then slowly lower the parachute. Continue playing until all the children have had a chance to run.

Sung to: "Row, Row, Row Your Boat"

Up, up, up it goes.
Down, down, down it comes.
If your name is Joshua,
Now's your turn to run.

Substitute the name of one of your children for *Joshua*.

Diane Thom

When the Parachute Goes Up

Sung to: "If You're Happy and You Know It"

When the parachute goes up,
Stomp your feet.
When the parachute goes up,
Stomp your feet.
When the parachute is high,
It floats up in the sky.
When the parachute goes up,
Stomp your feet.

Encourage your children to think of other movements to substitute for *stomp your feet.*

Diane Thom

He Sailed the Ocean Blue

Sung to: "The Farmer in the Dell"

He sailed the ocean blue,
He sailed the ocean blue.
Christopher Columbus
Sailed the ocean blue.

He sailed with three ships,
He sailed with three ships.
Christopher Columbus
Sailed with three ships.

He sailed to America,
He sailed to America.
Christopher Columbus
Sailed to America.

Gayle Bittinger

Christopher Columbus

Sung to: "I'm a Little Teapot"

Christopher Columbus sailed the sea.
Ships on the ocean, one, two, three.
When the trip was finished, he could see
America, the home of you and me.

Carla C. Skjong

Columbus Sailed Three Ships

Sung to: "I'm a Little Teapot"

Columbus sailed three ships across the sea,
Niña, Pinta, and Santa Maria.
They sailed away from sunny Spain as planned,
All the way to a great new land.

Susan A. Miller

Pumpkin, Pumpkin

Sung to: "Twinkle, Twinkle, Little Star"

Pumpkin, pumpkin on the ground,
How'd you get so big and round?
You started as a seed so small.
Now you are a great big ball.
Pumpkin, pumpkin on the ground,
How'd you get so big and round?

Diane Thom

The Roly-Poly Pumpkin

Sung to: "The Eensy Weensy Spider"

Oh, the roly-poly pumpkin
Went rolling down the hill.
Once it started rolling
It couldn't keep still.
It rolled and rolled and rolled
Until it bumped into a rock.
Then the roly-poly pumpkin
Rolled to a stop!

Diane Thom

Pumpkin Vine

Sung to: "Clementine"

In the garden by our school yard
Grows our lovely pumpkin vine.
Long and twisted, green and leafy,
Such a lovely pumpkin vine!

Yellow flowers start a-blooming
All along our pumpkin vine.
Soon the pumpkins will be budding
Underneath our lovely vine.

Oh, our pumpkin. Oh, our pumpkin.
Oh, our lovely pumpkin vine.
Long and twisted, green and leafy,
Such a lovely pumpkin vine.

Nancy Nason Biddinger

Have You Ever Seen a Spider?

Sung to: "Did You Ever See a Lassie?"

Have you ever seen a spider,
A spider, a spider?
Have you ever seen a spider
While it spins a web?
Spins this way and that way,
Spins this way and that way.
Have you ever seen a spider
While it spins a web?

Diane Thom

The Big Black Spider

Sung to: "Little White Duck"

Oh, the big black spider's
Web is on the wall.
Around her web she does crawl.
She might catch a bug,
Or she might catch a bee,
But the big black spider
Won't catch me!
Oh, the big black spider's
Web is on the wall.
Crawl, crawl, crawl.

Oh, the big black spider's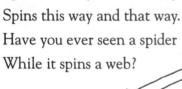
Web is on the tree.
It really is quite a sight to see.
She might catch a bug,
Or she might catch a bee,
But the big black spider
Won't catch me!
Oh, the big black spider's
Web is on the tree.
See, see, see.

Oh, the big black spider's
Web is on the door.
Every day she spins a little more.
She might catch a bug,
Or she might catch a bee,
But the big black spider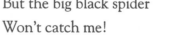
Won't catch me!
Oh, the big black spider's
Web is on the door.
Please spin more.

Jean Warren

Halloween
Sung to: "Mary Had a Little Lamb"

Who will be a funny clown,
Funny clown, funny clown?
Who will be a funny clown
For Halloween?

Substitute the names of other costumes
for the words *funny clown*.

Ann-Marie Donovan

Trick-or-Treat
Sung to: "Frère Jacques"

Trick-or-treat, trick-or-treat,
Halloween night, Halloween night.
In our costumes playing,
You will hear us saying,
"Trick-or-treat, trick-or-treat."

Gayle Bittinger

I'm a Jack-O'-Lantern
Sung to: "I'm a Little Teapot"

I'm a jack-o'-lantern, look at me!
I'm as happy as I can be.
Put a candle in and light the light.
I'll look great on Halloween night.

Betty Ruth Baker

THEMES • Fire Safety

Fire Safety Bulletin Board

Talk with your children about fire safety rules such as these: "Don't play with matches or lighters. Don't play with electrical cords or sockets. Keep away from things that are hot." Make a chart of the rules and hang it on a bulletin board. Let the children use red, yellow, and orange tempera paints to make fire pictures on pieces of black construction paper. Arrange the pictures around your fire safety chart to complete your bulletin board display.

Fire Prevention Badges

Cut badge shapes out of white index cards. Let your children decorate their badges with orange and yellow felt-tip markers. Use a black felt-tip marker to write these words on each child's badge: "(Child's name) does not play with matches or lighters." Then tape a safety pin to the back of the badge and pin it to the child's shirt.

Fire Safety Detectives

Around your room, place several pictures of matchbooks, lighters, candles, smoke detectors, fire extinguishers, and firefighters. Set out two boxes, one labeled "Things That Make Fires" and one labeled "Things That Stop Fires." Have your children search the room for the pictures of things that cause fires and put them into the appropriate box. Then have the children find the pictures of things that prevent fires and put them into the other box. Talk with the children about keeping away from the items that can start fires.

Stop, Drop, and Roll

Talk with your children about how they should "stop, drop, and roll" if their clothes catch on fire. Clear a large area in the room or take the children outside to a grassy area. Have the children start walking or running in place. At a given signal, have them stop what they are doing, drop to the floor or the ground, and roll over and over until the pretend flames are out.

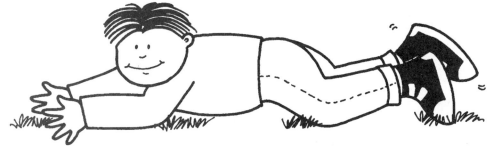

Never Play With Matches
Sung to: "Frère Jacques"

Never, never play with matches.
If you do, if you do,
You might burn your fingers,
You might burn your fingers,
That won't do! That won't do!

Never, never play with matches.
If you do, if you do,
You might burn your clothes,
You might burn your clothes,
That won't do! That won't do!

Repeat, substituting *lighters* for *matches*.

Leora Grecian

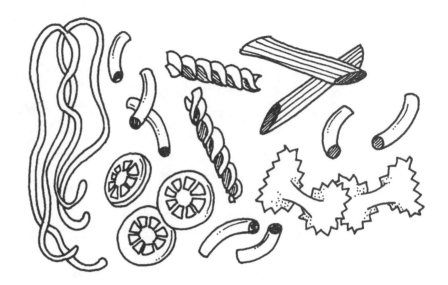

Celebrating Pasta Day

Celebrate Pasta Day any time during October, which is National Pasta Month. Pasta is a favorite food everywhere. It comes in many different shapes, ranging from macaroni to stars, from spaghetti to bow ties. So snack on some pasta while you and your children enjoy the following activities.

Dyeing Pasta

Put 2 tablespoons water and 10 drops food coloring into a resealable plastic bag. Add 1 cup uncooked pasta, seal the bag, and shake until the desired color is reached. Pour out the excess water and put the pasta on paper towels to dry.

Variation: Instead of dyeing pasta, use various flavors of pasta that come naturally in colors such as spinach, tomato, and whole-wheat.

Pasta Necklaces

Dye shapes of "stringable" pasta, such as salad macaroni, wheels, and rigatoni, in several different colors. Let your children string the colored pasta on pieces of yarn. Tie the ends of each child's yarn piece together to make a necklace.

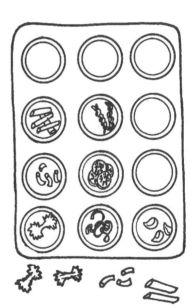

Sorting Pasta Shapes

Set out a muffin tin and a variety of small pasta shapes such as macaroni, wheels, bow ties, and shells. Let your children take turns sorting the pasta by shape into the muffin-tin cups. Then have them count the number of shapes in each cup.

Pasta Counting

Use a felt-tip marker to number 10 paper bowls from 1 to 10. Set out the bowls along with another bowl filled with pasta shapes such as shells or spirals. Let your children take turns selecting one of the bowls, identifying the number on it, and counting that number of pasta shapes into it.

Moving Like Pasta

Play music and encourage your children to move around the room like different types of pasta. Offer suggestions such as these: "Move like a tall, stiff spaghetti noodle; Move like a wet, limp spaghetti noodle; Move like a pasta wheel; Pretend that you are a piece of rigatoni and roll like a log; Move like a wavy lasagne noodle."

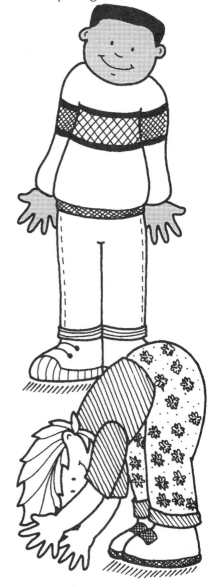

Pasta Shapes Song

Sung to: "Up on the Housetop"

I love pasta, yes, I do,
Noodles and twists are but a few.
Then there's spaghetti and bow ties,
Wheels and macaroni any size.
I love pasta, yum, yum, yum.
I love pasta in my tum.
Pasta is so fun to eat,
Pasta is a special treat.

Gayle Bittinger

THEMES • Learning With Owls

Facts About Owls

Although these facts are provided for the teacher's information, older children may enjoy learning a little more about owls.

- Owls have eyes on the fronts rather than the sides of their heads.

- Owls see very well in the dark.

- The circles of feathers around their eyes are what makes them look like "wise old birds."

- Owls have fluffy feathers on their bodies and wings.

- The "ears" on the tops of some owls' heads are actually little tufts of feathers.

- Owls are farmers' friends because they eat mice and harmful insects that destroy crops.

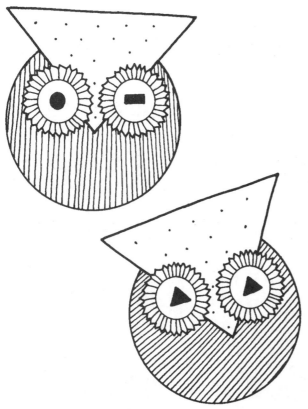

Owl Faces

Have your children paint the backs of paper plates brown. When the plates are dry, help each child glue yellow construction paper triangles on his or her plate to represent a beak and two ears. Then have each child glue two paper baking cups on either side of the beak for eyes.

Extension: Let your children experiment with changing the expressions on their owl faces. Cut out black construction paper circles, triangles, and rectangles small enough to fit inside the paper baking cups. Then let the children drop various shapes into the "eyes" of their owls. Depending upon the shapes, the owls will appear to be wide-eyed, sleepy, winking, etc. Let the children glue the shapes they like best in the bottoms of their baking cups.

Whooo Is It?

For this listening game, choose one child to be the Owl Parent. Ask the Parent to leave the room while you choose two or three other children to be Owlets (owl babies). Have all the children cover their mouths with their hands and ask only the Owlets to begin saying "Whooo, whooo." Then have the Owl Parent return to the room, listen carefully to the "whooo-ing," and try to find his or her babies. Continue the game, each time choosing different children to be the Owl Parent and the Owlets.

Wise Old Owl

Sung to: "Frère Jacques"

Wise old owl, wise old owl,
In the tree, in the tree.
Whoo-oo are you winking at?
Whoo-oo are you winking at?
Is it me? Is it me?

Jean Warren

Owl Snacks

Give each of your children a plate with a piece of bologna, a triangle cut out of a slice of cheese, and two round crackers on it. Let the children arrange their cheese slices on top of their pieces of bologna to look like ears and beaks. Then have them add their crackers for eyes.

"The Wise Old Owl" Story Patterns
Refer to page 305 for directions.

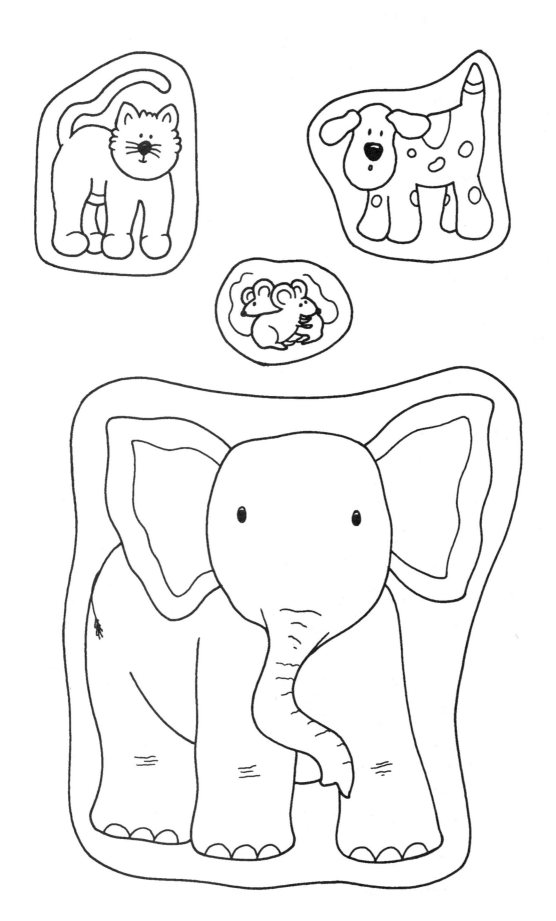

November

Turkeys in the Barnyard

Set out a large sheet of butcher paper. Fill shallow containers with red and brown tempera paint. Let your children make turkey handprints by having them use paintbrushes to paint their fingers and palms brown and their thumbs red. Then have them press their hands, painted sides down, on the butcher paper, leaving "turkey" prints. After the paint dries, let the children add eyes, beaks, legs, and feet with felt-tip markers. Hang the butcher paper on a wall or a bulletin board at the children's eye level. Add construction paper barnyard shapes, such as a large red barn, a fence, and a sun, to make a cheery barnyard mural.

Thanksgiving Quilt

Cut construction paper into 9-inch squares. Crease the squares diagonally both ways. Cut diamond shapes out of colorful paper and pieces of foil. Give each of your children one of the creased squares. Let the children glue colorful diamonds on the squares. Show them how to use the creases on the squares as guidelines for creating patterns. Arrange the squares in a rectangular shape on the floor and tape them all together. Carefully lift up the paper quilt and hang it on a wall or a bulletin board.

Thankful Turkey Mural

Cut feather shapes out of different colors of construction paper. Cut a large turkey body shape out of butcher paper or construction paper and attach it to a wall or a bulletin board at your children's eye level. Ask the children to tell you what they are thankful for. Write their answers on the feathers with a felt-tip marker. Then let the children glue their feathers to the turkey.

Variation: Instead of writing on the feather shapes, let your children tear out magazine pictures of things they are thankful for and glue them to the feather shapes.

Leaf Turkeys

For each of your children, cut a turkey shape out of brown construction paper. Let the children glue the turkey shapes onto sheets of yellow construction paper. Have them add eyes with black or brown felt-tip markers. Gather a variety of small leaves and let the children glue them to the tails of their turkeys.

Hint: Enlarge the turkey pattern on page 357 and use it as a guide for cutting out the turkey shapes.

Circle Turkeys

Cut 6-inch circles out of brown construction paper. Cut 1-by-7-inch strips out of colorful magazine pages. Give each of your children one circle and several strips. Have the children loop their magazine strips over the top halves of their circles and glue them in place to make feathers. Then let the children add construction paper head, beak, and foot shapes to their circles as shown. Let them use black felt-tip markers to add eyes to complete their turkeys.

ART • Weaving Fun

Chicken Wire Looms

To make each loom, tape the edges of a square of chicken wire. Tie one end of a piece of yarn to one of the wires and wrap the other end with tape to make a "needle." Show the children how to thread the yarn over and under the wires. Attach new pieces of yarn to the looms as needed.

Cardboard Tube Looms

Cut slits in the ends of a cardboard tube. Run yarn lengthwise between the slits to create a warp. (See illustration.) Make a loom for each of your children. Let the children weave additional pieces of yarn or ribbon over and under the warp around their tubes.

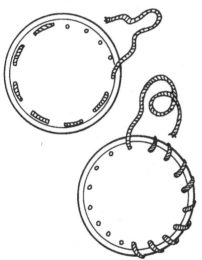

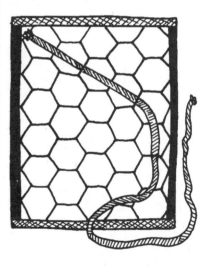

Plastic Lid Weaving

Use a hole punch to punch holes ¼ to ½ inch apart around the edge of a plastic lid. Tie a piece of yarn to one of the holes and wrap the other end of the yarn with tape to make a "needle." Prepare a lid for each of your children. Have the children weave the yarn around their lids.

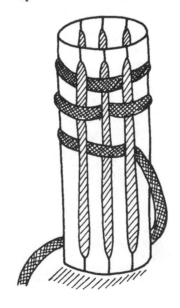

Fork Looms

Collect a fork for each of your children. Tie a piece of yarn to one tine of each fork. Show the children how to wrap the yarn in and out around the tines of the fork.

Potato Prints

Cut brown paper bags into large potato shapes. Cut real potatoes into various small shapes. Pour brown tempera paint into shallow containers. Let your children dip the potato pieces into the paint and use them as stamps to make designs on their paper potato shapes.

Corncob Prints

Peel the husks off corncobs. Allow the cobs to dry overnight. Let your children roll the cobs on paint pads and then roll the cobs across pieces of construction paper to make prints. Or let the children make prints with the ends of the corncobs.

Carrot-Top Painting

Purchase carrots with the tops attached. Cut the leafy tops off the carrots, leaving the stems attached. Let your children use the carrot stems like paintbrushes and paint designs on pieces of construction paper.

Making a Cube

Cut a 3-by-3-inch square out of cardboard. Trace around the square on heavy paper six times as shown to form a *T*. Cut out the shape and fold the sides to create a cube. Tape the edges together. Make as many cubes as desired. Decorate the cubes as directed in the following activities.

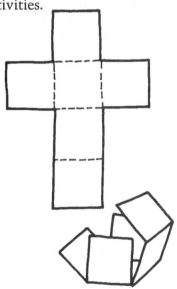

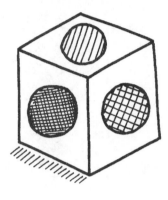

Color Cube

Use felt-tip markers to draw a different colored circle on each side of a cube. Let one of your children roll the cube and name the color that is pictured on top of the cube. Then have the children point to things in the room that are the same color.

Animal Cube

Draw or glue a simple picture of an animal on each side of a cube. Let your children take turns rolling the cube, naming the animal pictured on top, and making the sound of that animal.

Body Cube

Draw or glue a simple picture of a different body part on each side of a cube. Have your children take turns rolling the cube, naming the body part pictured on top of the cube, and touching that body part on themselves.

Fun With Pompons • LEARNING GAMES

Which One Is Different?

Put an assortment of pompons into a large bowl. Tell your children that you are going to take out all the yellow pompons. Start taking out yellow pompons, but quietly slip a red pompon out with them. Let the children notice that you've "goofed" and tell you which pompon is different. Repeat with other colors.

Hint: Pompons are available at most craft and variety stores.

Small and Large

Set out an assortment of small and large pompons, a small bowl, a large bowl, a pair of tweezers, and a pair of kitchen tongs. Have one of your children use the kitchen tongs to put the large pompons into the large bowl. Then let the child use the tweezers to put the small pompons into the small bowl.

Extension: Once the pompons are sorted by size, help your children count the number of pompons in each bowl and name their colors.

Measuring and Pouring

Fill a large container, such as a plastic dishpan or a plastic bathtub for infants, with pompons. Put cups and spoons into the container. Let your children experiment with the pompons and the cups and spoons. Ask them questions such as these: "How many spoonfuls of pompons fit in the large cup? How many spoonfuls fit in the small cup? How many pompons can you scoop up with the small spoon?"

LEARNING GAMES • Fun With Corn

Guessing Game

Place some corn kernels in a small, clear container. Show the container to your children and have them guess how many kernels are in it. After everyone has had a chance to guess, pour out the kernels and count them with the children. Repeat as many times as desired, varying the number of kernels in the container each time.

Measuring

Partially fill a plastic dishpan with cornmeal. Give one of your children a set of measuring cups. Let the child use the measuring cups in the cornmeal. Help him or her discover how many quarter cups or half cups it takes to fill the 1-cup measuring cup.

Sorting Game

Purchase a piece of colorful Indian corn. Carefully remove the kernels from the cob. Place the colorful kernels in a bowl. Set out the bowl and a muffin tin. Let your children take turns sorting the kernels by color into the muffin tin cups.

Feather Game

Collect a variety of colored feathers (available at craft stores) or cut feather shapes out of various colors of construction paper. Put the feathers in a paper bag. Let one of your children select a feather from the bag. Have the child name something he or she is thankful for that is the same color as the feather. Continue the game until each child has had a turn.

Color Roundup

Divide a box into four different colored sections to make a "color corral." Cut matching colored squares out of construction paper. Invite one of your children to play the roundup game. Give the "color cowboy" or "color cowgirl" a plastic drinking straw. Let the child suck up the colored squares and drop them into the matching sections of the corral.

Finger Colors

Use water-based felt-tip markers to draw a different colored dot on each finger of one of your children's hands. Use the same colors to mark the fingers of the child's other hand, but change the order of the colors. Ask the child to put both red dots together, then both green dots, then both yellow dots, etc. This finger-twisting game is bound to cause the giggles!

Extension: Reinforce listening skills by giving directions such as these: "Put a red finger on your nose. Put a green finger on your head."

The Little Red Hen

Adapted by Jean Warren

Sung to: "The Mulberry Bush"

Once there was a Little Red Hen,
Little Red Hen, Little Red Hen.
Once there was a Little Red Hen
Who found a grain of wheat.

"Who will help me plant this wheat,
Plant this wheat, plant this wheat?
Who will help me plant this wheat?"
Asked the Little Red Hen.

"We can't help you plant the wheat,
Plant the wheat, plant the wheat.
We can't help you plant the wheat,"
Said the Duck and Mouse and Pig.

"Who will help me cut the wheat,
Cut the wheat, cut the wheat?
Who will help me cut the wheat?"
Asked the Little Red Hen.

"We can't help you cut the wheat,
Cut the wheat, cut the wheat.
We can't help you cut the wheat,"
Said the Duck and Mouse and Pig.

"Who will help me thresh the wheat,
Thresh the wheat, thresh the wheat?
Who will help me thresh the wheat?"
Asked the Little Red Hen.

"We can't help you thresh the wheat,
  Thresh the wheat, thresh the wheat.
  We can't help you thresh the wheat,"
  Said the Duck and Mouse and Pig.

"Who will help me grind the wheat,
  Grind the wheat, grind the wheat?
  Who will help me grind the wheat?"
  Asked the Little Red Hen.

"We can't help you grind the wheat,
  Grind the wheat, grind the wheat.
  We can't help you grind the wheat,"
  Said the Duck and Mouse and Pig.

"Who will help me bake the bread,
  Bake the bread, bake the bread?
  Who will help me bake the bread?"
  Asked the Little Red Hen.

"We can't help you bake the bread,
  Bake the bread, bake the bread.
  We can't help you bake the bread,"
  Said the Duck and Mouse and Pig.

"Who will help me eat the bread,
  Eat the bread, eat the bread?
  Who will help me eat the bread?"
  Asked the Little Red Hen.

"We will help you eat the bread,
  Eat the bread, eat the bread.
  We will help you eat the bread,"
  Said the Duck and Mouse and Pig.

"Sorry, but it's just for me,
  Just for me, just for me.
  Sorry, but it's just for me,"
  Said the Little Red Hen.

Puppet Directions
Color and cut out the stick puppet patterns on page 356. Attach craft sticks to the backs of the figures to make stick puppets. Use the puppets as you sing the song, "The Little Red Hen."

Turkey in the Brown Straw

By Jean Warren

Sung to: "Skip to My Lou"

Turkey in the brown straw, ha, ha, ha,
Turkey in the brown straw, ha, ha, ha,
Turkey in the brown straw, ha, ha, ha,
Turkey in the straw my darling.

Turkey in the white snow, ho, ho, ho,
Turkey in the white snow, ho, ho, ho,
Turkey in the white snow, ho, ho, ho,
Turkey in the snow, my darling.

Turkey in the blue sky, hi, hi, hi,
Turkey in the blue sky, hi, hi, hi,
Turkey in the blue sky, hi, hi, hi,
Turkey in the sky, my darling.

Turkey in the red barn, harn, harn, harn,
Turkey in the red barn, harn, harn, harn,
Turkey in the red barn, harn, harn, harn,
Turkey in the barn, my darling.

Turkey in the yellow corn, horn, horn, horn,
Turkey in the yellow corn, horn, horn, horn,
Turkey in the yellow corn, horn, horn, horn,
Turkey in the corn, my darling.

Turkey in the green tree, hee, hee, hee,
Turkey in the green tree, hee, hee, hee,
Turkey in the green tree, hee, hee, hee,
Turkey in the tree, my darling.

Flannelboard Directions
Use the patterns on page 357 as guides for
cutting a brown turkey and a red barn out
of felt. Cut the following additional shapes
out of felt: a stack of brown straw, a pile of
white snow, a yellow bag of corn, and a green
tree. Cut a sky background out of light blue
felt. Arrange all of the shapes, except the
turkey, on a flannelboard. Then sing the
song on this page with your children and let
them take turns placing the turkey on the
appropriate shapes.

Some Families

Some families are big,
Some families are small.
Some families are short,
Some families are tall.

Some families live close,
Some live far away.
But they all love each other,
In their own special way.

Some families are happy,
Some families are sad.
But they still love each other,
Even when they are mad.

Some families you're born to,
Some families you're not.
But however you joined,
You are loved a whole lot!

Jean Warren

Family Album

Cut pictures of families out of magazines. Place each picture in a photo album. Let your children look at the pictures and discuss the many different kinds of families. You may wish to let each child draw a picture of his or her own family to add to the album. Or you may want to add photographs of each child's family.

All Kinds of Families

There are all kinds of families that I see,
Some are two and some are three.
  (Hold up two fingers, then three fingers.)
Some are eight and some are four,
  (Hold up eight fingers, then four fingers.)
And some are more and more and more!
  (Raise and lower all 10 fingers.)

Jean Warren

MY WORLD • Our Health

Tissue Power

Have each of your children place his or her hand on a piece of construction paper and trace around it. Let the children cut out their hand shapes. (Cut out the shapes for younger children.) Give each child another piece of construction paper and a facial tissue. Have the children glue their hand shapes to their papers and glue the tissues on top of them. Display the completed papers around the room or near the facial tissue boxes to remind the children to use tissue when they need to wipe or blow their noses.

Good Health Game

Place a variety of good health items, such as a comb, a brush, a washcloth, a bar of soap, a facial tissue, a jump rope, and an apple, on a tray. Have your children sit in a circle. Ask them how they feel when they are healthy and how they feel when they are not. Then go around the circle and let each child select an item from the tray, tell how it helps him or her stay healthy, and place the item in the middle of the circle.

Healthy Charades

Have your children sit in a circle. Ask one child to stand up. In the child's ear, whisper the name of an activity that promotes good health such as washing hands, brushing teeth, using facial tissue, eating nutritious foods, resting properly, or getting exercise. Then have the child act out the healthy activity and let the other children guess what it is. Continue until each child has had a chance to act out a healthy activity.

Keep the Germs Away
Sung to: "The Mulberry Bush"

This is the way we cover our sneezes,
Cover our sneezes, cover our sneezes.
This is the way we cover our sneezes
To keep the germs away.

Additional verses: This is the way we wash our hands; eat healthy foods; exercise.

Susan M. Paprocki

Sharing Boxes

Show your children a puzzle and a toothbrush. Ask them which one would not be healthy to share. Why? (The toothbrush is not healthy to share because it has been in someone's mouth.) Then set out two boxes, one marked with a happy face and the words "Healthy to Share," and the other marked with a sad face and the words "Not Healthy to Share." Place some familiar objects next to the boxes such as a crayon, a comb, a cup, a toy car, a piece of paper, a block, a spoon, and a plastic drinking straw. Let each child select an item and put it into the appropriate box.

Reflection Table

Collect a variety of items that your children can see their reflections in such as a mirror, an aluminum pie pan, a clear glass pie pan, a shiny plate, a metal bowl, a piece of aluminum foil, a baking pan with water covering the bottom, and a piece of shiny wrapping paper. Place the items on a table. Ask the children to find their reflections in each of the items. Which items show their reflections best?

Three-Dimensional Art

Set out a variety of small three-dimensional items (pine cones, rocks, shells, cotton balls, etc.). Give each of your children a piece of aluminum foil or metallic mylar mounted on a square of cardboard. Let the children glue the three-dimensional items onto their foil squares. Have them look at their finished artwork from several angles to see different reflections.

Variation: Have your children glue three-dimensional items onto aluminum pie pans.

Reflections Mural

Cut out magazine pictures that show reflections. Look for pictures of people looking in mirrors or dishes, scenery reflected in lakes, etc. Let your children glue the pictures on a large piece of butcher paper to make a mural. Ask them to name the reflective items in the pictures as they glue them on the paper.

A Reflection

Recite the poem below while your children take turns looking in mirrors and other reflective items.

A reflection is like a picture,
But it's not one you can keep.
You can see one in a mirror,
Or in some water deep.
You can see one in a window,
Or in the bottom of a pan.
Why don't you try to see yours?
I just know you can.

Diane Thom

Multiple Reflections

Collect three rectangular mirrors of similar size. Mount the mirrors onto a large cardboard rectangle that you've folded into thirds, one mirror in each section. Stand the cardboard on end. Let your children stand in front of the mirrors and look at their reflections. How many reflections can they see? Produce different effects by altering the angles of the mirrors. Move the mirrors closer together to let the children see more reflections.

Variation: Hang two mirrors at your children's eye level in a corner of your room so that the sides of the mirrors are touching each other. Let the children take turns standing in the corner and looking in the mirrors.

Getting Started

Children delight in play that involves their whole bodies. Not only are children having fun while engaging in these activities, they are also developing the coordination skills they will need to succeed in other areas of learning such as reading and writing. The following activities are designed for indoor play. Before starting, you will need to clear a large, open space. To help your children get the most out of the activities, be sure to stress the fun of participation rather than competition.

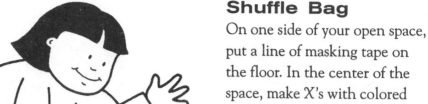

Shuffle Bag

On one side of your open space, put a line of masking tape on the floor. In the center of the space, make X's with colored tape. Have your children stand behind the line and try to slide beanbags onto the colorful X's.

Penny on the Shoe

Divide your children into two groups and have them line up on opposite sides of the room facing each other. Give a penny to the first child in one of the lines. Ask the child to carry the penny on his or her shoe to the child standing directly across the room without dropping the penny. Then have that child carry the penny on his or her shoe across the room to the next child in line. Continue until everyone has had a turn.

Cross Over

Divide your children into two groups and have them stand facing each other at least 10 feet apart. Then clap your hands and have the children try crossing from one side of the open space to the other side without bumping or touching anyone.

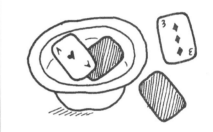

Beanbag March

Give each of your children a beanbag. Play some marching music and let the children march around the room, balancing their beanbags on their heads.

Variation: Let your children march while balancing the beanbags on their shoulders, elbows, feet, etc.

Indoor Basketball

Use masking tape to make a line on the floor. Place two or three empty trash cans 3 to 5 feet from the line. Let your children stand behind the line and take turns tossing beanbags into the cans.

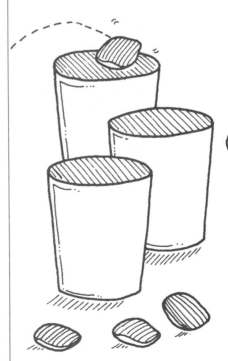

Cards in a Hat

Place a hat upside down on the floor and have your children sit 2 or 3 feet away from it. Distribute a deck of playing cards to the children and have them try tossing the cards into the hat.

MUSIC • Let's Be Thankful Songs

Let Us Now Give Thanks
Sung to: "Old MacDonald Had a Farm"

Thanksgiving Day will soon be here,
Let us now give thanks.
For the blessings of the year,
Let us now give thanks.
With a thankful heart,
With a thankful heart,
Thanksgiving Day we'll stop to say,
"For the blessings of the year,
We now give thanks."

Betty Ruth Baker

For My Friends
Sung to: "Mary Had a Little Lamb"

I'm thankful for my friends at school,
Friends at school, friends at school.
I'm thankful for my friends at school,
And my teacher, too.

I'm thankful for my family,
Family, family.
I'm thankful for my family,
And my home, too.

Let your children take turns saying what they are thankful for. Then make up new verses to the song.

Sue Brown

I'm Thankful
Sung to: "Row, Row, Row Your Boat"

I'm thankful for my friends
And my family.
I'm thankful for the food I eat,
I'm happy to be me!

Susan Hodges

On Thanksgiving Day
Sung to: "Mary Had a Little Lamb"

Turkey is so good to eat,
Good to eat, good to eat,
Turkey is so good to eat
On Thanksgiving Day.

Friends and family gather round,
Gather round, gather round.
Friends and family gather round,
On Thanksgiving Day.

For all these blessings we give thanks,
We give thanks, we give thanks.
For all these blessings we give thanks,
On Thanksgiving Day.

Maureen Gutyan

Smells Like Thanksgiving
Sung to: "Frère Jacques"

Smells like Thanksgiving,
Smells like Thanksgiving,
Mmmmm, so good. Mmmmm so good.
I can smell the turkey,
I can smell the pies,
Mmmmm, so good. Mmmmm so good.

Jean Warren

Thanksgiving Time
Sung to: "The Farmer in the Dell"

Thanksgiving time is here.
Let's give a great big cheer
For food and friends and family.
Thanksgiving time is here.

Gayle Bittinger

We Give Thanks

MUSIC • Turkey Songs

I'm Glad I'm Not a Turkey

Sung to: "Did You Ever See a Lassie?"

Oh, I'm glad I'm not a turkey,
A turkey, a turkey.
Oh, I'm glad I'm not a turkey,
On Thanksgiving Day.
They stuff you and bake you,
And then they all taste you.
Oh, I'm glad I'm not a turkey
On Thanksgiving Day.

Vicki Shannon

There's a Big, Fat Turkey

Sung to: "Little White Duck"

There's a big, fat turkey
Down on the farm,
A big, fat turkey
Who stays away from harm.
He's always gone on Thanksgiving Day.
For some odd reason he just runs away.
There's a big, fat turkey
Down on the farm.
Gobble, gobble, gobble.

Jean Warren

Where Is Turkey?

Sung to: "Frère Jacques"

Where is turkey? Where is turkey?
    (*Hold hands behind back.*)
Here I am. Here I am.
    (*Show hands, one at a time.*)
I will be hiding. I will be hiding.
    (*Hide hands behind back, one at a time.*)
You won't find me. You won't find me.

Barbara Vilet

Turkey Trot

Sung to: "Hokey-Pokey"

You put your right wing in,
  (Flap and move right arm as directed.)
You put your right wing out,
You put your right wing in,
And you shake it all about.
You do the Turkey Trot,
  (Flap both arms.)
And you turn yourself around.
  (Turn around.)
That's what it's all about!
  (Clap.)

Additional verses: You put your left wing in; drumsticks (legs); stuffing (stomach); wattle (head); tail feathers (rear); turkey body.

Micki Beckman, Tina Hubert,
Cynthia Kartsounes, and Julie Runge

Do the Turkey Hop

Sung to: "The Farmer in the Dell"

Do the turkey hop.
  (Hop in place.)
Do the turkey run.
  (Run in place.)
Do the turkey gobble.
  (Warble voice on gobble.)
It's a lot of fun.

Now flap your wings
  (Bend arms and flap them up and down.)
Like the turkeys do.
Run from the farmer
  (Run away.)
Before she catches you.

Diane Thom

Mr. Turkey

Sung to: "If You're Happy and You Know It"

Gobble, gobble, gobble, gobble, says the bird.
Gobble, gobble, gobble, gobble, says the bird.
Mr. Turkey gobble, gobbles,
And his feet go wobble, wobble.
Gobble, gobble, gobble, gobble, says the bird.

Becky Valenick

Vegetable Stew

Describe Vegetable Stew to your children. Discuss what ingredients are in it and how it is cooked. Then give each child a paper bowl. Let the children tear or cut pictures of vegetables out of magazines. Have them glue the pictures in their bowls to make "vegetable stew." Let the children take turns naming the vegetables in their bowls of stew.

Creating a Cornucopia

Have your children bring in fresh vegetables that they like or would like to try. Display them in a simple basket. Talk to the children about the vegetables. Encourage the children to describe the different colors, patterns, sizes, and weights. Ask questions such as these: "Which vegetable is the biggest? Which is the smallest? How many vegetables are green? How many are yellow?"

Which Vegetable?

Show your children the vegetables from the Creating a Cornucopia activity on this page. Ask the children to listen carefully as you describe a vegetable and then ask them to try to guess what it is. For example, you could say, "I'm thinking of a vegetable that is green. It has smooth skin and a stem. What is it?" (Green pepper.) Give as many clues as necessary.

Extension: Let your children take turns describing vegetables for the others to guess.

Sorting and Counting

Set out several sizes and colors of one kind of vegetable. For example, if you are using potatoes, set out small, medium-sized, and large potatoes with red, light brown, and dark brown skins. Let your children sort the vegetables by color or size. Then have them count how many are in each pile. If desired, have them arrange the vegetables in each pile from small to large.

Harvest Stew

Make a stew using the vegetables from the Creating a Cornucopia activity on the previous page. Early in the day, put 1 cup clear soup broth into a crock pot and turn the crock pot on high. Have your children help you wash the vegetables. Then let them help prepare the vegetables for eating. Place the vegetables in the hot broth and put the lid on the crock pot. Allow the stew to cook for 2 hours or longer. Spoon the stew into small bowls. When the stew has cooled, let your children enjoy their Harvest Stew.

Sharing With Nature

Save the vegetable peelings and scraps from the Harvest Stew activity on this page. Cut a grapefruit in half and remove the fruit, making two bowls. Cut the grapefruit into small pieces. Have the children mix the vegetable peelings and scraps with the fruit. Then let them fill the grapefruit bowls with the mixture and place them outside for birds and other animals. Have the children observe their bowls each day to see how they have changed.

Paper Bag Turkeys

Give each of your children a brown paper bag and several sheets of newspaper. Have the children crumple the sheets of newspaper and stuff them into their bags until the bags are half full. Twist the tops of the bags and tie them with pieces of yarn. To make tails for the turkeys, have the children make several cuts from the top edges of their bags down to the yarn. Let the children paint their turkey tails bright autumn colors. Then give each child a precut turkey head shape to decorate. Attach the head shapes to the fronts of the bags to complete the turkeys.

Paper Collage Turkeys

Cut turkey shapes out of brown construction paper. Give each of your children a turkey shape and scraps of colored construction paper. Let the children tear the construction paper into small pieces. Have them glue the torn pieces on their turkey shapes to make colorful feathers. Let the children use felt-tip markers to add eyes, mouths, or other features to their turkeys.

Hint: Enlarge the turkey pattern on page 357 and use it as a guide to cut out the turkey shapes.

Turkey Feather Game

Cut five turkey body shapes out of brown felt and 15 feather shapes out of red, yellow, and orange felt. Number the turkey body shapes from 1 to 5 and put them on a flannelboard. Place the feather shapes in a pile. To play the game, have the child select a turkey, identify the number on it, and add that many feathers to the turkey. Let the child continue playing until all the turkeys have feathers.

Stuff the Turkey

Make a large turkey by opening a large paper bag and rolling down the top edge three or four times. Set this bag aside, open side up. Stuff the bottom of two small lunch bags with newspaper, fasten the tops with twist ties, and mold them into turkey leg shapes. Attach the legs to the sides of the large bag. Give your children 6-inch squares of newspaper. Let them take turns "stuffing" the turkey by crumpling the newspaper squares and trying to toss them into the large grocery bag turkey.

Snacktime Fun

Scoop out the fruit from the center of an orange half. Dice the orange fruit along with ¼ apple and ¼ banana. Combine some chopped nuts with the fruits. Fill the empty orange half with the mixture. Add a toothpick for a neck, a round carrot slice for a head, and half a toothpick for a beak. Place two celery leaves in the back of the cup for feathers. Serve the fruit-cup turkey on a bed of lettuce. Makes 1 serving.

No-Lose Pin the Feather on the Turkey

Draw a turkey shape on a large piece of butcher paper. Hang the paper on a wall or a bulletin board at your children's eye level. Put loops of masking tape, sticky side out, on the backs of real or paper feathers. Place the feathers on a table close to the paper turkey. Have the children take turns choosing a feather from the table and then closing their eyes while they try to stick the feather on the turkey. (The crazy placement of all the feathers adds to the fun.)

Meet My Family

Explain to your children that some families live in one house together, while others live in more than one place. Encourage them to think and talk about where their own families live. Invite everyone to bring in photographs of their families.

Cut the shapes of different kinds of homes, such as houses, apartment buildings, duplexes, and mobile homes, out of construction paper. Cut a door in the front of each shape. Let each child select one of the home shapes. Have the children decorate their shapes however they wish. Then help them tape their family photographs behind their home shapes so that the photo is visible when the door is opened. Hang the homes where the children can open the doors and peek inside. Have them ask questions and share information about their families with one another.

The Family Tree Game

Explain that families differ in many ways. Some have a few members and some have many. Some have babies or older brothers and sisters, while some don't. Sometimes new people, such as stepparents, stepchildren, aunts, or uncles, join families. Let your children talk about the members of their families.

Gather in a circle and invite one child to stand in the center. Recite the chant below, pausing at the last line. Have the child in the middle select another child to join him or her and tell what member of the family that child is such as a mother, a brother, or a grandma. Then repeat the chant, letting the newest "family member" pick another child to join the circle until everyone is in the center. On the last line of the chant, substitute the name of the child's selected family member for *father*.

Thank, thank, thank you, Tree.
Thank you for my family!
I pick you, you pick me,
I pick a father for my Family Tree.

Lisa Feeney

Special Celebrations

Invite each of your children to draw a picture of his or her family at a celebration, a holiday, or a meal. (For younger children, set out precut pictures of adults and children. Let them glue the pictures on construction paper to represent their families.) Encourage the children to tell you about their pictures. Write down their explanations and attach them to their drawings.

Look at the pictures together and read your children's explanations. Discuss how families come together for many reasons such as birthdays, holidays, and meal times. Help the children make a list of things that family gatherings have in common. The list might include items such as: "We play games; We tell stories; We have family with us." Help your children illustrate and display the list.

Animal Families

Find an animal family to observe with your children. If pets or wild animals are not available, read a book or watch a video. While observing the animals, ask the children questions such as these: "Do animals have families? Who are the members of their families? What do the grown-ups do? What do the children do?"

Add props to your dramatic play area that might motivate your children to act out animal family scenarios. For example, if you observed a bird family, you might provide rags and strips of cloth for nesting materials, cotton balls and bits of yarn for food, and scarves and streamers for wings and feathers.

"The Little Red Hen" Story Patterns
Refer to page 337 for directions.

"Turkey in the Brown Straw" Patterns

Refer to page 338 for directions.

December

Homemade Stockings

Collect used, clean, hole-free socks in white or bright colors. (The longer the sock, the better.) Give one sock to each of your children. Let the children decorate their socks with red and green permanent felt-tip markers or by gluing on holiday ribbons, bows, rickrack, or lace.

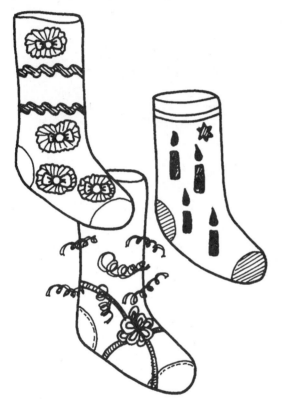

Pine Needle Envelopes

Give each of your children an envelope with several pine needles inside. Seal the envelopes after you have shown the contents to the children. Let the children hold the envelopes parallel to the floor and gently shake them to spread out the needles. Have them rub the long, flat sides of unwrapped crayons across the envelopes to create designs. Then have them create more designs by shaking the envelopes to move the pine needles around and rubbing over them again.

Little Lanterns

Cut 5-by-5½-inch rectangles out of aluminum foil. Cut colored tissue paper into small pieces. Set out the foil pieces, the tissue paper squares, bowls of diluted white glue, and brushes. Have your children brush glue over the foil pieces. Then let them cover the foil with the tissue paper squares. Allow the glue to dry. Secure each child's tissue-covered foil to an empty toilet-tissue tube. Punch holes in the tops of the tubes and attach pieces of yarn for hanging.

Holiday Stencil Cards

Use holiday cookie cutters to press shapes into clean plastic-foam food trays. Cut out the shapes with a craft knife and discard. Fold pieces of construction paper into cards. Let your children place the stencils over the fronts of the cards and use felt-tip markers to fill the centers.

Stamp It

Rubber stamps make it easy for your children to make "designer" notecards. Fold white paper into cards and set out an assortment of rubber stamps and stamp pads. Have the children stamp designs on the fronts of the cards and add self-stick foil stars for a festive touch.

Recycled Cards

Provide your children with bits of wrapping paper, ribbons, and pictures cut from leftover greeting cards. Let them glue these materials to folded heavy paper to make their own unique cards.

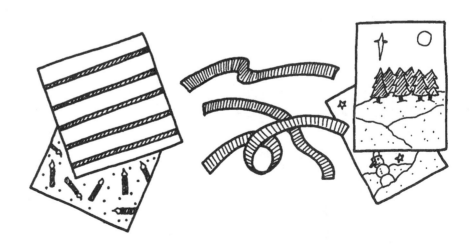

Christmas Tree of Hands

Give each of your children a piece of green construction paper and a pencil. Help each child trace around one of his or her hands and cut out the shape. Use the hand shapes to make a large tree on a bulletin board. Starting at the bottom of the tree shape, overlap the hands in progressively shorter rows with the fingers pointing down. If you wish, add an outdoor scene or holiday decorations to the tree.

Triangle Tree Mural

Cut 12-inch triangles out of green construction paper. (You will need a total of four, nine, or sixteen triangles to complete a tree.) Give each of your children one of the triangles and six foil cupcake liners. Have the children flatten their liners and glue them shiny side up on their triangles. Let the children decorate their triangles. Arrange the decorated triangles in a tree shape on a wall or a bulletin board. If you have four triangles, place three on the bottom (alternating point up, point down). Then place the fourth triangle on the top, point up. For nine triangles, add a row of five to the bottom. For sixteen triangles, add an additional row of seven to the bottom. Add construction paper shapes such as a tree trunk, a star, and packages to complete the mural.

Italian Glove Puppets

For each of your children, cut two puppet shapes out of felt as shown in the illustration. Sew or glue each pair of shapes together, leaving the bottom edges open. Let your children decorate their puppets by gluing on fabric scraps, ribbons, lace, buttons, or sequins.

Mexican Tin and Bead Necklaces

Make "tin" shapes by cutting 2-inch triangles out of posterboard and covering them with aluminum foil. Punch a hole in the bottom two corners of each triangle. Set out containers of beads. Give each of your children a piece of string. Let the children thread beads and triangles on their strings until their necklaces are the desired length. Tie the ends of each child's necklace together.

Jewish Dreidels

Give each of your children a small milk carton. Help them tape down the tops of their cartons to form boxes and let them paint their boxes. (To make paint that will adhere to waxed-cardboard milk cartons, mix powdered tempera paint with liquid hand soap.) When the boxes are dry, help each child poke a sharpened pencil through his or her carton to make a dreidel. Show the children how to spin their dreidels.

Picture Match-Ups

Select a wrapping paper with small, repetitious designs. Cut out three or four pairs of different designs. Cover each design with clear self-stick paper for durability. Mix up the designs and let your children take turns finding the matching pairs.

Greeting Card Puzzles

Select several cards with interesting pictures. Cut the front of each card to fit inside a plastic-foam food tray. Cut each card into three or four puzzle pieces. Let your children take turns putting the puzzles together in the food tray holders.

Lotto Game

Select a wrapping paper with large, simple pictures. Make a gameboard from a 14-by-14-inch piece of cardboard. Cover the cardboard with some of the wrapping paper. Cover the wrapping paper with clear self-stick paper for durability. From the remaining wrapping paper, cut out pictures that match those pictures on the gameboard and cover them clear self-stick paper for durability. Give one of your children the gameboard and the individual pictures. Have the child match up the pictures by placing the cutouts on top of the matching gameboard pictures.

Sewing Cards

Cut the fronts off sturdy greeting cards. Punch holes around the edges of the cards and tie a shoestring to one of the holes on each card. Give the cards to your children. Let them use the shoestrings to "sew" around the cards.

Measuring With Ribbon

Cut leftover ribbon into different lengths. Have your children find the longest and shortest ribbons. Then let them put all the ribbons in order from short to long.

Variation: Cut pairs of ribbons into various lengths. Let your children find the matching pairs.

Plastic Shapes

Collect old plastic ribbons used on outdoor wreaths. Cut the ribbons into various shapes. Let your children use the shapes to create pictures on smooth surfaces such as windows or mirrors.

Nesting Game

Select three or four boxes that fit inside one another. Let your children take turns separating the boxes and fitting them back together.

Tree Scene

Draw a simple Christmas tree scene on a large piece of paper. Make each object in the scene a definite shape. For example, draw a triangular tree with a square trunk, round ornaments, and rectangular presents. Show the scene to your children. Call out the names of shapes and let the children take turns pointing to those shapes in the scene.

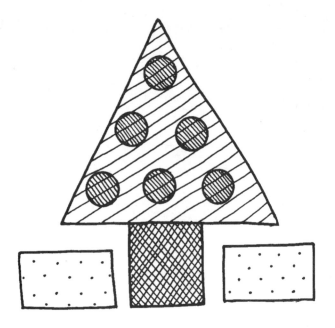

Tree Matching

Use a green felt-tip marker to draw a simple triangular tree shape on each of 10 index cards. Divide the cards into pairs. Use other felt-tip markers to decorate the pairs of trees differently with such items as a simple yellow star, three red bulbs, or a purple garland. Mix up the cards. Let your children take turns finding the trees with the matching decorations.

Tree Calendar

Cut a large Christmas tree shape out of construction paper. Cut small ornaments out of various colors of construction paper, one ornament for each day left before Christmas. Attach the tree to a larger piece of paper. Put a loop of tape on the back of each ornament and attach the ornaments to the paper below the tree. Each day before Christmas, have one of your children place an ornament on the tree. Tell the children that when all the ornaments are on the tree, the next day will be Christmas.

What Is It?

Take photographs of parts of common objects such as the tire on a car, the doorknob on a door, and the legs of a chair. Show the photos to your children and let them guess what they are.

Photo Match

Take a photograph of each of several different kinds of fruits and vegetables. Set out the photos and one of each of the fruits and vegetables pictured. Let your children take turns matching the photos to the real fruits and vegetables.

Backward Photos

Take a photograph of the back of each of your children. Have a picture taken of your back too. Display the developed photos. Let the children look at them and guess whose back is in each photo.

Photo Fun

Hide a photograph of one of your children's favorite activities somewhere in your room. Have the children hunt for the photo. After the photo is found, let them do the activity pictured in it.

Toys

Let your children complete these open-ended sentences. Answers may be serious or silly. Accepting all answers as "correct" fosters children's creativity and self-esteem.

I am shopping for a toy.

The biggest toy I see is a _____.

The funniest toy I see is a _____.

Some toys can move.
The one I like best is a _____.

The smallest round toy I see is a _____.

The softest toy I see is a _____.

Some toys you can play with outside.
The one I like best is a _____.

Some toys you can play with inside.
The one I like best is a _____.

Some toys you can play with by yourself.
The one I like best is a _____.

Some toys you need other people to play with.
The one I like best is a _____.

The toy I would most like to buy is a _____.

Jean Warren

My Wagon

Have your children act out the following rhyme as you read it. Pause after the first two lines to let them tell you which toys they are putting into their wagons.

I have a little wagon I pull around with me.
I fill it with my toys, so everyone can see.
I love my little wagon; sometimes I jump inside.
Then I push with my two feet and give my
    toys a ride.

Jean Warren

Eight Little Candles

Use the menorah, candle, and flame shapes from the Hanukkah Is Coming Soon activity on this page. Place the menorah and candle shapes on a flannelboard. Put a flame shape on the center candle. Then recite the following rhyme, pausing after each verse to let one of your children place the flames on the appropriate number of candles. After each verse, let the child "blow out" the candles by removing all the flames.

The first night we light candle number one,
Hanukkah time has now begun.

The second night we light candles one and two,
Hanukkah's here—there's lots to do.

The third night we light all up to three,
Hanukkah's here—there's lots to see.

The fourth night we light all up to four,
Each now a part of the Hanukkah lore.

The fifth night we light all up to five,
Helping our Hanukkah come alive.

The sixth night we light all up to six,
Happy candles—happy wicks!

The seventh night we light all up to seven,
The glow of each candle reaches to heaven.

The eighth night we light all up to eight,
Hanukkah's here—let's celebrate!

Jean Warren

Hanukkah Is Coming Soon

Cut a menorah shape, nine candle shapes, and nine yellow candle flame shapes out of felt. Place the menorah with the nine candles standing in it on a flannelboard. Put a flame shape on top of the middle candle. Explain to your children that with a real menorah, the candle in the center would be used to light the other candles. Recite the rhyme below, placing a flame shape on each of the remaining candles as you say each number.

Hanukkah is coming soon.
Light each menorah light.
One, two, three, four,
Five, six, seven, eight—
One for every night.

Jean Warren

The Tree

Adapted by Jean Warren from a story by Dee Dee Crockett

In the woods, not far away,
Some children came one winter day
To decorate a tree right there
With gifts the animals could share.

They covered it with bells and berries
And other things to make it merry.
Flowers, nuts, and pretty string
For the animals they did bring.

The tree felt very, very proud
And wanted so to shout out loud
And say, "How beautiful am I!"
When a mother deer walked slowly by.

With gentle eyes, she blinked and stared,
And then so cautiously she dared
To take the bells off of the tree.
She said, "I'll take these home with me.

I'll put them on my baby deer
So I will know that he is near.
The bells will tinkle if he strays,
And I will find him right away."

Then as she set out for her house,
There scampered up a little mouse.
He spied the berries red and sweet,
And said, "I'll take these home to eat."

Just then, the tiny mouse, he heard
The flutter of a winter bird
Who perched up high so she could see
The string that hung down from the tree.

She took the string so soft and gold
To line her nest, to warm her cold.
But just before her wings were spread,
She saw a black-and-white-striped head.

A skunk approached with tail held high.
His nose was up, he wasn't shy.
He saw the flowers pink and green
And said, "They smell so rich and clean.

"I think I'll wear one by my ear.
Perhaps my friends will then come near.
I don't know why they run away
Whenever I come out to play."

The skunk ran quickly through the trees.
The wind picked up and with the breeze
The snow began to dance and swirl,
And through the snowflakes came a squirrel.

She scurried round and searched the ground
For any food that could be found.
And when she came upon the tree,
Great big nuts she then did see.

She took them slowly, one by one,
And walked away. She did not run.
She did not want to lose her treat
The children left for her to eat.

Soon all the treats were gone that day,
But the animals came back to play.
What a lovely time of year,
When treats are shared and friends are near.

Flannelboard Directions
Use the story patterns on pages 386 and 387
as guides for cutting the following shapes
out of felt: tree, deer, mouse, skunk, and
squirrel. From felt scraps cut out shapes of
silver bells, red berries, gold string, pink and
green poinsettia flowers, and brown nuts.
Read the story on this page to your children,
placing the shapes on a flannelboard as
they are mentioned.

Sharing the Fun at Holiday Time

Sharing and holidays go together. Below are some suggestions of ways your children can share with others during the holiday season.

- Let your children make special holiday treats and deliver them to friends and family.

- Have your children make cards and pictures to take or send to a nursing home.

- Take your children caroling through the neighborhood or to local businesses.

- Have your children sprinkle birdseed outside for the birds.

- Take your children to a local park and let them clean up the litter they find.

- Let your children make picture books that show ways they can help out at home. Have each picture be a promise to do that particular task such as sweeping or picking up toys.

- Make thank you cards for neighborhood helpers such as police officers, mail carriers, firefighters, and garbage collectors.

Trail Time

Draw a simple trail on a piece of butcher paper. Divide the trail into equal sections, one section for each hour or half hour the children are with you. Hang the butcher paper on a wall at your children's eye level. After the designated amount of time has gone by (an hour or half hour), select two or three children to work together to color in the first section of the trail. After each period of time, select another group of children to color in the next trail section. Point out the progress of the trail to the children. Encourage them to notice if there are more colored-in sections or more blank sections. Ask them to tell you when half the time is over. Explain that when the trail is completely colored in, it will be time to go home.

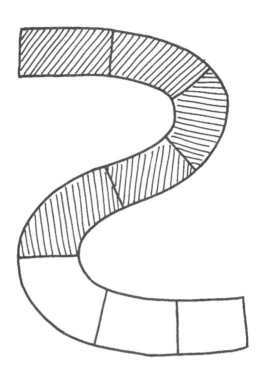

School Clock

Cut a large circle out of posterboard. Draw simple pictures around the edge of the circle to represent the events of the day. Attach a construction paper arrow shape to the center of the circle with a brass paper fastener. Show the clock to your children. Talk about each activity that is represented on the clock. Explain to the children that after the last activity is completed, your time together will be over. Show the children how to move the arrow around the clock. Ask one child to point the arrow to the activity that is going on now. Hang the School Clock where everyone can see it. As each part of the day is completed, select a different child to move the arrow to the next activity.

Simon Says "Feelings"

Play Simon Says with your children, substituting feeling phrases for the usual directions. For example, give directions such as these: "Simon says, 'Look happy'; Simon says, 'Look angry'; or Simon says, 'Look brave.'" In between the directions, ask the children to tell you when they have those kinds of feelings.

Feelings Masks

Set out materials for making masks such as paper plates, paper bags, construction paper scraps, yarn, glue, crayons, and felt-tip markers. Have your children use the materials to make Feelings Masks. Let each child make as many masks as he or she wishes. Have the children wear their masks when you talk about feelings.

Feelings

Sung to: "Twinkle, Twinkle, Little Star"

Sometimes on my face you'll see
How I feel inside of me.
A smile means happy, a frown means sad,
And when I grit my teeth, I'm mad.
When I'm proud, I beam and glow,
But when I'm shy, my head hangs low.

Have your children act out the feelings as they are described in the song.

Karen Folk

Paper Tear

Unfold sheets of newspaper and put them into a pile in the middle of the floor. Have each of your children take a sheet of the newspaper. Then say, "Show me how you would tear your newspaper if you were feeling happy." Have the children tear their newspapers "happily," taking new sheets of paper as they like. After a while, change the mood to mad, sad, frustrated, or any other feeling you have been talking about. Be sure to include a final, "Show me how you would put the newspaper in the recycling box if you were feeling _____."

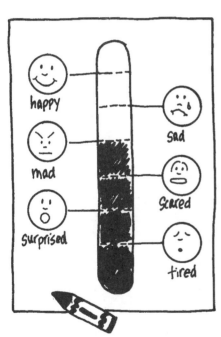

Feelings Thermometers

Draw a picture of a thermometer with different feelings on it, as shown in the illustration. Make photocopies of your drawing. Give a copy to each of your children. Have the children color in the "mercury" on their thermometers until it stops at how they feel. Let them fill in new thermometers as their feelings change.

Feelings Tape

Write out a question about feelings such as one of these: "How do you feel if someone pushes you? You see someone crying? You stay up past your bedtime? Your best friend comes to play?" Read the question to your children and place it near a tape recorder. One at a time, have the children record their answers on tape. Play back the responses when all the children can listen to them.

Santa's Toys

By Jean Warren

Tell your children the following story about toys on Christmas Eve. Let them pretend to be the toys in the story and act out the movements as they are described. If you wish, extend the story with additional verses about other toys.

One Christmas Eve, Santa was getting ready to pack up all the toys for the girls and boys. Before he put them into his sack, however, he decided to test them one last time. He took a small music box out of his pocket and opened the lid. It played a delightful tune. (Hum "Frère Jacques.")

First the music woke up the ballerina doll. She got up and started to sing the following song while she danced around.

Sung to: "Frère Jacques"

I am dancing, I am dancing,
Round and round, round and round.
First I go one way.
Then I go the other way.
Touch the ground, now sit down.

Santa was pleased with the way she danced, so he wrapped her up and put her in his sack. Next the toy airplane got up and started flying around while it sang this song.

Sung to: "Frère Jacques"

I am flying, I am flying,
Round and round, round and round.
First I go one way.
Then I go the other way.
Touch the ground, now sit down.

Santa was pleased with the way it flew, so he wrapped it up and put it in his sack. Now all his toys were tested, and he flew off with his reindeer to deliver them to all the little girls and boys.

Bag Game

Fold an old sheet in half widthwise and stitch up the two sides to make a large bag. Have several of your children climb into the bag. Then ask them to move the bag across the room while they stay in it. Offer the children suggestions as needed.

Mirror Partners

Divide your children into pairs. Have the children in each pair face each other. Ask one child in each pair to move his or her hands slowly while the other child mirrors his or her movements. Then have the children reverse roles.

Musical Cooperation

Place carpet mats, one for each of your children, on the floor in a circle. Ask each child to stand on one of the mats. Begin playing some music and have the children walk around on the mats. Take away one of the mats. When you stop the music, have each child find a mat to sit on or touch in some way (with a foot, a hand, an elbow, a knee, etc.). In order to do this, at least two children will have to share a mat. Continue to start and stop the music, removing one mat each time. As the game progresses, the children will be sharing fewer and fewer mats. Encourage them to work together to find ways for all of them to touch a mat. When you have one mat left and all the children are sharing it, the game is over.

Holidays of Light
Sung to: "Jingle Bells"

Christmas time, Christmas time,
Holiday of light.
Time to sing and celebrate—
Gifts and cards to write.
Christmas time, Christmas time,
Season of delight.
Decorations to put up—
What a pretty sight!

Additional verses: Kwanzaa time, Kwanzaa time;
Hanukkah, Hanukkah.

Diane Thom

'Tis the Season
Sung to: "Deck the Halls"

'Tis the season to be giving,
Think about the gifts that you can give.
Did you know your special smile
Brightens up the day for quite a while?
Help someone pick up a toy.
Helping's always sure to spread some joy.
Don't forget the best of all,
Let your laughter ring from wall to wall.

Virginia Colvig

Happy Times
Sung to: "Jingle Bells"

Happy times, happy times,
Holiday time is here.
We are, oh, so busy
At this time of year.
Making this, making that,
It's a lot of fun.
We'll have so many gifts to give,
When all our work is done.

Substitute the words *Christmas, Hanukkah,* or *Kwanzaa*
for the word *holiday.*

Barbara Paxson

Happy Hanukkah
Sung to: "Frère Jacques"

Spin the dreidel, spin the dreidel,
Round and round, round and round.
Maybe I'll be winning,
When it stops spinning.
Happy Hanukkah! Happy Hanukkah!

Jean Warren

Light the Candles Bright
Sung to: "The Farmer in the Dell"

Oh, light the candles bright,
And dance around the light.
Heigh-ho the derry-oh,
It's Hanukkah tonight.

Additional verses: Spin the dreidel round, And watch it
falling down; Latke treats to eat, And family to greet.

Gillian Whitman

Sing a Song of Hanukkah
Sung to: "Did You Ever See a Lassie?"

Oh, sing a song of Hanukkah,
Hanukkah, Hanukkah.
Sing a song of Hanukkah,
Happy holiday!
With presents and presents,
On every night, presents.
Oh, sing a song of Hanukkah,
A happy holiday.

Gillian Whitman

MUSIC • Christmas Songs

I'm a Little Christmas Tree

Sung to: "I'm a Little Teapot"

I'm a little Christmas tree, short and green.
Here are my branches, the cutest you've seen.
When I get all decorated, hear me cheer,
"Merry Christmas and Happy New Year!"

Vivian Sasser

Christmas Bells

Sung to: "The Muffin Man"

Oh, do you hear the Christmas bells,
The Christmas bells, the Christmas bells?
Oh, do you hear the Christmas bells?
They ring out loud and clear.

Oh, can you see our Christmas tree,
Our Christmas tree, our Christmas tree?
Oh, can you see our Christmas tree?
It fills the room with cheer.

Oh, do you smell the gingerbread,
The gingerbread, the gingerbread?
Oh, do you smell the gingerbread?
I'm glad Christmas is here.

Maureen Gutyan

A Sunny Christmas

Sung to: "Jack and Jill"

There is no ice,
There is no snow,
At Christmas time in Florida.
But I can play
In the sun all day,
On Christmas Day in Florida!

Substitute the name of your sunny city, town, or state for *Florida*.

Nancy Nason Biddinger

Kwanzaa Songs • MUSIC

Celebrate

Sung to: "Frère Jacques"

Celebrate, celebrate,
I can't wait, I can't wait!
Soon it will be Kwanzaa,
Soon it will be Kwanzaa.
I can't wait to celebrate.

Jean Warren

Kwanzaa's Here

Sung to: "Three Blind Mice"

Red, green, black. Red, green, black.
Kwanzaa's here. Kwanzaa's here.
The decorations are quite a sight—
We light a candle every night.
The holiday is filled with light.
Kwanzaa's here.

Jean Warren

Soon It Will Be Kwanzaa

Sung to: "Down by the Station"

Soon it will be Kwanzaa,
And we'll celebrate
With our friends and family
Gathered all around.
See our Kwanzaa bush,
And watch us light the candles.
Dancing, singing,
What a joyous sound!

Gayle Bittinger

Paper Collages

Discuss with your children how paper is made from trees. Talk about all the different kinds of paper they use. Let your children each color a picture of a tree in the center of a piece of construction paper. Then set out different kinds of paper for them to tear into pieces and glue around their trees in collage form.

A Tree for Birds

Let your children help decorate a tree for the birds. Discuss how difficult it is for birds to find food in the winter, especially when there is snow on the ground. Have the children string O-shaped cereal pieces on 8-inch lengths of yarn and tie the ends of yarn together to make loops. Let the children also cover pine cones with peanut butter and sprinkle on birdseed. Attach loops of yarn to the cones for hanging. Then, as a group, go outside and decorate a tree with the cereal loops and pine cones.

Four Seasons

A deciduous tree looks different in each of the four seasons. Help your children understand this by having them make four trees, one for each season. For each child, you will need four short cardboard tubes and two paper plates. Cut two slits, directly opposite each other, in one end of each of the cardboard tubes. Cut the paper plates in half. Have your children paint their cardboard tubes brown. Then have each child use crayons or felt-tip markers to decorate one paper plate half with pink blossoms, one with green leaves, one with red and orange leaves, and one with bare branches. When the children have finished, help them insert their decorated plates into the slits in the tubes to make trees. Talk about the four seasons represented by the trees.

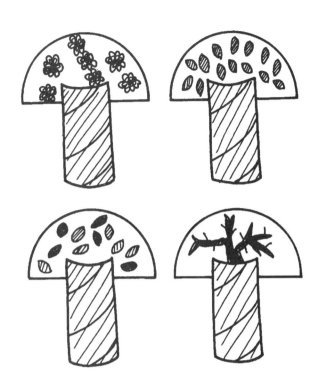

Plant a Forest Game

Paint a shoe box brown and cut six slits in the lid of the box. Number the slits from 1 to 6. Make six trees out of craft sticks by attaching paper tree shapes to them. Number the stick trees from 1 to 6. To play the game, let your children take turns identifying the numbers on the trees and inserting the trees in the matching numbered slits.

Tree Charades

On index cards, draw simple pictures of things you can do in a tree (climb, pick apples, etc.), things you can do under a tree (rake leaves, pick up pine cones, etc.), and things you can do with a tree (decorate it, chop it up for firewood, etc.). Have one of your children select a card and show it to the others. Then have all the children act out together the activity pictured on the card. Repeat until each child has had a chance to choose a card.

Rudolph Faces

Give each of your children a piece of brown or yellow construction paper. Have the children trace around their hands on their papers. Let them cut their hand shapes out—these will be the antlers. Give each child a brown paper triangle to place in front of him- or herself with the point facing down. Help each child fold down the two upper corners of the triangle to make ears. Have the children glue their hand shapes at the tops of their triangles. Then let them add black paper circles for eyes and red paper circles for noses.

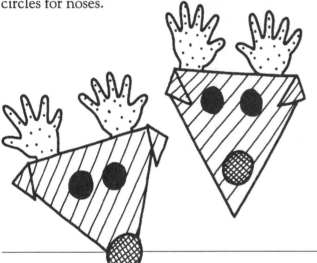

Antler Painting

Set out small tree branches, shallow containers of tempera paint, and large pieces of construction paper. Let your children paint using the branches as "antler" brushes. Have the children dip the tips of their antlers into the paint and gently move them across their papers.

Reindeer Tracks

Discuss with your children the kinds of tracks different animals make. Show them pictures of reindeer tracks and other animals' tracks. Talk about how the tracks are made in the snow or mud. Then let them make their own Reindeer Tracks. Give the children stamps with reindeer track shapes, ink pads, and paper. (To make reindeer track stamps, cut sponge pieces into reindeer track shapes and glue them to small pieces of wood, as shown in the illustration.) Let the children print reindeer tracks by pressing the stamps on the ink pads and then on their papers.

Sandwich Fun

To make four reindeer snacks, you will need one slice of bread, eight celery sticks, peanut butter, eight raisins, and four red berries. The night before, remove the crust from the slice of bread and cut it twice diagonally to make four triangular pieces. Freeze the cut pieces of bread. (It is easier for young children to spread peanut butter on frozen bread.) Slice each of the celery sticks halfway down and refrigerate them overnight in a bowl of water. The sliced halves of the celery sticks will curl outward to look like antlers. The next day, have the children spread the peanut butter on their frozen bread pieces. Then have the children place the points of their triangles downward and let them each add two raisins for eyes, a berry for a nose, and two celery sticks for antlers to make a reindeer-shaped sandwich.

Reindeer Warm-Ups

Discuss with your children the many different ways that people and animals can run. Have the children pretend to be reindeer. Ask them to experiment with different ways of moving such as fast, slow, backward, in slow motion, in place, in a circle, on tiptoe, side-by-side with a friend, and in the snow. Then let them act out the movements described in the following rhyme.

Reindeer, reindeer, jump up high,
Reindeer, reindeer, across the sky.

Reindeer, reindeer, softly land,
Reindeer, reindeer, if you can.

Reindeer, reindeer, turn around,
Reindeer, reindeer, touch the ground.

Reindeer, reindeer, now run slow,
Reindeer, reindeer, still far to go.

Reindeer, reindeer, now run fast,
Reindeer, reindeer, home at last.

Jean Warren

Cooperative Quilt

Give each of your children a long strip of adding machine tape. Let the children use crayons or felt-tip markers to decorate their strips any way they wish. Hang half of the decorated strips vertically on a wall or a bulletin board. Then help the children weave the remaining strips horizontally over and under the hanging strips, taping them in place as needed.

Hint: Purchase rolls of adding machine tape at office supply stores or check with a local business about collecting used tape.

Taping Stories

Divide your children into small groups. Have each group work together to record a familiar story on tape. Play back the stories for everyone to hear.

Hint: The week before you plan this activity, read stories at storytime that would be suitable for young children to retell. At the time of the tapings, set out the week's worth of books for your children to look at, if needed, while they tape their stories. If necessary, assign each group a story.

Cooperation Game

Give each of your children a 3-foot piece of rope. Have the children work in small groups, combining their ropes to form letters, numbers, shapes, or simple pictures.

Cooperation
Sung to: "Yankee Doodle"

Cooperation is the thing
We all must learn to do,
It makes life, oh, so nice,
And gets the work done, too.
Let's cooperate today
In our work and play,
Who knows what we can do
If we all work this way.

Jean Warren

Let's Find Our Shoes
Have each of your children give you one of his or her shoes. While the children wait out of sight, hide the shoes around the room. When you are ready, call out, "One, two, buckle your shoe!" Let the children look for their shoes. Encourage them to cooperate in helping one another find and put on their shoes.

Putting the Pieces Together
Separate your children into groups of three or four. Give each group a puzzle. Have the children divide the puzzle pieces among themselves and cooperate in putting the puzzles back together.

"The Treee" Story Patterns
Refer to page 371 for directions.

Contributors

Betty Ruth Baker, Waco, TX

Mary A. Barich, Whittier, CA

Mickie Beckman, Downers Grove, IL

Ellen Bedford, Bridgeport, CT

Nancy Nason Biddinger, Orlando, FL

John Bittinger, Everett, WA

Janice Bodenstedt, Jackson, MI

Elizabeth Bossong, Highland Park, NJ

Fawn Bostick, Allentown, PA

Sally Braun, Elmhurst, IL

Josette Brown, Bridgeport, WV

Sue Brown, Louisville, KY

Susan Burbridge, Albuquerque, NM

Judith Taylor Burtchet, El Dorado, KS

Susan Carpenter, Elberfeld, IN

Mary Cheetam, Santa Ana, CA

Vicki Claybrook, Kennewick, WA

Patty Claycomb, Ventura, CA

Sharon Clendenen, Syracuse, NY

Tamara Clohessy, Eureka, CA

Virginia Colvig, Albion, WA

Jennifer Contaya, Arlington, TX

Pat Cook, Hartford, VT

Patricia Coyne, Mansfield, MA

Dee Dee Crockett, Marshfield, WI

June Crow, Weaverville, NC

Frank Dally, Ankeny, IA

Marjorie Debowy, Stony Brook, NY

Cindy Dingwall, Palatine, IL

Ann-Marie Donovan, Framingham, MA

Allane and Jennifer Eastberg, Gig Harbor, WA

Laura Egge, Lake Oswego, OR

Ruth Engle, Kirkland, WA

Lisa Feeney, Pawling, NY

Barbara B. Fleisher, Glen Oaks, NY

Barbara Fletcher, El Cajon, CA

Karen Folk, Franklin, MA

Paula C. Foreman, Lancaster, PA

Sue Foster, Mukilteo, WA

R. Hardy Garrison, Stevens Point, WI

Nancy H. Giles, Key West, FL

Connie Gillilan, Hardy, NE

Rosemary Giordano, Philadelphia, PA

Eloise Gray, San Francisco, CA

Leora Grecian, San Bernardino, CA

Maureen Gutyan, Williams Lake, BC

Jean Hack, Bedford, OH

Judy Hall, Wytheville, VA

Tami Hall, Owasso, OK

Gemma Hall-Hart, Bellingham, WA

Peggy Hanley, St. Joseph, MI

Judith Hanson, Newton Falls, OH

Kim Heckert, Arian, MI

Susan Henry, Dallas, OR

Mildred Hoffman, Tacoma, WA

Heather Hogg, Sussex, NB

Tina Hubert, Downers Grove, IL

Colraine Hunley, Doylestown, PA

Joan Hunter, Elbridge, NY

Linda Irwin, London, ON

Barbara Jackson, Denton, TX

Ellen Javernick, Loveland, CO

Linda Kama, Pittsburgh, PA

Cynthia Kartsounes, Downers Grove, IL

Karel Kilimnik, Philadelphia, PA

Wendy Kneeland, Incline Village, NV

Margery Kranyik, Hyde Park, MA

Alison Lang, O'Fallon, IL

Paula Laughtland, Edmonds, WA

Martha T. Lyon, Ft. Wayne, IN

Joyce Marshall, Whitby, ON

Nancy McAndrew, Shavertown, PA

Kathy McCullough, St. Charles, IL

Leigh McCune, Tuscon, AZ

Judith McNitt, Adrian, MI

June Meckel, Andover, MA

Joleen Meier, Wausau, WI

Rose Merenda, Warwick, RI

Carol Metzker, Oregon, OH

Susan A. Miller, Kutztown, PA

Debbie Monts de Oca, Winter Haven, FL

Donna Mullennix, Thousand Oaks, CA

Micki Nadort, Coquitlam, BC

Ann M. O'Connell, Coaldale, PA

Lois Olson, Webster City, IA

Sharon Olson, Minot, ND

Paula Omlin, Maple Valley, WA

Susan M. Paprocki, Northbrook, IL

Barbara Paxson, Champion, OH

Melinda Perry, Alta Loma, CA

Susan Peters, Upland, CA

Dawn Picollelli, Wilmington, DE

Lois E. Putnam, Pilot Mountain, NC

Beverly Qualheim, Marquette, MI

Polly Reedy, Elmhurst, IL

Judi Repko, Topton, PA

Barbara Robinson, Glendale, AZ

Kay Roozen, Des Moines, IA

Debbie Rowley, Redmond, WA

Julie Runge, Downers Grove, IL

Sara Salzberg, Brighton, MA

Vivian Sasser, Independence, MO

Paula Schneider, Kent, WA

Debbie Scofield, Niceville, FL

Vicki Shannon, Napton, MO

Betty Silkunas, Lansdale, PA

Kathy Sizer, Tustin, CA

Carla C. Skjong, Tyler, MN

Beth Smalley, Celina, OH

Karen Smith, Bluemont, VA

Connie Jo Smith, Bowling Green, KY

Jane Spannbauer, South St. Paul, MN

Priscilla M. Starrett, Warren, PA

Betty Swyers, Cuyahoga Falls, OH

Diane Thom, Maple Valley, WA

Martha Thomas, Lake Clear, NY

Margaret Timmons, Fairfield, CT

Kathleen Tobey, Griffith, IN

Carolyn Tyson, Ann Arbor, MI

Stephanie Kidd Tyus, Cleveland Heights, OH

Becky Valenick, Rockford, IL

Barbara Vilet, Cortland, IL

Karen Vollmer, Wauseon, OH

Kristine Wagoner, Puyallup, WA

Cynthia Walters, Mechanicsburg, PA

Kathleen Weber, Allentown, PA

Gail Weidner, Tustin, CA

Betty Loew White, South Beechwold, OH

Gillian Whitman, Overland Park, KS

Sherilyn Wilson, Norwich, CT

Nancy Windes, Denver, CO

Saundra Winnett, Lewisville, TX

Peggy Wolf, Pittsburgh, PA

Bonnie Woodard, Shreveport, LA

Jane Woods, Sarasota, FL

Yosie Yoshimura, Gardena, CA

Joy Zomerdyke, Freehold, NJ

Deborah Zumbar, Alliance, OH

Index

Art

Language

Learning Games

Movement

Music

My World

Themes

TOTLINE BOOKS

PIGGYBACK® SONGS
SERIES *Repetition and rhyme*
New songs to the tunes of childhood favorites. No music to read.

Piggyback Songs
A seasonal collection of more than 100 original songs in 64 pages.
WPH 0201

More Piggyback Songs
More seasonal songs—180 in all—in this 96-page collection.
WPH 0202

Piggyback Songs to Sign
Signing phrases to use each month along with new Piggyback songs.
WPH 0209

Holiday Piggyback Songs
More than 250 original songs for 15 holidays and other celebrations.
WPH 0206

Piggyback Songs for School
Delightful songs to use throughout the school day, such as songs for getting acquainted, transitions, storytime, and cleanup.
WPH 0208

Animal Piggyback Songs
More than 200 songs about farm, zoo, and sea animals.
WPH 0207

Piggyback Songs for Infants and Toddlers
A collection of more than 170 songs just right for infants and toddlers. Also appropriate for children ages 3 to 5.
WPH 0203

1•2•3 SERIES
These books emphasize beginning hands-on activities—creative art, no-lose games, puppets, and more. Designed for children ages 3 to 6.

1•2•3 Art
Open-ended art activities emphasizing the creative process are included in this 160-page book. All 238 activities use inexpensive, readily available materials.
WPH 0401

1•2•3 Games
Each of the 70 no-lose games in this book are designed to foster creativity and decision making for a variety of ages.
WPH 0402

1•2•3 Colors
160 pages of activities for "Color Days," including art, learning games, language, science, movement, music, and snacks.
WPH 0403

1•2•3 Shapes
Hundreds of activities for exploring the concept of shapes—circles, squares, triangles, rectangles, ovals, diamonds, hearts, and stars.
WPH 0411

1•2•3 Science
Fun, wonder-filled activities to get children excited about science and help develop early science skills such as predicting and estimating.
WPH 0410

1•2•3 Rhymes, Songs & Stories
Capture the imaginations of young children with these open-ended rhymes, songs, and stories.
WPH 0408

1•2•3 Math
This book has activities galore for experiencing number concepts such as sorting, measuring, time, and ages.
WPH 0409

1•2•3 Reading & Writing
Ideas for meaningful and non-threatening activities help young children develop *pre-reading* and *pre-writing* skills.
WPH 0407

1001 SERIES
These super reference books are fill with just the right solution, prop, poem to get your projects going. Creative, inexpensive ideas await you in these resources for parents and teachers of young children.

1001 Teaching Tips
Busy teachers on limited budgets will appreciate these 1001 short-cuts to success! Three major sections include curriculum tips, roc tips, and special times tips. Plus a subject index!
WPH 1502

1001 Rhymes & Fingerplays
A complete language resource for parents and teachers! Rhymes for all occasions, plus poems about self-esteem, families, the environment, special needs, and more.
WPH 1503

1001 Teaching Props
The ultimate how-to prop book! A comprehensive materials index makes it easy to create projects by using readily available recyclable materials. Now it's easy and fun t plan projects and equip centers.
WPH 1501

TOTLINE® BOOKS

THEME-A-SAURUS® SERIES
Handy resources for meaningful learning experiences that cover around-the-curriculum activities.

Theme-A-Saurus
Grab instant action with more than [?] themes from Apples to Zebras, and more than 600 activity ideas.
WPH 1001

Theme-A-Saurus II
New opportunities for hands-on learning with 60 more theme units that range from Ants to Zippers.
WPH 1002

Toddler Theme-A-Saurus
[?]0 teaching themes that combine safe and appropriate materials with creative activity ideas.
WPH 1003

Alphabet Theme-A-Saurus
Giant letter recognition units with hands-on activities that introduce young children to the ABCs.
WPH 1004

Nursery Rhyme Theme-A-Saurus
Capture children's enthusiasm with nursery rhymes and related learning activities.
WPH 1005

Storytime Theme-A-Saurus
This book combines 12 storytime favorites with fun and meaningful hands-on activities and songs.
WPH 1006

SNACK SERIES
A most delicious series of books that provides healthy opportunities for fun and learning.

Multicultural Snacks
75 recipes from 38 countries let children get a taste of many cultures. Each chapter features one food and different ways to prepare it.
WPH 1604

Super Snacks
Recipes for treats that contain no sugar, honey, or artificial sweeteners! Nutritional analysis and CACFP information included.
WPH 1601

Healthy Snacks
Over 100 recipes for healthy alternatives to junk-food snacks at home and school! Each recipe is low in fat, sugar, and sodium. Nutritional analysis and CACFP information.
WPH 1602

Teaching Snacks
Use snacktime to promote basic skills and concepts through cooking and extend learning into snacktime!
WPH 1603

BUSY BEES SERIES
Fun for Two's and Three's Hands-on projects and movement games are just right for busy hands and feet of two- and three-year-olds!

Busy Bees—Winter
Enchant toddlers through the winter months with a wealth of ideas for learning fun from movement ideas to hands-on projects.
WPH 2406

Busy Bees—Spring
With a focus on spring, more than 60 age-appropriate activities enhance the learning process for busy minds and bodies.
WPH 2407

Busy Bees—Fall
Fun ideas for fall activities include simple songs, rhymes, snacks, art, movement, and science projects.
WPH 2405

PLAY & LEARN SERIES
Hands-on activities explore the versatile play and learn opportunities of a familiar object. For ages 3 to 8.

Play & Learn with Photos
Educational and meaningful photo activities to enjoy with young children.
WPH 2303

Play & Learn with Magnets
Fun and inexpensive ideas for using magnets in learning games, art, storytime, and science.
WPH 2301

Play & Learn with Rubber Stamps
Around-the-curriculum fun with simple rubber stamps. Ages 3 to 8.
WPH 2302

BEAR HUGS® SERIES
Positive approaches to dealing with potential problem times in groups.

Nap Time
Tips to guide reluctant children into a quiet, restful mood.
WPH 2509

Meals and Snacks
These Bear Hugs quiet young ones enough so they can eat without dampening their spirits.
WPH 2507

Cleanup
Encourage cooperation and speedy work efforts for fun cleanup times.
WPH 2508

Remembering the Rules
These simple rule reminders are fun and nonthreatening.
WPH 2501

Staying in Line
Make staying in line fun, quiet, and safe.
WPH 2502

Circle Time
Help children get focused, interested, and involved in circle time.
WPH 2503

Transition Times
Help your children smoothly shift focus from one activity to the next.
WPH 2504

Time Out
Encourage quiet, reflective, and therapeutic time outs with results.
WPH 2505

Saying Goodbye
Ease separation anxiety with gentle distractions.
WPH 2506

Make storytime come alive with
Cut & Tell Cutouts

Enjoy instant storytime fun with these full-color, inexpensive folder stories. Each one contains a traditional nursery tale or rhyme retold by Jean Warren; beautifully illustrated, full-color cutouts ready to turn into flannelboard and magnet board props or stick puppets; songs; poems; and learning games.

NEW!

COLOR RHYMES

Cobbler, Cobbler
WPH 2219

Hickety, Pickety
WPH 2220

Mary, Mary, Quite Contrary
WPH 2221

The Mulberry Bush
WPH 2222

The Muffin Man
WPH 2223

The Three Little Kittens
WPH 2224

NUMBER RHYMES

Hickory, Dickory Dock
WPH 2207

Humpty Dumpty
WPH 2208

1, 2, Buckle My Shoe
WPH 2209

Old Mother Hubbard
WPH 2210

Rabbit, Rabbit, Carrot Eater
WPH 2211

Twinkle, Twinkle, Little Star
WPH 2212

NURSERY TALES

The Gingerbread Kid
WPH 2201

Henny Penny
WPH 2202

The Three Bears
WPH 2203

The Three Billy Goats Gruff
WPH 2204

Little Red Riding Hood
WPH 2205

The Three Little Pigs
WPH 2206

The Big, Big Carrot
WPH 2213

The Country Mouse and the City Mouse
WPH 2214

The Elves and the Shoemaker
WPH 2215

The Hare and the Tortoise
WPH 2216

The Little Red Hen
WPH 2217

Stone Soup
WPH 2218

Make instant nursery-tale manipulatives out of sturdy cardstock. ▼ Outside spread

Enjoy the related activities and songs, plus reproducible pages. ▼ Inside spread

CUT & TELL SCISSOR STORIES

Each book has eight original stories and patterns and directions for cutting a paper plate into a fun prop. Each story has extenders: art, music, movement, and learning games. Each 80 pp.

Scissor Stories for Fall
WPH 0301

Scissor Stories for Winter
WPH 0302

Scissor Stories for Spring
WPH 0303

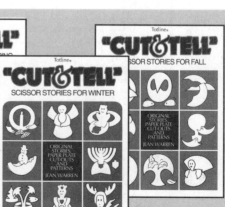

TOTLINE BOOKS

Teach the year with Huff & Puff!

JANUARY
Huff & Puff's Snowy Day
Themes: Snow, Winter, Helping Others
PB: WPH 2019 • HB: WPH 2020

FEBRUARY
**Huff & Puff
 Groundhog Day**
Themes: Shadows, Groundhogs, Spring
PB: WPH 2023 • HB: WPH 2024

MARCH
Huff & Puff's Hat Relay
Themes: Wind, Occupations, Hats
PB: WPH 2013 • HB: WPH 2014

APRIL
Huff & Puff's April Showers
Themes: Rain, Flowers, Mother's Day
PB: WPH 2005 • HB: WPH 2006

MAY
Huff & Puff's Hawaiian Rainbow
Themes: Rainbows, Colors, Hawaii
PB: WPH 2015 • HB: WPH 2016

JUNE
Huff & Puff Go to Camp
*Themes: Outdoor Activities,
Being Afraid*
PB: WPH 2017 • HB: WPH 2018

JULY
Huff & Puff on Fourth of July
*Themes: July Fourth, Thunder,
Lightning, Fireworks*
PB: WPH 2021 • HB: WPH 2022

AUGUST
Huff & Puff Around the World
Themes: Transportation, Foreign Lands
PB: WPH 2007 • HB: WPH 2008

SEPTEMBER
Huff & Puff Go to School
Themes: School, Numbers, Colors, Shapes
PB: WPH 2009 • HB: WPH 2010

OCTOBER
Huff & Puff on Halloween
Themes: Halloween, Being Afraid
PB: WPH 2001 • HB: WPH 2002

NOVEMBER
Huff & Puff on Thanksgiving
Themes: Thanksgiving, Families
PB: WPH 2003 • HB: WPH 2004

DECEMBER
Huff & Puff's Foggy Christmas
Themes: Christmas, Fog, Curiosity
PB: WPH 2011 • HB: WPH 2012

- Delightful stories written by Jean Warren
- Beautifully illustrated!
- BONUS! Each story comes with 16 pages of related activities & songs
- Perfect as a Read-Aloud for ages 2 to 6
- Great as an Easy-Reader for ages 6 to 8
- Each book 32 pp.
- Available in paperback and hardback

Huff and Puff books are available at parent-teacher stores and some book stores

Delightful Stories

Related Activities & Songs

Instant Hands-on Ideas!

Totline Newsletter and **Super Snack News** are the ideal resources for busy teachers and parents who work with young children. Both newsletters are developed by the publisher of Totline Books. Help your children feel good about themselves and their ability to learn by using the hands-on approach to active learning found in these two newsletters!

Totline Publications
P.O. Box 2250, Dept. Z,
Everett, WA 98203

To receive your FREE copy of *Totline Newsletter* or *Super Snack News*, or for additional information, call 1-800-609-1724.

Totline Newsletter

This newsletter offers creative hands-on activities that are designed to be challenging for children ages 2 to 6, yet easy for teachers and parents to do. Minimal preparation time is needed to make maximum use of common, inexpensive materials. Each bimonthly issue includes • seasonal fun • learning games • open-ended art • music and movement • language activities • science fun • reproducible teaching aids • reproducible parent-flyer pages and • Good Earth (environmental awareness) activities. *Totline Newsletter* is perfect for use with an antibias curriculum or to emphasize antibias values in a home environment.

6 bimonthly issues per year

Super Snack News

This newsletter is designed to be reproduced!

With each subscription you are permitted to make up to 200 copies per issue! They make great handouts to parents. Inside this monthly, four-page newsletter are healthy recipes and nutrition tips, plus related songs and activities for young children. Also provided are category guidelines for the CACFP reimbursement program. Sharing *Super Snack News* is a wonderful way to help promote quality childcare.

12 monthly issues per year